# SILVER BOXES

**A selection of Vesta cases:** See page 52.

# SILVER
# BOXES

## ERIC DELIEB

ANTIQUE COLLECTORS' CLUB

*Proverbs* XXXI 26

She openeth her mouth with wisdom

And the law of kindness is on her tongue.

ISBN 1 85149 313 1

British Library Cataloguing-in-Publication Data
A catalogue record for this book is available from the British Library

Origination by Antique Collectors' Club Ltd., Woodbridge, England
Printed and bound in The Czech Republic

# Contents

# Acknowledgements

The writer wishes to express his deep indebtedness to the anonymous collectors who kindly permitted him to illustrate articles from their collections and to the following for kind advice and technical assistance:

The Worshipful Company of Barbers and J. H. L. Trustram, MBE, MA, the Clerk and Solicitor. The Birmingham Assay Office: H. A. Westwood, Esq., Assay Master, Miss D. E. Dudley, Secretary to the Assay Master, A. Cartland, Warden, Michael Roberts, Photographic Records Department. Birmingham Central Reference Library: Miss D. McCulla and Miss D. N. Norris and the staff of the Local Studies Library. H. E. Brocksom. Mrs Shirley Bury, Victoria & Albert Museum. Miss M. E. Cliff. Edward Croft-Murray, MBE, Keeper of the Department of Prints and Drawings, British Museum. Rev. R. Dunwell, Rector, St Peter's Church, Cogenhoe, Northamptonshire. William R. Fletcher and Keith R. Fletcher. Monseigneur R. J. Foster, Rector of St Mary's College, Oscott, Warwickshire and Thomas Fenwick, Sacrist. The Board of General Purposes, Freemasons' Hall and A. R. Hewitt, Librarian and Curator and John Groves, Assistant Curator, Grand Lodge Museum, Freemasons' Hall, London WC2. L. H. Gilbert. The Wardens of the Worshipful Company of Goldsmiths and Miss Susan Hare, Librarian to the Company. Rev. W. A. Hepher, MA. Mrs G. E. P. How. Victor Joliffe and William Hathaway of Messrs Brown & Co., Birmingham. Derek Keen. E. Kish. F. L. Lancaster of Messrs. G. H. Lancaster Ltd., Birmingham. Mrs Beryl Linwood of Sandringham, Victoria, Australia and the late Charles Linwood. Mrs J. S. Martin of the Department of Coins and Medals, British Museum. O. T. Miles. Dr George Mitchell. Maurice Newbold. Charles C. Oman. Professor J. J. Plumb, D. litt D.FSA. H. Rubin. Bez Swinton-Berry. The Trustees of the Wellcome Medical Historical Museum and J. K. Crellyn, Curator and Robin Price, Assistant Librarian. The photographs of the enlarged Birmingham Makers Marks appended to the Genealogical sections are by Michael Roberts of the Photographic Records Department, Birmingham Assay Office. With the exception of Plate 156 which is by Peter Parkinson, AIBP, and Plate 110 by Otto Auer of Lisbon, the colour photographs are by Michael Plomer and Tim Ferguson. Black and white illustrations are by Christopher Ashdown, Raymond Fortt and Peter Parkinson.

In compiling this second edition, I have received widespread advice, instruction and support from many generous private collectors, museum authorities, specialist libraries and trade colleagues. Many contributors requested anonymity, and simply appear as names in a schedule. The remainder may be overtly identified:

Mrs. Anne Al-Shahi. The library staff of the Royal Institute of British Architects. David Beasley, Librarian, Goldsmiths' Company. Peter Brown, Curator, Fairfax House, York. Nigel Bird, Director, Reginald Bridges, Samuel Redknap, Messrs. Searle & Co. Alexis Butcher. Peter Cameron. Dr. Helen Clifford. Sim Comfort, Sim Comfort Associates. Edward Donohoe. Dr. Richard Edgecumbe, Department of Metalwork, Victoria & Albert Museum. Henry Gillett, Archivist, The Bank of England. The staff of the Guildhall Library. Miss Eileen Goodway, Silver Department, Sotheby's. Christopher Hulme. Grayham Hunt. Roger Hudson. Brand Inglis. Richard Inglis. Miss Lorraine Jones, Museum Assistant, the Royal Pharmaceutical Society. Mrs. Diana Keggie. Mrs. Sanda Lipton. Timothy Millett, Director, A. H. Baldwin & Son, Ltd. Clive Moss. Miss Claire Nagle, New Jersey. Miss Tina Prentice, Department of Antiquities, National Maritime Museum, Greenwich. Mr. Michael Prevezer, Director, Silver Department, Phillips. Eric I. G. Smith. Miss Juanita Waterson.

# Preface

In 1968, when writing the peroration to the preface of this work's first edition, I hoped my mission of bringing a new appreciation of the genus 'box' to collectors and book-lovers alike would be successful.

Happily, *Silver Boxes* was generously greeted by the collecting public, and received enthusiastic reviews from international antiques journalists. The book became a much quoted reference work, with further editions requested, hence the 1979 Ferndale Editions re-issue.

Now, after thirty further years of dealing in and handling these superb pieces, discussing, studying and researching obscure aspects, notoriously unwilling to give up their secrets, I have the pleasant opportunity of publishing a second edition, and at the publisher's request, have greatly widened the scope and introduced new parameters.

Having proved itself, my ploy of attacking arcane subjects from oblique angles can be further pursued. So, although the original text remains more or less intact, the book has been painstakingly revised, errors in ascription and typography amended, and fresh illustrations added.

Particular care has been taken with captioning, but again, there are no pages bristling with footnotes; as a dedicated reader and student, I find these disturbing. All bibliographical references and credits appear at the end of the book. Where a comment is required, this is incorporated in the text.

I discuss manifold types and styles of the Box, its applied ornament, unusual and rare varieties, and touch on gold and platinum boxes. Several topographical reference works and architectural views of cathedrals, country houses and castles appear, to assist collectors trying to identify a scene (usually illustrated from an obscure angled prospect) on a box-lid, earlier customs – snuff and snuff-taking, calling cards, and the background to vesta cases.

It will be noted that several recipes appear in the text. Their inclusion seeks to elevate the silver box in the same way that fine decor in a magnificent mansion enhances its appearance. These beautiful receptacles, sadly now without their original contents – sweetmeats, aromatic vinegars, perfumes and snuff moistening scents, are thus restored to their former glory.

Perhaps I should clarify why I refer to the 'castle-top' specimen as a *die-struck* or *repoussé* lidded box. The Birmingham makers elevated the craft of die-engraving and stamping to great heights, and their efforts deserve mention, and although the type frequently *does* illustrate castles, other examples depict diverse architectural features, such as country houses, palaces, ruins, cathedrals and historical and remarkable buildings.

Again, I am deeply indebted to the kind antiques lovers both anonymous and named, who opened their vitrines to me to furnish the beautiful illustrations. Much welcome counsel, too, has been given.

No preface on Old English Silver can be complete without some words of gratitude to the celebrated antiques specialists whose important works of reference have so enriched our vision. Without their help, many would have stumbled in the dark.

They are, of course, the doyen of English Silver, Mr. Arthur G. Grimwade, FSA, and Mr. John Culme, writing on Makers' Marks and Victorian Gold and Silversmiths, respectively. One might also mention the captioning staff of many of our leading auction houses, who instead of providing one-line ascriptions, now write fascinating articles packed with profound knowledge, erudite museum curators whose monographs and books so inspire public awareness, and the competent antiques journalists writing in newspapers and magazines.

I have been fortified and assisted by generous international correspondence, as well as personal encouragement, and think it appropriate to thank the Lord for allowing me to complete the reissue of this labour of love.

# CHAPTER 1
# Special Purpose Boxes

What is a box? Certainly it is a receptacle with a lid, hinged or otherwise. The shape matters little, but the function of the article is all-important. On the point of etymology lexicographers tend to disagree. Some, like Dr Johnson, distinguish the 'box' from the 'chest', as 'the less from the greater' – he supplies a quotation from Sir Philip Sidney's *Arcadia* (*circa* 1586) – 'a magnet, though put in an ivory box, will, through the box, send forth his embracing virtue to a beloved needle'. Others, notably Bartholomew de Glanville (*circa* 1360) define the term as originating with the material from which, at the time, boxes were usually made, the wood of the box-tree (*Buxum Sempervirens*). He mentions, in passing, other uses for the box than as a mere receptacle 'also of boxe that boxes made to kepe in musk and other spicerve'.

## *The Pyx*

The more logical origin for the term is the Greek πύξις a pyx, from the Christian practice of using a consecrated wafer in the communion service as a symbol of the body of Christ. The thread of religious persecution which runs through English history, often inspired by the whims of monarchs, has served to bond many Roman

**Plate 1** Commonwealth Pyx, formed as a circular box, reeded around the rim, and engraved on the lid. Scratched on the back with contemporary initials 'IM' and the date '1649'. Unmarked, *circa* 1635-49, probably the latter date, although Charles Oman in his *English Church Plate 597-1830* inclines to the former on stylistic grounds. 2in. (5.1cm) in diameter by 1in. (2.5cm) deep.

**Plate 2** Small Charles II pyx of oval shape, primitively engraved in contemporary characters. The back with 'Ecce Agnus Dei' and with similar ecclesiastical 'Lamb with Flag' motif, the lid (not shown) engraved 'In Hoc Signo Vinces'. Unmarked and undated, but thought to be *circa* 1660. 1⅝ in. (4.1cm) in diameter by ¾in. (1.9cm) deep.

*Courtesy of Monseigneur R J Foster, Rector of St Mary's College, Oscott, Warwickshire*

**Plates 3 and 4** Large Victorian silver-gilt pyx, the back engraved with the 'Agnus Dei' and fleurs-de-lis in a neo-Gothic cartouche, and the front (not shown) with The Crucifixion and sorrowing angels. It has a 'snap' fastener and five-lugged hinge and hangs from a cast and pierced loop. Inside the lid is engraved The Sacred Monogram in Pugin's neo-Gothic script. John Hardman & Co Birmingham 1849. 3in (7.6cm) in diameter by ½in (1.3cm) deep.

*Courtesy of Monseigneur R J Foster, Rector of*
*St Mary's College, Oscott, Warwickshire*

Catholics to their faith, and thus historical references abound which indicate the wide use of the pyx from the earliest times.

Both Ranulf Higden, a Benedictine monk of Chester, author of the famous 'History' of his time (*circa* 1299-1363), the *Polychronicon*, and John Bale, who was a bitter enemy of the Monastic system, and was known as 'Bilious Bale' for his vicious writings against the monks (among them *The Actes of the Englysh Votaryes, comprehending their unchast practices… Reade but laugh not…*, [*circa* 1495-1563]) relate of King Stephen's Coronation that 'the pyx in which the sacrament was contende, brekynge the chene, did falle, which was a prognostication contrary to the victory of the kynge' (Trevisa's translation) and, 'they tell of kynge Stuen, that the pixte fell out of hys tabernacle, at his coronacion' (Bale).

Pyxes were widely used in monasteries: an inventory of 1536 (the year in which the Henry VIII Act was passed for the dissolution of the lesser monasteries) contains '190 Divers Pyxides of Ivory (another version lists 'one pyx evere') with clasps and without them, of silver, with many relicks'. The Inventories of Church Goods for the Counties of York, Durham and Northumberland cite various pyxes which were similarly impounded, and one item entered in an inventory at Hunmanbie, in the East York Riding in 1552 states: 'This bill indented, maid the xvjth daie of August, 6 Edward VI: Item: 1 pyx of silver'. The Act of 1536 gave to Henry VIII the ornaments, jewels, goods and chattels of such foundations, and although it was not specifically mentioned in the Act of 1539 for dissolving the greater monasteries, their goods were also undoubtedly seized under it.

As a result of this legalised robbery, much important sacramental plate was melted down, and very few authentic English boxes (pyxes, caskets and the like) of pre-Reformation times survive. There may well be a few in private possession, but Charles Oman in his *English Church Plate 597-1830* (OUP, 1957) cites only five. The most impressive of Mr Oman's illustrations is the superb gold pyx at Westminster Cathedral, but as this present work is dedicated to the study of 'Silver Boxes', it was decided to restrict illustrations to those boxes made in silver and silver-gilt. Thus, three specimens are shown: two of early provenance, and one in Pugin's 'Mediaeval Revival' style.

At this juncture it ought to be pointed out that there are many foreign pyxes extant, in Limoges champlevé enamels, bronzes, and copper-gilt, but these escaped the Reformation, or were possibly imported as substitutes. The reason that the English pyx has been elected to open this survey of English Silver Boxes is that it is the earliest surviving silver receptacle of actual 'box-form'.

Of the two early pyxes shown, the circular example is the more interesting (see Plate 1). It is of undoubted English origin, and bears the scratched date '1649' and the owner's initials 'IM' on the back. It is a simple little box, engraved on the lid with a band of arabesque foliate motifs, interspersed with primitive Tudor Roses. Engraved within this band are the Sacred Monogram and Heart pierced with Nails. There is a primitive five-lugged hinge, and a loop, which perhaps engaged upon a hook or other type of fastener. The inside of the box was left 'unplanished', that is, it was not polished, and was permitted to retain the 'flaws' often found in unwrought silver. Obviously, there are no hallmarks – the Puritans' reaction to a communicant's application would have been unpleasant, to say the least! Notwithstanding his haste to finish the box, however, the unknown silversmith found time to fashion a band of 'reeding' enrichment around the rim.

The pyx in Plate 2 is somewhat later in date, being *circa* 1660, although it is completely undated and unsigned. The front bears an engraved crucifix with the Sacred Legend 'In Hoc Signo Vinces' (Constantine the Great's watchword – 'In this Sign shalt thou conquer') and the back with the Agnus Dei motif, and the Sacred Legend 'Ecce Agnus Dei'. The Agnus Dei, of course, symbolises Christ as the 'Lamb of God'. The shape is slightly oval, and the lid has a five-lugged hinge and a suspensory loop, so it was probably intended for use by an itinerant celebrant. The rim is 'wriggle-engraved' and there is a band of twisted wire gadroon enrichment around the body, probably to serve as a strengthener, and a 'hook' fastener.

Finally, there is Pugin's beautiful silver-gilt pyx (Plates 3 and 4). This is much larger than the other specimens, being probably intended for ceremonial use at St Mary's Roman Catholic College, at Oscott, near Birmingham. Augustus Welby Northmore Pugin, son of a French architect who had worked for Nash, George IV's famous protégé, was converted to Roman Catholicism in 1834, and his 'neo-Gothic' designs attracted the attentions of Bertram Arthur, 17th Earl of Shrewsbury, himself a Catholic and a great patron of St Mary's, Oscott. Under his patronage, Pugin designed and 'Gothicised' much of the college, and eventually collaborated with the Birmingham craftsman (now a stained-glass manufacturer), John Hardman. This silver-gilt pyx is a product of their joint design: Pugin provided the 'neo-Gothic' influence, complete with fleurs-de-lis and Gothic characters for the Sacred Monogram, and Hardman made the article in 1849.

The pyx is engraved on the front with the Crucifixion and sorrowing angels, and the Agnus Dei is placed within a cartouche surrounded by a band of matt-chased and engraved fleurs-de-lis. This, in turn, is encircled with a band of neo-Gothic floral motifs on an engraved ground. Pugin and Hardman collaborated to create the 'Mediaeval Court' at the Great Exhibition of 1851, and received great praise for their reintroduction of mediaeval designs and methods.

# Sweetmeat Boxes

One essential constituent of 'dry sweetmeats' (as Samuel Johnson epitomises the group) was a natural dulcifier and, of course, natural honey was the purest of these. In Anglo-Saxon times, honey was widely used and the wild honey found in the English woods became an article of importance in the Forest Charter (Carta de Foresta – hotly contested common law and forest law rights were among the grievances which united the barons and the people against King John). It would appear, from contemporary records, that the existence of this natural product was the reason why sugar was not brought to England in any great bulk until the 15th century.

Sugar was at first regarded as a spice, and was introduced as a substitute for honey after the Crusades (there is a contemporary record of the use of sugar in the household of Simon de Montfort, 1208-1265). It was sold by the pound in the 13th century, and was obtainable in even such remote towns as Ross and Hereford. In an early account of Anglo-Venetian trade, *circa* 1319, there is an account of a shipment made at Venice for England of 10,000 pounds of sugar-candy.

The actual preparation of sweetmeats in England is mentioned by a variety of writers. Caxton, in *The Game and Playe of the Chesse* (1474), refers to the confectioners as 'they that make confeccions and confites and medecynes', and Bacon's *Naturall Historie* (1627) states: 'They have in Turkey and the East certain confections which they call serverts [sherberts?] which are like to candied conserves, and are made of sugar and lemons'.

The monumental *The Jewels and the Plate of Queen Elizabeth I*, taken from the Inventory of 1574, edited by A. Jeffries Collins, 1955, includes an intriguing entry (page 584, item 1557): 'One Cvmfett box Sylver gylte Fasshyoned Lyke a Tortoyes with a Lyttle folding Sponne ther in poiz. [weight] vj oz. qyarter'. Mr Collins states that Queen Elizabeth 'received a number of other comfit boxes for sweetmeats as New Year's gifts. They do not appear in this inventory, however, because they were classed as jewellery, not as plate, and were committed to the charge of the Gentlewomen of the Privy Chamber. Thus the 'littill box of gold to put in cumphetts, and a litill spone of golde', presented by Blanche Parry in 1578, and the 'Comfett box of mother of pearles gar. w$^{th}$ gold and sett w$^{th}$ small sparks of Rubies', received from Lord [Henry] Seymour in 1589, were entrusted respectively to Lady Howard of Effingham, later Countess of Nottingham, and Mistress Mary Radclyffe. The present box was also originally in the keeping of Lady Howard. It appears towards the end of both copies of the inventory of the jewellery for which she was responsible thus: 'A Comfitt Box of Siluer gilt Fashioned lyke a Tortes w$^{th}$ vij stones iij of them Christalles the ground painted with flowers, the iiij other stones being Conelians (sic) and a Lytle siluer Spoone, geven by M$^r$ Arthur Frogmorton'. This 'little tortois box' with the other plate still in the Upper Jewel-house at the Tower, fell into the hands of the Parliament in August 1649.

As a result of Commonwealth sequestration, very few 'comfit or sweetmeat boxes' of true provenance remain extant: it is only possible, by study of the form of the box itself, its closely fitting lid, the 'drop-over' or 'snap' fastener, and, sometimes, a contemporary mention, to arrive at its probable use. Thus, the Exhibition of Royal and Historic Treasures, held at 145 Piccadilly in 1939, contained (item 3, page 49, in the catalogue) 'One comfit box belonging to Lord Darnley with his initials 'H.S.' engraved on it'. The item was loaned to the Exhibition by the Earl of Galloway. Henry Stuart, Lord Darnley (1545-1567) was the second husband of Mary, Queen of Scots, and the father of King James I of England. He was deeply involved in both political and personal intrigues, and died in highly suspicious circumstances.

The delightfully austere oval Sweetmeat Box in Plate 6 was wrought in 1651 and, on reflection, is a surprising manifestation of Puritan indulgence: at a time when

**Plate 5** A very rare Charles II small rectangular lift-off lid comfit box, crudely wrought and primitively engraved with a Tudor rose and other bands of 'wreath' motifs. Unmarked, *circa* 1670-80. 1in (2.5cm) by ⅝in (1.6cm) by ½in (1.3cm) deep. The box is roughly fashioned, and has not been planished on the base, thus pointing to the work of an itinerant silversmith or tinker, but a certain amount of skill has been devoted to making the bezels, and the interior is crudely silver-gilt. The lid is astonishingly close-fitting.

**Plate 6** Commonwealth large oval elliptical sweetmeat box of austerely plain form. The lid is of the 'stepped' variety, that is, the top ellipse is slightly higher than the rim. With 'drop-over' fastening.
A.F. in shield (J3, p.121, line 18), London 1651. 7½in (19cm) by 5¾in (14.6cm) by 2½in (6.4cm) deep. Weight: 17 ozs. 8 dwts. (542gr.). Contemporary initials and the date '1652' are pricked on the lid. *Courtesy of the Worshipful Company of Goldsmiths*

**Plate 7** Charles II circular moss-agate comfit box, with heart-shaped mounts and on a filigree base. The lid has a three-lugged hinge, 'snap' fastener, and floral filigree finial. Unmarked *circa* 1675. 2⅞in (7.1cm).

most sumptuous plate was frowned upon as 'frivolous luxury' the commission of, and execution by, a Commonwealth craftsman of such a beautiful article, is inexplicable. The silversmith obviously attempted to conform to the austerity of the times, as the receptacle is really nothing more than a hinged-lid box with a massive 'hinge-drop' fastening and, with the exception of the pricked initials and date '1652' in a primitive floral device, there is no other embellishment. As the article is fully hallmarked, there can be no question that it was clandestinely wrought: it was made with the full sanction of the Commonwealth authorities. The only other possible explanation might be that its intended function was disguised in some way – it might have been originally described as a 'bible-box', but this is highly conjectural, and very unlikely.

From *A Queen's Delight: or the Art of Preferving, Conferving, and Candying Candies.* Printed by R. Wood for Nath. Brooke, at the Angel, in Cornhill, 1660:

### TO CANDY SUCKETS OF ORANGES, LEMONS, CITRONS AND ANGELICKA

Take, and boil them in fair water tender, and fhift them in three boilings, fix of feven times, to take away their bitternefs, then put into as much fugar as will cover them, and fo let them boil a walm[1] or two, then take them out, and dry them in a warm oven, as hot as Manchet[2], and being dry, boil the fugar to a Candy height, and fo cast your Oranges into the hot fugar and take them out again fuddenly, then lay them upon a lettice of wier (sic) on the bottom of a fieve in a warm oven after the bread is drawn, ftill warming the oven till it be dry, and they will be well candied.

---

1. Walm: a spell of boiling.
2. Manchet: a ring-shaped cake of the finest wheaten bread. A 1620 work says 'Our manchet is of fine flower of wheat, hauving in it no leauen, but insteede thereof a little barme (yeast).

# Oval Amatory Spiceboxes

As far as may be presently ascertained, this type of container has always been taken for granted as a receptacle for spices. The term somehow attached itself although, except for the country of origin of the motifs, as will be shown, there is little provenance to link this object with spice.

The type is well-known: it is a little oval box with 'pinch-sides', that is, a device whereby, on pressing the sides, the slightly convex, tightly fitting lid is 'sprung' open, although there is no actual spring inside the lid. It is usually engraved on the top with a primitive 'Cherub' subject and some sort of motto in either Latin or French, and normally possesses only a maker's mark of the 1685-95 period.

Yet, on closer examination, there are some very interesting aspects which invite careful scrutiny. The first question to be investigated is that of the origin of the *genre*, that is, the source from which the style was taken or copied. Before this may be undertaken, however, it is essential to describe the type of engraving which may be encountered: the majority of such boxes illustrate single cherubs or 'amorini', usually against a background of landscape or architecture, and sometimes these figures bear 'love-arrows' or gaze on a 'heart upon a burning altar', or at a rosebush. All such boxes bear mottoes 'scratch-engraved' within 'motto-ribbons' at the top, usually in Latin, French or, very occasionally, in English.

The essential clue to this enigmatic group lies in the 'emblems' engraved on the lids, for the term 'emblem' signifies 'a picture expressing a moral fable or allegory', and such subtle messages were very much admired throughout the 17th century. There was even a group of poets known as 'The Emblematists', and one of the most famous of these, though not necessarily the most profound, was the English writer, Francis Quarles (1592-1664). His work consisted of a series of paraphrases from Scripture, expressed in ornate and metaphorical language, followed by a passage from the Christian Fathers, and concluding with an epigram of four lines. This type of 'emblem' was defined as 'Sacred', but there were also 'Profane Emblems' which copied the work of Quarles and his contemporaries, but which introduced amatory subjects into the text.

The mottoes were very innocent (except perhaps to the recipient) and consisted of such messages as *To the most faithful*, or, *With you as my leader, I am not blind* and, sometimes, where a burning heart is shown upon an altar, the message might be: *I shun, but I burn*, (*Arceo sed ardeo*). These mottoes are mostly in French and Latin – English versions are rarer.

**Plate 8** William III oval engraved lid spicebox, with a five-lugged 'stand-away' hinge, and soldered with 'side-ovals' (the pressing on which eased the tension on the lid for opening) and with a 'snap' catch inside. The lid is engraved with an 'Emblemata Amatoria' motif depicting a cherub pointing arrows at an altar bearing a heart aflame, and the motto 'Vn sevl me blesse' – 'One alone injures me'. IG crowned, London 1695 (J3 p.141, line 2). 1¾in (4.4cm) by 1¼in (3.2cm) by ⅝in (1.6cm) deep.

**Plate 9** William and Mary small oval spicebox, engraved with a foliate cartouche on the domed lid, with a stand-away hinge, and a foliate motif on base. I.A. (not known), London *circa* 1690. 1in (2.5cm) by ¾in (1.9cm) by ⅝in (1.6cm) deep.

**Plates 10 and 11** Charles II oval 'Emblemata Amatoria' spicebox, with a 'stand-away' hinge and engraved on the lid with a 'Cherub leading a serpent' motif and on the base with a 'scratched' portrait of King Charles I and the initials 'C R' in a debased laurel wreath frame. The motto on the lid reads 'Envy Follow Me'. Unmarked *circa* 1675-80. 2½in (6.3cm) by 1⅜in (2.6cm) by ⅝in (1.6cm) deep. This type of spicebox usually has Latin or French mottoes, and an English one is uncommon.

It is now possible to return to the question of the original *genre*, and the subject may perhaps best be tackled from an historical angle. It is well-known, for instance, that love emblems flourished throughout Holland in the 17th century, and the distinguished Jacob Cats (1577-1660) wrote his *Emblemata* in 1618. The great Flemish painter, and Master of Rubens, Otto Van Veen (otherwise known as 'Vaenius') engraved a series of 'Emblemata' known as *Amorum Emblemata*, published in Antwerp in 1615, and which was, in turn, based upon the renowned engravings by Crispin van de Passe the Elder (1565-1637) which were known as *Thronus Cupidinis*; this group of engravings was far more elaborate than the simply 'scratched' amorini appearing on the boxes, but the *genre* is thus established.

Much more to the point, however, both from a practical point of view and because the 'Love Poems', as they are called, are printed in four languages: Latin, English, Italian and French, and illustrated by simpler engravings, is a little book entitled *Emblemata Amatoria,* or *Cupid's Adresse to the Ladies*; the poems were penned by Philip Ayres (1638-1712) the author of numerous books and pamphlets, who was active in the latter part of the 17th century, and the engravings were by an artist whose enigmatic cypher has been variously interpreted as that of Isaac Beckett of London, or Jan Van Vianen (*circa* 1660, died after 1719), who was known as an engraver of historical subjects.

The book was published in London in 1683, about the same time as the oval silver 'spiceboxes' appeared. It would have been too much to expect that the very mottoes and love poems which Ayres wrote in his charming little book should appear within the motto-ribbons on the boxes, but the gist is often very similar. Where, for instance, the engraving depicts a cherub plucking roses, the poem is headed 'The Difficult Adventure' and states:

> 'While wanton love in gathering Roses strayes
>   Blood from his hands, and from his eyes drop tears,
> Let him poor Lovers pitty, who tread wayes,
> Of bloody prickles, where no Rose appears.'

This verse, simply paraphrased, would be 'No Rose without Thorns' which motto indeed appears on one of the oval boxes illustrated, and the subject, with a simplified architectural scene in the background, could be the very example used!

It has, then, to be borne firmly in mind that the original engravings from which these 'emblems' are taken, are of Low Countries origin, although some specimens bear mottoes in French (which was then, as now, an international language) because this provenance might have yet another important bearing upon the design of the article. It has been noted that as opposed to purely English oval boxes which were 'hand-raised', that is, beaten up from a single sheet of silver, these little boxes are often composed of three layers of metal: the concave base, an elliptical 'middle' and the convex lid, all subtly soldered together to constitute the whole, and frequently engraved around the ellipse with a band of that primitive 'debased laurel' motif which is such a feature of most oval boxes of the period. The motif itself, namely, the 'laurel' wreath running round the rim, has ancient Chinese origins, and is even found on mid-16th century Turkish pottery of the Isnik region of Asia Minor, and was applied to the 'spiceboxes' in order to disguise the joint between the portions.

Oval 'amatory pinch-sides' boxes had important secondary uses other than spicing wines and punch with cinnamon, cloves and nutmegs.

They also held certain medicinal powders, very favourably regarded by gentlemen in the 17th and early 18th centuries. These included 'Cardinal's Powder', also known as 'Pope's Powder'; 'Duke of Portland's Gout Powder' (see below); 'Lady Moor's Drops' and 'Countess of Kent's Powder' for the plague. At a time when sanitation and clean water were unknown, man was afflicted with fevers and fits, much to the delight of the quacks who 'prescribed' all manner of dangerous cures.

A 20th century writer comments: 'Quacks endlessly dropped names. A "High German Doctor" headed his bills "By the KING and QUEEN'S Authority", and other spurious vendors claimed they had cured Kings, Queens and Dukes of various maladies.'

It came then as a great relief when, in the middle of the 17th century, the Jesuits introduced a safe medical substance taken from the 'Peruvian Bark', the important vegetable alkaloid eventually known as 'quinine', found in the Cinchona Tree, ground into powder and taken as a successful febrifuge.

It was named for the wife of the Spanish Viceroy of Peru, Countess Ana of Chinchon (a town forty miles from Madrid), who was cured of a fever in 1638 by the bark, which had been brought to Lima by Jesuit missionaries. On the Viceroy and his wife's return to Spain in 1640, their physician imported large quantities of the bark, and it was soon successfully curing sufferers of the fevers, against medical opposition. In 1649 the Procurator-General of the Jesuit Order, Father (afterwards Cardinal) John de Lugo (1583-1660) on a journey to Paris found Louis XIV suffering from an intermittent fever, and recommended the use of the bark – the King quickly recovered.

Peruvian Bark was introduced into England by the Cambridge apothecary Robert Talbor, who in 1672 wrote *Pyretologin*, an account of the cause and cure of agues or fevers. In May 1680, when Charles II, harried by the Monmouth Affair and the fight for the Succession, fell ill with ague, violent fits and a fever, Talbor was sent for, administered quinine, and the King was cured. In his excellent biography of *King Charles II* Bryant adds 'by a quaint irony the Popist cure saved his life'. Talbor was knighted, and appointed a royal physician with a salary of £100 per year.

Talbor's Powder was sold in London in the 1670s, at 4 shillings per ounce, or £3 per lb. He then went to Paris, changed his name to Talbot, was received at court and sent for when the Dauphin was dangerously ill with a fever in 1680, cured him with quinine, and became the King's favourite. Louis XIV bought the formula and an annual pension was granted to Talbot, who was also made a Chevalier.

In passing, it should be added that there was a great controversy in the 1680s as to whether the epidemic sickness known as the 'ague' should be treated with Peruvian Bark.

### The Duke of Portland's Gout Powder

This remedy was originally devised by the 6th century Greek physician Aetius, from a number of herbs, a modification of whose compound comprising birthwort root, gentian root, the tops and leaves of germander, ground pine and centaury, came to the attention of William Henry Cavendish (1738-1809), third Duke of Portland.

The Powder had a great reputation from the middle of the 18th and well into the 19th century as a cure for gout. One drachm (27½ grains or 1/16th of an ounce, avoirdupois) was to be taken every morning, fasting, for three months, and then ½ drachm for the rest of the year. The result was so satisfactory that the Duke of Portland had the formula and the diet directions printed on leaflets, and these were given to anyone who asked for them.

The medicine was not always successful, however. Some practitioners were accused of quackery. The novelist Henry Fielding (1707-1754), suffering from gout in August 1753, found no relief with 'The Duke of Portland's Medicine', prescribed for him by the rough-mannered sergeant-surgeon to George II, John Ranby.

A memoir on Fielding says that he admiringly introduced the character of the

**Plate 12** Charles II oval spicebox of large size, engraved on the domical lid with a cherub holding a rose, and the motto (in English) 'No rose without thorns'. With a stand-away hinge. Pricked inside the lid is a fine contemporary cyphered monogram. 'DS Crowned', *circa* 1700. 1½in (3.8cm) by 1¼in (3.2cm) by ⅝in (1.6cm) deep.
[Mr Grimwade ascribes this well-known small worker to 'Daniel Shelmerdine, first mark entered 1697' (AGG 499). Entered 1717 as a 'sword cutler' at the Golden Dagger, in New Street, by Shoe Lane, St. Bride's Parish.] However, this mark has been noted on a fully marked trefid three-pronged fork, dated 1689.

former barber-surgeon Ranby (1703-1733) into his novel *Tom Jones*, but this belief is surely pure supposition, as in real life Ranby's 'cure' almost killed the novelist, and it is highly unlikely that Fielding felt any love for him!

Yet another aspect, which has been noted after careful comparative study is that the majority of Dutch and Flemish boxes possess 'stand-away' hinges, that is, instead of the 'integral hinge' which is such a feature of the 18th century French boxes, where the hinge is completely hidden from view, the Netherlands specimens have wide flanges, or rims which stand away from the bezel of the box itself, thus permitting the lid to open much wider. The 'integral hinge' has been noted on jewelled book-covers, caskets and belt-buckles as far back as Anglo-Saxon times, so it is nothing new, but it might be opportune to devote some space to a survey of 'the hinge through history' at the end of this chapter.

## *Nutmeg Graters*

The use and manufacture of nutmeg graters spanned 1650-1865. Early types were either of heart-shaped or teardrop form, being of small size but large enough to contain a nutmeg inside the box, which had hinged lids, top and bottom, one to permit access to the punched steel grater and the other to remove the grated spice. Another popular type was the tubular variety which had a pull-off circular lid and a silver 'sleeve' grater inside, which was removed for use and replaced. A third, rarer, type consisted of a primitively silver-mounted cowrie-shell. The silver grater was mounted by 'strapwork' bands to the body of the shell and the grated nutmeg was shaken through a small hole pierced at the apex of the container. This type dates from circa 1690 and is never marked. In the 18th century egg-shaped, barrel and keg shaped and mace shaped specimens were produced, other varieties included goblets, urns, walnuts, shoes and strawberries. Late Georgian, William IV and Victorian specimens possessed engine-turned decoration and at this point the container reverted to box form.

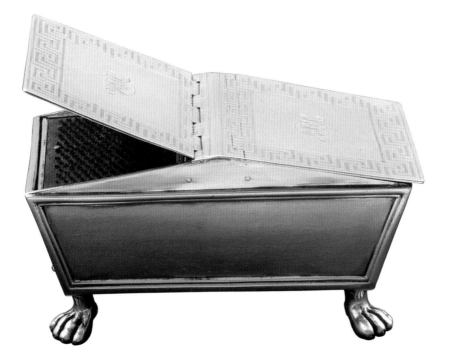

**Plate 13** George III table spice-box cum nutmeg grater, formed as a rectangular sarcophagus with tapering sides and sloping lids, which have superbly fitted integral-hinges. On four claw feet, the lids engraved with 'Greek Key' motifs and contemporary monograms. The steel graters are set in brass frames, and are hinged to permit access to the grated nutmeg. John Edwards III, London 1805. 5in (12.7cm) by 2½in (6.3cm) by 2½in (6.3cm) deep.

Plate 14 Victorian cushion-shaped nutmeg grater of rectangular form, with a blued steel grater. The spice-compartment is on the side, with a hinged lid, and the lid of the grater is engraved to simulate a smaller lid at the other side, in order to provide continuity of design. The reeded base has a finely concealed 'integral hinge' and the lids have scrolling thumbpieces. It is engraved with contemporary monogram. Charles Wallingford and Shirley Deakin, Birmingham, 1863. Marked in lid, inside base, and with lion passant on side. 4¾in (12cm) by 1¼in (3.2cm) by 1in (2.5cm) deep.

Plate 16 George II acorn-shaped nutmeg grater, the screw-off lid mounted by a medallet of George I's coronation. The Royal Arms struck on the obverse are worn but the reverse, depicting the King's head, is in brilliant state. The grater is blued steel. Edward Bennett I, London *circa* 1740. 3½in (8.8cm).

Plate 15 George III cylindrical nutmeg grater, with reeded bands on the body and near the rim, and with a gadrooned rim on top of the blued steel grater. With contemporary crest. Matthew Boulton, Birmingham 1795. Small articles from Boulton's factory, especially at this date, are uncommon.

*Courtesy of the Birmingham Assay Office*

Plates 17 and 18 George III shaped nutmeg grater formed as a 'snail', the lid and base, as well as the sides, with 'corrugated concentric' enrichment, and a projecting thumbpiece. Matthew Linwood V, Birmingham 1804. 1¼in (3.2cm) by 1in (2.5cm) by ¾in (1.9cm) deep.
George III oval elliptical nutmeg grater with a stand-away hinge and finely bright-cut with foliate motifs on a 'threaded' ground. The base has a fine integral-hinge. Peter and Anne Bateman, London 1795. 1¾in (4.4cm) by 1⅛in (2.8cm).

**Plate 19** George III 'keg' nutmeg grater, bright-cut and engraved with foliate motifs. Joseph Taylor, Birmingham 1799. 1⅜in (3.5cm).

**Plate 20** George II egg-shaped nutmeg grater, with spice compartment in apex, plain but with band of reeding. David Field, London *circa* 1750. 2in (5cm).

**Plate 21** William and Mary large silver-mounted East Indies stag cowrie shell formed into a nutmeg grater with a simple loop handle. It has 'scratch-engraved' straps around body, the joints secured by a pin, and a simple silver-hinged grater, lifting to reveal the natural 'teeth' of the shell. The powder was shaken through a small hole at the apex. Unmarked, *circa* 1690. 4¼in (10.8cm).

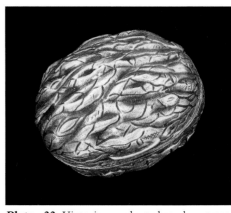

**Plate 22** Victorian walnut-shaped nutmeg grater. With blued steel grater. By Joseph Willmore, Birmingham 1842. 2in (5.1cm).

**Plate 23** A George III large heart-shaped table nutmeg grater with a silver punched grater, top and bottom lids with five lugged hinges. Scrolling contemporary monogram on lid. Unmarked, *circa* 1770. 2⅞in (7.1cm).

# Counter Boxes

Another small yet highly important silver box is the familiar 'Counter Box'. These little circular containers are well-known to all collectors of 17th century *bibelots*: they are usually about 1¼in (3.2cm) high by 1¼in in diameter, and when fully complete, contain between twenty and thirty-seven counters. The designs on these very thin 'coin-like' discs vary considerably; some have floral motifs of Dutch or Flemish influence, others bear the portraits of English Sovereigns, a very few have Biblical themes (scenes from the Gospels) there is even a full set of the 'Cries of London' from the period of Charles I, based on a 'broadside' of the period, and enumerating such delightful occupations as: 'Bandstringes for hankercher buttons; Buy my Hartichokes Mistris; Matt for a bed buy a Doore matt; Maribones Maides Maribones; I have Screens if yow desier to keep yˢ. Buty from yˢ fire; Radishes or lettis tow bunches a peny'. The itinerant sellers are dressed in mid-17th century costume and are all of sombre disposition.

It would, in this connection, be quite wrong to plagiarise the work of the late Miss Helen Farquhar (1859-1953) whose superbly researched articles on counters appeared from time to time in *The Numismatic Chronicle*, but some of her researches coincide so exactly with aspects in this present work, that they must, for this reason, be included here.

Miss Farquhar, basing her theories on her own wise observations and on the earlier work of G. F. Hill of the British Museum, concluded that many of the superlatively engraved counters found within Charles I 'counter-boxes' were not, in fact, hand-engraved, as had been quite legitimately believed hitherto, but the work of the clever Dutch medallist Simon van de Passe (*circa* 1595-*circa* 1637), who had invented a method whereby a steel die was cut and wafer-thin discs of silver were struck with the motifs, thereby imitating engraving by hand. Grueber's *magnum opus: Medallic Illustrations of the History of Great Britain and Ireland*, published by the British Museum between 1906-11, in the notes referring to Plate XXXIV (where counters struck between 1625-38 appear) states: 'These are stamped in imitation of engraving. They were used as markers or counters for reckoning and for play…' The period over which the issue of these pieces ranges is from 1616 to 1638, the earlier date corresponding with that when Simon Passe commenced his portraits of various members of the Royal Family and others. When the present work comes to the analysis of 19th century ornament the connection with Miss Farquhar's discoveries will become apparent. It becomes necessary to examine their probable use. To pass them off as mere 'gaming counters' would be highly inviting (and possibly even partially correct) but there is much more to these little objects than a purely frivolous use.'

**Plate 24** Stuart filigree tubular counter box and 29 filigree counters. *Circa* 1670. 1½in (3.8cm).

**Plate 25** A George III shallow circular box, the lid engraved with an 'amoeba' motif on a dotted ground. It contains four gilt medallets, by an unknown artist, struck circa 1805, commemorating the Battle of St. Vincent, 1797; the Battle of the Nile, 1798; the Battle of Copenhagen, 1801 and the Battle of Trafalgar, 1805.
Samuel Pemberton, Birmingham 1805.
¾in (1.9cm) in diameter.

Thomas Snelling's treatise *A view of the Origin, Nature and use of Jettons, or Counters*, printed in London, 1762, defines the term 'counter' literally, a disc which was used as a 'counting device' by an ignorant person unskilled in mathematical calculation. After citing various European terms for these 'counters' – he traces the word from the French verb 'jet(t)er', to cast or throw – Snelling enumerates the instances, made towards the close of the 15th century, of gifts of jettons, at public expense, to various dignitaries, in magnificent purses and silver boxes ornamented on the lids with the Arms of the Province or the City of Origin, and each example bore emblems, inscriptions and Royal Portraits. This practice is of course, yet another manifestation of the Biblical adage 'Unto every one that hath shall be given' – these counters were originally intended to serve the poor ignorant peasant, and became eventually a magnificent New Year's gift for the mighty.

The famous numismatist Francis Pierrepoint Barnard in his *The Casting Counter and the Counting Board* (this last was a device whereby the drudgery of counting by hand could be speeded up) cites many historical origins for counter boxes. In 1496 and 1540 a 'nest of counters' is mentioned, in 1583 'a case of lyon counters' (presumably because they had lions struck on their surfaces), and in 1628, 'a box and counters'. In a footnote, Barnard suggests that the box of van de Passe's counters exhibited at the New Gallery in 1889 as part of the Exhibition of the Royal House of Stuart, 'probably contained play-pieces'. This statement is of great service to the student as it establishes, once and for all, the fact that where counters are in pierced and die-struck circular boxes (such as those illustrated on page 72) these were probably used by the nobility during gambling games, and where the box-lid has a die-struck portrait of either Charles I or Charles II, this was intended as a clandestine allusion to the Martyrdom of the House of Stuart.

It is interesting that whereas English counter-boxes are almost invariably completely circular, the Dutch and French examples tend to taper towards the base; it may be possible that several sizes of counters were in use on the continent, the smaller being placed at the bottom of the box, and the larger at the top. In passing, Barnard tells the amusing anecdote recounted by Ouville (*Les Contes aux Heures Perdues*, Volume II of the 1644-52 edition) that a bridegroom, who had tried in vain to sum up his expenses on his fingers, in desperation forgot all about the expectant bride, and, drawing jettons from his pockets, set himself to cast his account with their aid.

# *Patchboxes*

Much has been written elsewhere (vide *Investing in Silver*, pp.104-5) about the fascinating little object, the patchbox, but recent researches have revealed further interesting material: The very earliest use of the 'patch' as a cosmetic aid was in classical Rome, and it was a general practice amongst women in the closing years of the Empire; men apparently also used patches to excite the curiosity of their ladies, for Henry Glapthorne (working between 1639-43) in his *Lady's Privilege*, 1640, says: 'If it be a lover's part you are to act, take a black spot or two. I can furnish you; 'twill make your face more amorous, and appear more gracious in your mistress' eyes'. Finally, in a volume issued in 1658 called *Wit Restored*, the following allusion to 'patching' appears:

'Her patches are of every cut,
    For pimples or for scars;
Here's all the wandering planet's signs,
    And some of the fixed stars;
Already gummed to make them stick,
    They need no other sky.'

The 'death-knell' of the practice appears to have come during the mid-18th

**Plate 26** William III circular patchbox, the slightly domed lid engraved with a primitive Tudor rose motif and slant gadroon rim. Thomas Kedder, London, *circa* 1695. Maker's mark only. 1⅛in (2.9cm) in diameter by ½in (1.3cm) deep.

**Plate 27** Queen Anne small circular patchbox, the lid engraved with a Tudor rose. Unmarked, *circa* 1710. 1¼in (3.2cm).

**Plate 28** George III circular patchbox, with a stand-away hinged lid of the 'three-lugged' variety and a slightly domical lid. Peter and Anne Bateman, London, 1795. 1⅛in (2.9cm) in diameter by ¼in (6.3mm) deep. Fully marked in 'cruciform formation' on base.

**Plate 29** Charles II large circular patchbox, engraved on the pull-off lid with a tulip motif. Maker, BC (not known to Jackson) *circa* 1660. Diameter 2in by ¾in deep.

**Plate 30** William III small heavy gauge circular patchbox, engraved on the side with a barrel-staves motif. 'TN' in monogram struck in lid and base, *circa* 1695. Diameter ⅞in (2.2cm) by ⅝in (1.6cm) deep. A nutmeg grater with the same mark is illustrated in Elizabeth B Miles' *The English Silver Pocket Nutmeg Grater* (page 21).

**Plate 31** William and Mary small circular patchbox: magnificently engraved on the pull-off lid and the base with 'Emblemata Amatoria' motifs. On the lid is a cherub firing an arrow at a pair of flaming hearts on an altar, and on the base a cherub is placing a 'flaming heart' in a basket containing other hearts, with amatory mottoes in French. It has debased laurel wreath borders. Diameter 1in by ¼in deep.

century: a writer in *The World* of 1754, speaks of the patch increasing in size as to almost overwhelm the face.

Some patchboxes are quite large, and during the 17th and early 18th centuries only lift-off lids have been noted, none hinged. One delightfully engraved English example (below), though embellished with a Dutch-inspired 'tulip motif', appears by virtue of the maker's mark and the primitiveness of the engraving, its date may be tentatively set as of *circa* 1660. Other patchboxes were very small, no more than ¾in (1.9cm) in diameter and quite shallow, but of heavy gauge metal and ranging in date between 1680 and 1720. While it is possible that foreign specimens infiltrated into England, most of the examples noted have been of purely English provenance; some have contemporarily engraved cyphers or initials and, occasionally, a date roughly 'scratched' on the base; others have unimpeachable English makers' marks struck several times, both on the base and inside the lid.

## Skippet Boxes & Sealing Wax

Curiously enough, while many thousands of steel, bronze and silver dies for seal matrices, that is, the finally cast seal, remain extant, little is known about the boxes which eventually preserved the actual wax impressions (originally very brittle) and then traditionally encased them for ceremonial reasons in metal 'skippets' or boxes. Early references to 'skippet boxes' are scant; primarily, the term of which several variations are known, chiefly 'skibbet', refers to a small box or compartment in a chest, used for the preservation of documents or seals. The Caxton version of Guillaume de Guilleville's poem *The Pylgremage of the Sowle* (written about 1330 and printed *circa* 1483) states; 'In her hond she brought a Skypet, and she took forth the Charter'.

That tireless researcher, Edward Alfred Jones, in a short article in *Apollo Magazine* of December, 1934, illustrated a superbly engraved oval elliptical skippet box, with the plaited tassel which normally runs through the seal (and provision for which is made in the base of the box by means of a slit at either end) still attached. This oval silver box is engraved with the Arms of the University of Cambridge and the coat-of-arms of the Duke of Albermarle, quartering Monck, Plantagenet, Grey and Talbot within the Garter. 'From the fact that the second Duke was Chancellor of the University from 1682 until his death in 1688' says Jones, 'it is assumed that the box was provided for him'. A local antiquarian researcher, A. S. F. Gow, Esq., Fellow of Trinity College, discovered in the accounts for the

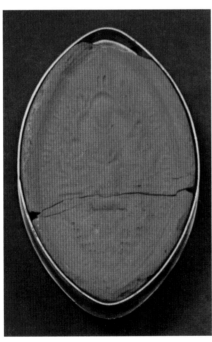

**Plate 32** A pair of George III skippet or seal boxes of oval elliptical form, the lids engraved with typical mid-Georgian scrolling cartouches containing the Arms of Oxford University. The seal illustrated is that of a medieval Chancellor of the University. There are slits at the top and bottom of the boxes to permit the tassels or seal-strings to protrude. 'RG' in Gothic characters (see text for full details of this mark). 3in (7.6cm) by 2¼in (5.7cm) by ½ in (1.3cm) deep.

making of the box, the name of a local Cambridge goldsmith, one Samuel Urlin, an apprentice (1647-54) of the London goldsmith, Robert Welstead. Some five years after his admission as a Freeman of the Goldsmiths' Company, Urlin settled in Cambridge and worked there until his death in 1698, when he was succeeded by his son, Samuel.

Another University Sealbox had been supplied and probably made by another Cambridge goldsmith, John Disbrow, who had been apprenticed to the London goldsmith, John Ward, from 1661 to 1668, and this particular specimen was made for the Duke of Monmouth in 1674.

The two skippet boxes illustrated bear the early 19th century coats-of-arms of the University of Oxford, and one contains a medieval seal of the Chancellor of the University. Mr Grimwade explains (p.519-20) that the mark RE in Gothic characters (AGG 3769a) was an oversight or misunderstanding of the cutter, the 'G' wrongly cut

**Plate 33** George IV large circular silver-gilt sealbox with an oakleaf motif border and stand-away hinge, embossed and chased with the Royal Coat-of-Arms of George IV embracing the Order of the Garter and with the 'George' pendant below. John Bridge, London, 1826. 6in (15.2cm) in diameter by 1⅜in (3.5cm) deep.

as an 'E'. Robert Garrard II was entered at Goldsmiths' Hall in April 1818.

Even less is known of the materials which constituted 'sealing wax', not the modern 'shellac' variety, but the medieval and early 16th century types. Only John Beckmann, Professor of Economy at the University of Göttingen in Hanover, whose fascinating *History of Inventions, Discoveries and Origins*, published originally in German, *circa* 1780-1805, examined the substance thoroughly, and traced the origins from Egyptian Dynastic times, to the Romans, and the Byzantine emperors. It would appear that coloured sealing wax was already in use in 1524, when Charles V granted a Dr Stockamar of Nuremberg the privilege of using blue wax in seals. The oldest mention of sealing wax which Beckmann had noted in printed books was the work of Garcia ab Orto, *circa* 1563, and the oldest printed recipe for making sealing wax appeared in a work by Samuel Zimmerman, citizen of Augsburg, printed in 1579; the following is an extract:

> 'To make hard sealing-wax, called Spanish wax, with which if letters be sealed they cannot be opened without breaking the seal: – take beautiful clear resin, the whitest you can procure, and melt it over a slow coal fire. When it is properly melted, take it from the fire, and for every pound of resin add two ounces of vermillion, pounded very fine, stirring it about. Then let the whole cool, or pour it into cold water. Thus you will have beautiful red sealing wax. If you are desirous of having black wax, add lamp-black to it. With smalt (finely pulverised glass of azure pigmentation) you may make it blue, with white lead white, and with orpiment (yellow arsenic) yellow. If, instead of resin, you melt purified turpentine in a glass vessel, and give it any colour you choose, you will have a harder kind of sealing-wax, and not so brittle as the former.'

Finally, the imposing circular silver-gilt seal-case by John Bridge of London, 1826, with the embossed Royal coat-of-arms of George IV on the lid was probably intended to accommodate an Ambassadorial Seal, but all provenance has been lost. Certainly, it is an impressive container worthy of His Britannic Majesty's Ambassador to any nation in the world!

# Dental Boxes

It is always very difficult to be dogmatic about the original use of an article many generations after the deaths of the people who invented it. Many such 'inventions' of which, no doubt, their owners were justly proud, are now nothing more than an irritating enigma to present-day researchers. Yet it has to be continually borne in mind that all the curious, unusual and useful boxes illustrated within these covers were once owned and cherished by normal, respectable people. When, in the course of time, they bequeathed their treasures to their heirs, these might have been stolen, mistreated, or finally and ignominiously sent to the saleroom by indifferent beneficiaries, and their real function temporarily lost to posterity.

Thus, who is to say, for instance, that the delightfully bright-cut rectangular containers described here as 'toothpick cases' are, in fact, of dental origin? 'Perhaps', some sceptical reader might retort, 'they were originally patchboxes?' Perhaps they were: it is possible that the silversmiths of the late 18th-early 19th centuries had finally arrived at the conclusion (not yet amounting to 'all-out mass-production') that one type of article might, if fitted out individually, have several different uses. The fact remains that most of the elliptical and rectangular cut-corner shallow boxes, lined with fading red velvet, which were intended as patchboxes, have tiny mirrors set within their lids, in much the same way as the modern ladies' powder compacts have in theirs. On reflection, a fully, or even partially filled patchbox of this type has never been noted, presumably because the patches were fragile and brittle, and, in any case, were probably used up long ago by their avid possessors. Very similar boxes, however, also with red velvet linings, but without mirrors, have been noted which contained several ivory toothpicks (and, occasionally, an ivory bodkin needle) still reposing inside them.

Strangely, very few 18th and 19th century toothpicks in precious metals appear to have survived in English boxes, although French and sometimes Swiss specimens are occasionally encountered. The toothpick, apart from many mentions in classical literature, particularly Greek and Roman, was well-known to the Court of The Virgin Queen, and fascinating accounts of this specialised 'toilet accessory' appear in the aforementioned *Inventory of the Jewels and Plate of Queen Elizabeth I*, for instance,

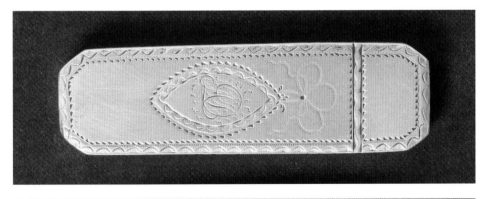

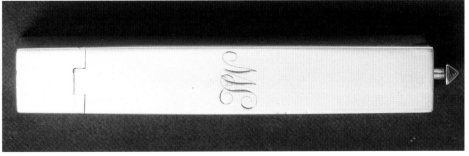

**Plate 34** George III 'vertical opening' toothpick case, the rims bright-cut with 'wriggle-motifs', the centre of the lid with an oval escutcheon containing a contemporary monogram, the hinge of the hidden-integral type. It has a velvet lining and a mirror in the lid. Samuel Pemberton VI Birmingham 1812. 3¾in (9.5cm) by 1in (2.5cm) by ¼in (6.3mm) deep.

**Plate 35** George III 'toothpowder' box of plain rectangular form, with a sunken-integral hinge and a diamond-shaped lifting handle at the base. It is engraved with a contemporary monogram. Phipps and Robinson, London, 1799. 4in (10.2cm) by ½in (1.3cm) by ¼in (6.3mm) deep. This item was probably originally one of a set contained in a case.

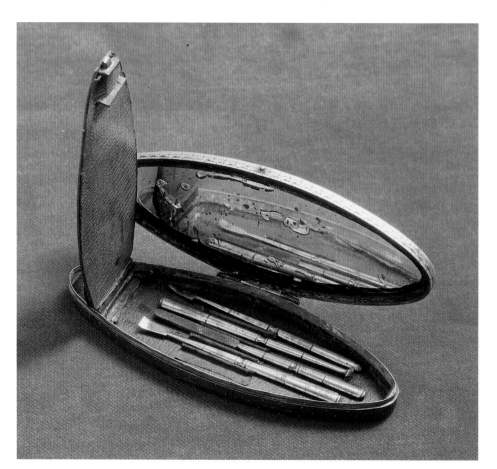

**Plate 36** George IV oval elliptical 'Dental Instruments' case containing scaling instruments of steel and lined with green morocco on the inner lid and red morocco on the outer. Set in the centre of the lid is an oval plaque bearing hallmarks and a mirror inside the lid. The rim is delicately bright-cut with 'wriggle-motifs'. The top of the inner lid is hinged and has a 'snap' fastener. It is probable that toothpicks could be accommodated on the top surface of this inner lid. No maker's mark, Sheffield 1825. 4in (10.2cm) by 1½in (3.8cm) by ¼in (6.3mm) deep.

'Item foure Touthe pickes of golde gevon by M$^{rs}$ Snowe at new yers tide Anno predicto poiz all iiij d.wait. dim'. As Mr Collins' footnote could hardly be improved upon, it is here given in full (apart from a few parenthetical genealogical references): 'Mistress Snowe seems to have been a widow, a Gentlewoman of the Privy Chamber who died in 1587. Rarely did she fail to offer a New Year's gift. In 1577 she produced "vj Tothe pickes of golde and vj smale Clothes to wype Teeth wrought w$^{th}$ blacke silke" (to replace the tooth-cleaning appliances given the previous year) and in 1574 she had given six toothpicks, one of which was lost by the Queen'. It has been said that the Queen suffered from defective teeth (F. Chamberlin, *Private Character of Elizabeth.* pp. 86-7, etc). Earlier in the *Inventory* (No. 1368) mention is made of a 'Touthe picke and Eare picke of like siluer guilt' which had been made for Queen Mary, but which had disappeared.

Plate 36 is a charming little elliptical box of undoubted dental provenance. Quite apart from its unusual design – it has an inner lid, hinged about one inch from the end of the ellipse, and with a steel 'snap' fastener at the other, the lid and base lined in green morocco leather – it still contains a set of 'scaling' instruments, one of which is a file, to cleanse between the upper front teeth, and the other a 'scaler' to remove tartar from the enamel, with further green morocco leather 'separators' between the instruments and a very clear mirror set in the lid. Careful scrutiny of the hall-marks struck on an elliptical cartouche on the red morocco leather lid has determined that the place of origin is Sheffield (quite normal as the instruments are of finely wrought steel) and the date 1825. The maker's mark, for some reason, has been deliberately obliterated. There is a band of beautiful bright-cut ornament around the top of the lid, and the whole receptacle is of delicate yet purposeful appearance. Presumably, the mirror in the lid had something to do with dental practice; it is even possible that it was used by the practitioner as a form of primitive dental mirror, but this is pure conjecture.

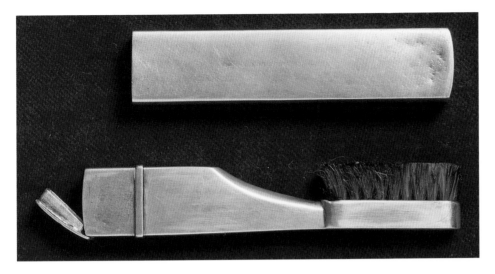

In early dental references two commentators stand out: *Paulus Aegineta*, a celebrated Greek surgeon of between the 4th and 7th centuries AD, who *inter alia* mentions a small raspatory (file) used for removing tartar from the teeth and adds: 'The scaly concretions which adhere to teeth we may remove with the scoop of a specillum, or with a scaler or a file'; and the earlier court physician to the Emperor Claudius, *Scribonius Largus* (A.D. 47) mentions an excavator for similar purposes.

The toothbrush, as a substitute for the toothpick, appears to have developed during the second half of the 17th century. The very earliest toothbrushes were nothing more than a bundle of semi-abrasive animal hairs such as hog bristles set in a primitive tubular handle, and late 18th century specimens have been noted where a piece of ivory has been fashioned into a 'handle-like' instrument with a circular indented pad at one end, into which, presumably, the hairs were inserted (by the time the brushes were noted, nothing remained of the bristles).

The ingenuity of the European silversmith in creating new implements to the commission of his customers is legendary and towards the end of the 18th century, in both England and France, a new type of toothbrush appeared. This had, again, a simple silver shaped handle, but with a rectangular frame at one end, into which a 'brush-pad' already wired with segmented bristles could be placed, and removed for

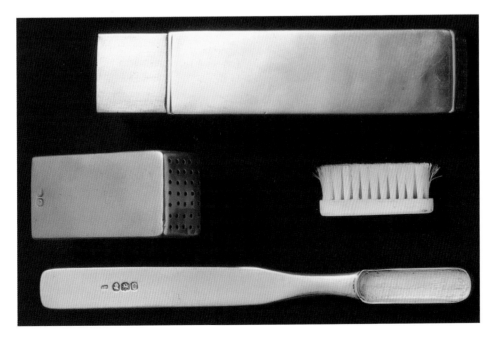

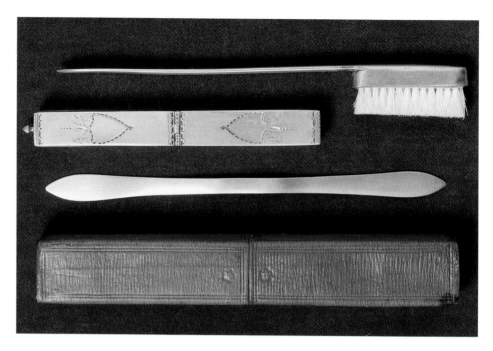

**Plate 39** George III 'Tooth Etui' comprising a toothbrush, with removable ivory brush-pad and plain tapering handle, double-ended tongue-scraper, and toothpowder box with double compartments hinged in the centre with a three-lugged integral-hinge and with a diamond-shaped lifting-handle on the base. The lids are bright-cut with 'shield and festoon' motifs. In a fitted red morocco contemporary case. Joseph Taylor, Birmingham 1795. Toothbrush and tongue-scraper 4½in (11.4cm), toothpowder box 4in (10.2cm) by ½in (1.3cm) by ¼in (6.3mm) deep, case 6in (15.2cm) by 1⅜in (3.5cm).

easy cleaning. The type is well-known, and Napoleon had one in his elaborate travelling necessaire. The 'brush-pad' of the fine toothbrush in Plate 38 has been deliberately removed to show its form. Toothbrushes, once in existence, required further containers, and a specimen of this type of silver box is also illustrated.

Finally, what of the dentifrice powders used by these early hygienists? Most of the early 19th century 'toothbrush kits' (a fine specimen, in its contemporary red morocco case, Plate 39) had, in addition to the toothbrushes and tongue-scrapers (necessary items in an imbibing society) a little rectangular box with double hinges, disguised at the central hinge with a hint of fine bright-cutting. This was for a slightly abrasive tooth-powder. The 'toothbrushing enthusiast' of the mid-17th century, however, was less lucky than his later counterpart. Here, taken from Brooke's *A Queen's Delight* (London, 1660), is a recipe for 'MR FERENE OF THE NEW EXCHANGE, PERFUMER TO THE QUEEN, HIS RARE DENTIFRICE, SO MUCH APPROVED AT COURT':

'First take eight ounces of Irios [sic] roots, also four ounces of Pomistone [a highly abrasive mineral more usually employed in erasing ink from parchments], and eight ounces of Cutel bone [the shell of the cuttlefish, yet another abrasive, perhaps put in to mystify the credulous, as the shell was rarely available], also eight ounces of mother of pearle, and eight ounces of Corral, and a pound of brown sugar candy and a pound of brick if you desire to make them red, but he did oftener make them white, and then instead of the brick did take a pound of fine Albablaster [sic]; after all this being thoroughly beaten, and sifted through a fine sieve, the powder is then ready prepared to make up in a paste, which must be done as follows:

TO MAKE THE SAID POWDER INTO PASTE

Take a little Gum Dragand [tragacanth] and lay it in steep twelve hours, in Orange water or Damask rose-water, and when it is dissolved, take the sweet gum, and grind it on a marble-stone with the aforesaid powder, and mixing some crumbs of whitebread, it will come into a paste, the which you may make dentifrices, of what shape or fashion you please, but long rolls is the most commodious for your use.'

Although later recipes were a trifle more merciful to the delicate tooth-enamel, and consisted mostly of chalk, camphor and borax, it is small wonder that very few people of the 17th and 18th centuries had healthy teeth. Might it be too much to presume that the unsophisticated country lads and lasses died with the teeth they had been born with, and that the cultured 'men about town' who followed fashion so devotedly, were left toothless; in fact, the higher the rank, the ranker the mouth?

# Toilet Boxes

Only two pre-Restoration Toilet Boxes have been noted: the first appears, once again, in *Queen Elizabeth's Inventory* as No. 1363: 'Item oone lie potte of siluer and guilt with a purslane hedde in the fore part thereof with a Couer [cover] standing in the backe thereof with a Coure having a round pece wherein is a Christall in place of a glasse enamelid vnder it with a shutting before the same poiz xxxv oz. iij quarters dim'. Once again, the footnote is highly enlightening: 'A "lye-pot" was an ornamental vessel to hold lye (alkalized water, usually a solution of potash) for use as a hair-wash'. The term, incidentally, is noted as far back as *circa* 1000. This 'lye-pot' is another form of toilet container which is not normally mentioned, and the Inventory cites two other specimens, one of which was made for Queen Mary.

The second mention appears in the catalogue of the famous 'Magniac Collection sale', held at Christie's in July, 1892, and appears as No. 344 in the catalogue: 'A circular Flat-shaped Toilet Box and Cover, of silver-gilt engraved with band of Tudor Rose and other flowers, foliage and trellis ornament, London Hall-mark, 1589. 1¼ inches high'. Magniac was one of the most eminent collectors of *objets de vertu* of his day, and there is no reason to doubt his ascription.

What is interesting, and entirely absorbing, is the enigma of what was placed within the perforated lidded toilet boxes (Plate 40 is a late example). A superlative oval box by David Willaume, dated London 1720, was sold in a London saleroom in 1964, which possessed, in addition to the sturdy gauge box (the weight was 9 ozs. 8 dwts) a charmingly pierced rising-domed lid enriched with scroll motifs. Perhaps the answer lies in the fact that Willaume was a Huguenot craftsman and was thus influenced by some French custom – possibly a washing cloth was placed within the box and the perforated lid permitted it to air – it is hardly likely that such a large container would be used to hold perfume or soap (which, in any case, had its own spherical 'box'), similarly, the English silversmith who fashioned the opulent rectangular box with florally pierced centre panel, also made a complete 'Toilet Service' (this item is but one piece from it) in which there were other receptacles for toothbrushes, etc.

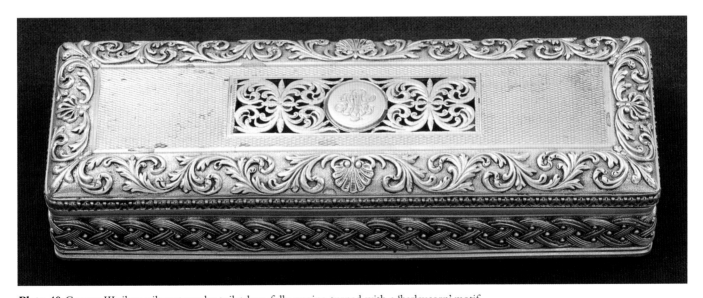

**Plate 40** George III silver-gilt rectangular toilet box, fully engine-turned with a 'barleycorn' motif and with a cast 'egg and dart' rim. The sides are enriched with an appliqué 'basketwork' motif, the lid embellished with scrolling acanthus and shell foliage. The centrally placed pierced panel is finely conceived. With an 'integral hinge'. William Pitts, London, 1815. 7in (17.8cm) by 2¼in (5.7cm) by 1⅜in (3.5cm) deep. This workshop specialised in fine castings.

# Medical Boxes

**P**erhaps one of the most fascinating of all the boxes illustrated within this group is the wholly delightful 'medicine box' (Plate 41), which so greatly resembles a 17th century octagonal watch, complete with a delicately engraved florally enriched 'dial' and 'scratched' Roman numerals from I to XII. There is a typical five-lugged hinged octagonal lid, and the device is repeated on the back, with the exception that there are no 'works' inside the case. The box was originally made to contain powdered potions, and the user would set the 'hands' to the time of the next dosage. The 'acorn-shaped' baluster finial and the 'snap' type fastener are typically English in style.

Another rare receptacle illustrated is a 'Caul Case' (Plate 42). It occasionally occurs that a baby is born with a 'caul' or remnant of membrane enveloping the head at birth; for some unknown reason, widespread superstitions became associated with the 'caul', and the most famed of all the fallacies connected with this is the belief that the owner of a caul would be preserved from drowning. An advertisement appearing in *The Times* as late as 1813 stated: 'To persons going to sea. A child's caul in a perfect state, to be sold cheap. Apply at 5 Duke Street, Manchester Square, where it may be seen'. This caul case is heart-shaped and bears the owner's name and date of birth.

**Plate 41** Charles I octagonal 'watch-shaped' medicine box: the domed octagonal lids with five-lugged stand-away hinges. The 'dial' engraved with Roman numerals and foliate motifs. The single 'hand' was moved to indicate the time of the next dosage, and the compartment at the back contained the pills or potions. With a snap catch fastener and baluster terminal. Unmarked, *circa* 1630-40. 1⅞in (4.8cm) by 1¼in (3.2cm) by 1in (2.5cm) deep.

**Plate 42** William IV Caul case formed as a heart, with a suspensory loop. Engraved with foliate motifs on front and back, and secured by tiny 'butterfly nuts', that is, with wings to be turned by thumb and finger. Contemporary inscription: 'Henry Rogers, born March XVIII, MDCCCXXVI (1826). Joseph Hicks, Exeter, 1830.
*Courtesy of the Birmingham Assay Office*

# Lancet or Phlebotomy Cases

**T**he surgical practice of 'bleeding', or Phlebotomy, has very ancient origins indeed and, quite often, was done with no thought of its therapeutic value. It is recorded, for instance, that there were 'four bleedings per annum' in the Cistercian abbey of Pipewell in Northamptonshire, and that in some monasteries the brethren were bled five times a year: in September, before Advent, before Lent, after Easter, and at Pentecost, which 'bleeding lasted three days'. This last practice was obviously connected with 'mortification of the flesh' and, as such, has no place here, but it is of interest, nevertheless.

In his *Early History of Surgery*, W J Bishop mentions that primitive peoples

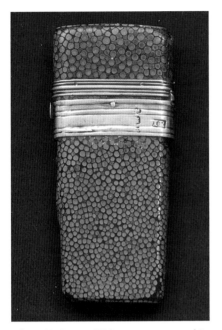

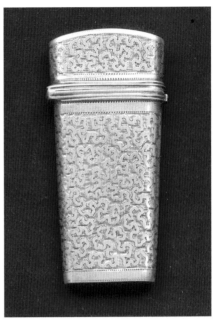

**Plate 43** George III lancet case covered in shagreen, with silver mounts. Containing two lancets. John Reily, London 1797. 3in (7.6cm) by 1½in (3.8cm).

**Plate 44** Victorian lancet case, silver-gilt and engine-turned with 'basketweave' motifs and with cast foliate borders. Containing one lancet. Taylor and Perry, Birmingham 1845. 3in (7.6cm) by 1¼in (3.2cm).

**Plate 45** Victorian lancet case of shallow type, containing two lancets. Engraved with 'abstract' motif and with reeded rim. No maker's mark, Birmingham 1843. 3in (7.6cm) by 1½in (3.8cm).

practiced various methods of 'bleeding' without any training in surgery, and enumerates three methods used which almost exactly emulate medieval surgical practice. Of these – venesection – the direct opening of a vein, is widely popular. As early as 1380-1400, a Latin poem translated by Furnivall on 'The Manners and Meals in the Olden Time', and printed in the famous *Babees Book*, states:

'Phlebotomy clears the eyes, purifies

The minds & the brain, makes the marrows warm'

The great Milanese surgeon Lanfranc, whose standard work *Chirurgia Magna et Parva* was first printed *circa* 1490, gave surgeons a guide to phlebotomy: 'Indications

**Plate 46** Victorian lancet case of the rectangular 'sliding lid' variety, engraved with foliate motifs on an engine-turned 'fox's head' ground. Containing two lancets. Thomas Dones, Birmingham 1853. 3in (7.6cm) by 1¼in (3.2cm). Thomas Dones entered his mark at Birmingham in 1850.

**Plate 47** Victorian gold lancet case containing six lancets, enriched overall with scrolling foliate motifs and with cast foliate borders. Joseph Willmore, Birmingham 1841. 3in (7.6cm) by 2¼in (5.7cm).

for blood letting: a vein in the forehead is cut against headache and frenzy. A Blood-letting on the temples is good against Megrim [the medieval term for the modern 'migraine']. Give the patient a slice of bread and wine before the operation. Blood letting shall be used if a man eats and drinks too much, in cases of gout'.

A most interesting account of mid-17th century phlebotomy appears in Gladys Scott Thomson's *Life in a Noble Household* 1641-1700, which is a domestic history of the First Duke of Bedford, William Russell. The book itself is entirely fascinating, and the contemporary material contained therein of the utmost absorption. In the chapter headed 'In Sickness and in Death' (chapter XVI) the author cites two particular instances involving phlebotomy. The Earl Russell, then in his last years, took regular lettings of blood ('the health precautions' explains the author, 'customary at the time'). Furthermore, mention is made of Sir Edmund King, (who, as Dr King, was a Court Physician) who was summoned to Whitehall when Charles II showed symptoms of what proved to be his last illness. While Dr King was in the room, Charles fell down in a fit, whereupon King immediately bled him and the royal patient recovered consciousness. The other physicians, coming in, exclaimed that Dr King had undoubtedly saved His Majesty's life, and the Privy Council, hearing of this, recommended a gratuity of a thousand pounds. It was never paid, for before the warrant could be signed, Charles was dead... Further details of domestic 'bleeding' appear in the account-books of the family, and on various occasions, the surgeon charged 2 shillings and 6 pence for 'opening a vein'.

The practice of phlebotomy, as can be discerned, went on well into the Victorian era, as many of the finely wrought lancet cases stem from this period; most still have sets of razor-sharp lancets inside them, and some are most delicately enriched in the contemporary style of engraving.

**Plate 48** William IV lancet case engraved with foliate motifs, containing two lancets. Taylor and Perry, Birmingham 1836. 3in (7.6cm) by 1½in (3.8cm).

**Plate 49** Victorian lancet case containing six lancets, the sides bright-cut with foliate motifs on a 'double-dot' scored ground. Taylor and Perry, Birmingham 1845. 3in (7.6cm) by 2¼in (5.7cm).

**Plate 50** William IV lancet case containing two lancets, silver-gilt and engine-turned with basketweave motifs and cast foliate borders, and with a stand-away hinge. Ledsam, Vale and Wheeler, Birmingham 1830. 3in (7.6cm) by 1½in (3.8cm).

*Courtesy of the Wellcome Medical Historical Museum*

# Surgical Instrument Cases

A letter which appeared in the correspondence columns of *Country Life* magazine on 30th December, 1954 under the heading 'Surgical Bygones' is of particular interest to the present survey for two reasons: one, that the photograph accompanying the letter illustrated a shagreen instrument case almost exactly duplicating the specimen shown in Plate 52, and two, that all the instruments were still intact, and, moreover, one was hall-marked for 1672. Thus a form of provenance is established between the two items, for very few complete surgical cases remain extant, and such as do might easily be mistaken for French or Low Countries examples. Also in the collection of the Wellcome Historical Medical Museum (from which the fine shagreen case originates) is an Italian silver mounted tortoiseshell instrument case containing lancets, forceps, a needle, a tongue depressor and a director. This article is dated *circa* 1707, from the contemporary inscription on the base.

In the *Country Life* specimen, there were no fewer than nine instruments – the usual forceps and scissors, directors (guiding devices for bullet probes) – but in addition, a dental scraper for scaling teeth, an ointment spatula, a measuring spoon (for removing ointment from a bottle) and, finally, a tapering tubular 'caustic holder' for holding a stick of silver nitrate at one end, and with a little lidded box for containing red oxide of mercury at the end. There was also a most interesting tongue depressor, which to all but the very initiated, looked like a modern 'all-purpose sardine-tin opener', with an ornamental inverted heart-shaped handle at one end, and a flat vertically pierced blade at the other. The silver mounts on both boxes are very primitively 'scratched' with floral motifs, and the hinges are simple 'book-clasp' types, pinned to the shagreen. Presumably the drawer in the base held the 'edge' tools, to prevent them from loss of sharpness.

**Plate 51** A Charles II surgeon's scalpel case, of tapering 'cannon-barrel' type. The five-lugged domed lid is engraved 'Robertus Perkes Chirugus 1710' with an engraved Tudor rose in the centre. The lid has a 'push piece' and steel spring opening. 'HH' conjoined, a fleur-de-lis and pellets below, London 1677-78. (J3 134) The Perkes or Parkes were an old Shropshire family. 3¼in (8.2cm).

**Plate 52** A Charles II rectangular shagreen-covered instrument case with silver stand-away mounted hinges engraved with 'debased laurel' and floral motifs, and engraved on the pierced clasp with a 'sunflower' motif. The lid opens by means of a 'push-piece' button. The interior is lined with leather. Unmarked, *circa* 1680. 6in (15.2cm) by 2½in (6.3cm) by 1½in (3.8cm) deep. Shagreen was made from untanned leather; it had a rough granular surface, and was prepared from horse or ass hide, or from sharkskin or sealskin. It was frequently dyed green but naturally coloured specimens have been observed.

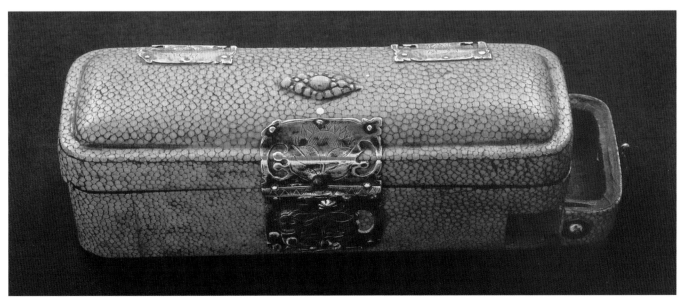

# Vinaigrettes

These charming little sponge-boxes, made in precious metals – gold, silver, enamels, silver-mounted glass, etc. – were introduced to alleviate problems with personal hygiene. Their delightfully pierced grilles also increased the owners' appreciation.

Nowadays it is assumed that 18th century fashionable trends led to 'the vapours', that dreaded fainting and depressive sickness suffered by fragile ladies. The *Oxford English Dictionary* clarifies this: 'A morbid condition supposed to be caused…by the *exhalations rising by natural causes from the ground or from some damp place*'. This discomfort, then, had nothing to do with a feeling of unexplained sickness.

The vinaigrette owed its invention to quite another cause. From the 1770s the modes and attire of female English and Continental followers of fashion became severely challenging. Few people realise to what lengths that late 18th-early 19th century lady was driven by its dictates. She was frequently 'laced' into a gown with a cruelly pinched-to-the-waist bodice, with inserted busks (rigid strips of whalebone or wood, often lovingly carved with geometric, floral or naval motifs and presented as love gifts), which were sewn into the corset to stiffen the garment.

The fine contemporary print above is taken from a watercolour by John Collet (1725-1780) and graphically illustrates the extremes a lady of fashion underwent. The little monkey at bottom right points to a book entitled *Fashion, Victim and Satire*. At least two people had to tug her into this imprisonment.

This 'tight-lacing' and later, the bustle, had at times disastrous results. As late as 1844, for instance, *The Times* reported that a young trainee milliner, aged twenty-two, working

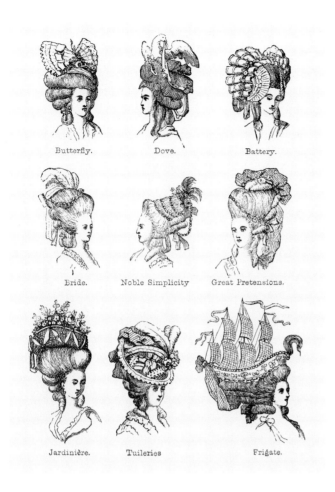

Butterfly.  Dove.  Battery.

Bride.  Noble Simplicity  Great Pretensions.

Jardinière.  Tuileries  Frigate.

in Lower Grosvenor Street, died as a result, according to the doctor, of the 'tightness of her corset, which was 1 foot 11 inches round on her body. It would not meet in the smallest part by 2 inches'!

From 1775 further tortures to be endured were the elaborately constructed coiffures comprising, as one writer put it, 'a crazy conglomeration of false hair, feathers, ribbons, and scarves, and, as if this were not enough, it is surmounted by models, in blown glass, etc., of windmills, ships, a coach-and-four, and the like'.

Eugene Rimmel's *Book of Perfumes* illustrates two pages of 18th century coiffures and cites a squib from the *London Magazine* for 1777:

> 'Give Chloe a bushel of horse hair and wood,
> Of paste and pomatum a pound;
> Ten yards of gay ribbon to deck her sweet skull,
> And gauze to encompass it round.'

*The Lady's Magazine*, March 1774, commenting on these artificial coiffures, states 'The fashion was most uncleanly, and the general unpleasantness was increased by the fact that "making" a head was a long and expensive business not to be undertaken too often, even by a woman of means, and consequently these structures sometimes remained "set" for weeks on end. It was said that three weeks was as long as a woman might go in comfort during the hot weather without her having her head opened…'

It can come as no surprise, therefore, that many of the skilful gold and silversmiths elected to enrich their *bijouterie* with beautiful ornament and interesting topographical views – and successfully disguised the real function of a tightly-lidded container whose aromatic acids greatly refreshed and revived their users.

**Plate 53** Horn-shaped vinaigrette with a finely intertwined monogram on the lid and a suspensory chain. Sampson Mordan, London 1886. 4in (10.2cm).

**Plate 54** A rare finely wrought Victorian globular vinaigrette with a suspensory coronet, delicately pierced coronet-shaped rim and a finely pierced fleur-de-lis grille. H W Dee, London. 1¼in (3.2cm) in diameter. Height including coronet, 1½in (3.8cm). *Circa* 1870 - badly struck.

**Plate 55** *Left:* George III vinaigrette with diaper bright-cut lid and bright-cut leafage on the base. Filigree grille. John Shaw, Birmingham 1810. 1in (2.5cm) by ⅞in (2.2cm).
*Right:* George III silver-gilt reeded vinaigrette with a florally pierced grille. Thomas Holford, London 1801. 1¼in (3.2cm) by ¾in (1.9cm).

**Plate 56** Victorian shaped vinaigrette: formed as a 'cane-top'. The knob is of octagonal shape, and has an integral-hinged domed lid. Engraved with foliate motifs, and with simply pierced floral grille. Unmarked, *circa* 1850. 1½in (3.7cm) by 1¼in (3.2cm).

**Plate 57** William IV realistically cast cow vinaigrette, fully marked on the grille. Henry Wilkinson & Co., Sheffield 1834. 2½in (6.3cm).

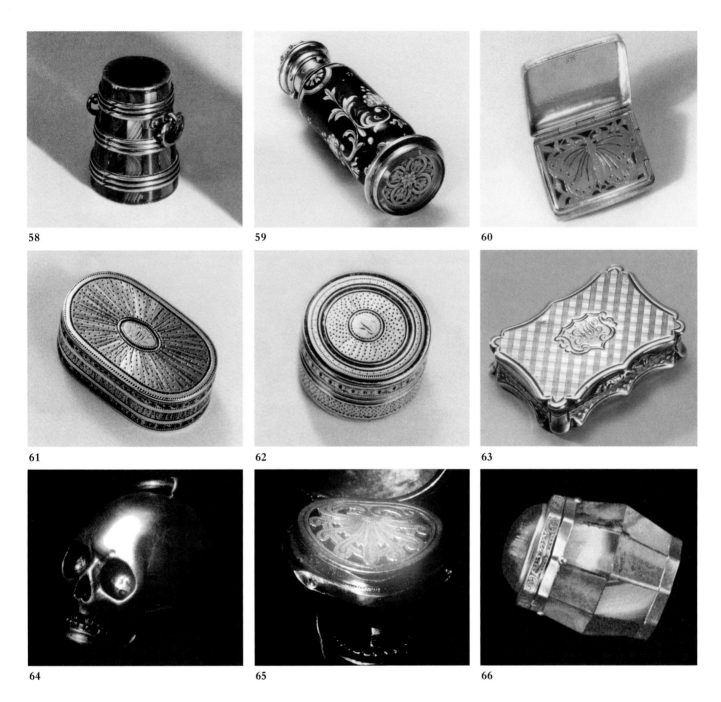

58

59

60

61

62

63

64

65

66

**Plate 58** Victorian silver-mounted Scottish vinaigrette formed as a milk churn, the sides set with panels of semi-precious stones: bloodstone, cornelian, agate, cairngorm, etc. The base is silver-gilt, with simulated 'hoops' and drop-down handles. The hinged lid is set with a panel of bloodstone, the grille pierced with a snowdrop motif. Charles Robb, Edinburgh 1855. 1½in (3.8cm).

**Plate 59** Victorian scent bottle-cum-vinaigrette, the body with enamel scrolling shells and foliage, the lid appliquéd with a contemporary monogram, the base a bevelled glass cover, and finely pierced quatrefoil grille. H W Dee, London 1872. 3¼in. (8.2cm).

**Plate 60** George III rectangular vinaigrette, the grille pierced with butterfly motif. Richard Lockwood & John Douglas, London 1800. 1in (2.5cm).

**Plate 61** George III oval vinaigrette, the lid decorated with raying bright-cutting, the centre with an oval cartouche. Phipps & Robinson, London 1796. 1½in (3.8cm).

**Plate 62** George III circular vinaigrette, the lift-off lid engraved with a raying bright-cut circlet inside a plain frame. Phipps & Robinson, London 1795. 1in (2.5cm).

**Plate 63** William IV Scottish rectangular vinaigrette, the lid applied with tartan engine-turning. James Naysmith, Edinburgh 1833. 1¼in (3.2cm).

**Plate 64** Victorian cast 'memento mori' skull-shaped vinaigrette, the fan-shaped hinged grille set in the lower jaw. With a gold suspensory loop. H W Dee, London 1877. 1in (2.5cm).
**Plate 65** Grille to No 12.

**Plate 66** Victorian gold-mounted Scottish 'pebble' vinaigrette of octagonal section, comprising multi-coloured agates, with a moss agate top. Unmarked, *circa* 1840. 2¾in (6.9cm).

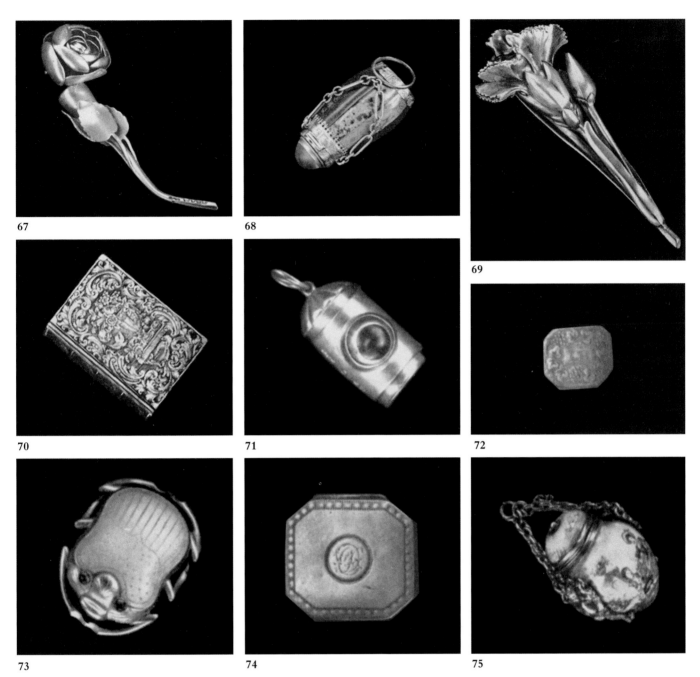

**67**

**68**

**69**

**70**

**71**

**72**

**73**

**74**

**75**

**Plate 67** Victorian silver-gilt rose vinaigrette, the flower-head bending back to reveal a tiny grille. Henry William Dee, London 1867. 3in (7.6cm).

**Plate 68** Victorian gold-mounted Scottish 'pebble' reticule, with a carrying ring. Etched with floral motifs. Deep receptacle, with a small circular grille. Unmarked, *circa* 1840. 2in (5.1cm).

**Plate 69** Victorian cast carnation vinaigrette, the grille hidden in a petal. Edward H Stockwell, London 1878. 3½in (8.9cm). Weight: 2oz (62.207g).

**Plate 70** Victorian finely acid-etched book vinaigrette, the covers with floral motifs and foliate cartouches, with 'Affection' engraved on the spine. Rawlings & Summers, London 1845. 1½in (3.8cm).

**Plate 71** A French lantern-type vinaigrette, with a tiny grille set in the base, *circa* 1840.

**Plate 72** George III very small cut-corner bright-cut vinaigrette. Richard Buckton, London 1818. ⅝in (1.6cm).

**Plate 73** A silver-mounted agate 'scarab' vinaigrette with ruby eyes, *circa* 1840.

**Plate 74** George III rectangular cut-corner simple bright-cut vinaigrette. Phipps and Robinson, London 1800. 1½in (3.8cm).

**Plate 75** A Viennese multi-chrome scent bottle cum vinaigrette, *circa* 1870.

**Plate 76** Victorian walnut-shaped vinaigrette, the pierced grille with a central 'starburst' and with a suspensory loop. Sampson Mordan, London, *circa* 1860. 1¾in (4.4cm).

**Plate 77** A French pinchbeck hurdy-gurdy vinaigrette, *circa* 1830, size 1¼in (3.1cm).

**Plate 78** A superb George III *pietra dura* oval top depicting butterflies and engraved with scrolling motifs. Alexander James Strachan, London 1827. 1¾in (4.4cm).
**Plate 79** The 'toxophile' grille.

**Plate 80** Filigree, The 'diaper' is from a French specimen, *circa* 1784.

**Plate 81** Victorian finely cast Tiger's Head vinaigrette, the jaws and fangs superbly delineated, the vinaigrette formed of the inside of the head, with a simply pierced floral grille. The circular lid is set with bloodstone, and the head has a suspensory loop. Sampson Mordan, London, 1860. 1in (2.5cm) by ¾in (1.9cm).

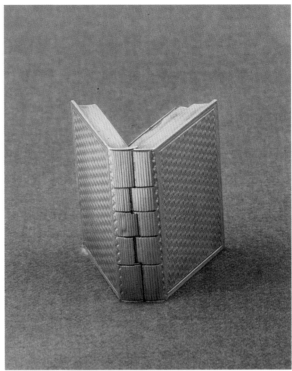

**Plate 82** Victorian shaped vinaigrette formed as a 'Policeman's Lamp', the conical lid with 'clasp' lifts up to reveal the grille. Sampson Mordan, London 1877, 2½in (6.3cm) by ⅞in (2.2cm) in diameter.

**Plate 83** George III silver-gilt shaped vinaigrette: formed as a superlatively designed book. John Reilly, London 1809. 1¼in (3.2cm) by 1in (2.5cm).

**Plate 84** A Victorian vinaigrette formed as a 'cauldron' on tripod legs with a swing handle. The lid has a baluster terminal. Thomas Johnson, London 1865. 1¼in (3.2cm) diameter.

Plate 85 An old label showing Fribourg & Treyer's sign of the rasp and crown, and also a carotte of tobacco at the left hand side at the top. Taken from *An Old Snuff House* by George Evans.

# Snuff and Snuff-taking

The practice of grinding leaves of tobacco for personal use, by inhaling the powder, is first mentioned in the 1650 'Letters' of James Howell, the noted 17th century lexicographer.

An advertisement in the *Spectator*, August 8th 1711 reads: 'The exercise of the Snuff Box, according to the most fashionable Airs and Notions in opposition to the exercises of the Fan will be taught with the best plain or perfumed Snuff at Charles Lillis's &C'.

Early snuff-taking had its own rituals: the snuffbox was taken from the pocket by the left hand, the fingers of the right gave the cover three taps, the box was opened and a pinch of snuff placed on the back of the left hand or on the thumbnail enclosed by the forefinger, and inhaled.

Fortunately for students of English snuff-taking, it is possible to have a 'look behind the scenes' of an early 18th century London tobacconist. In 1921 George Evans, a member of the well-known St. James's tobacco and snuff dealers Fribourg & Treyer of 34 The Haymarket, established in 1721, wrote a history of the firm celebrating its bicentenary. An account appears of some of its notable customers, prices, recipes for snuff-fragrances, and informative notes on how they were made.

Undoubtedly, their most prestigious client was the Prince of Wales, later George IV. The King and members of the Court stored large quantities of plain and scented tobaccos in special rooms, inspecting stocks from time to time, and replenishing their supplies.

86

87

Plate 86 George III Scottish snuffmull, the elongated receptacle of finely figured natural horn, the oval hinged lid set with polished agate in a scalloped bright-cut rim with a scrolling thumbpiece. Unmarked, the lid engraved with the owner's name, 'W. Innes'. *Circa* 1790. 5½in (14cm).

Plate 87 George III heavy ridged top snuffbox. Matthew Linwood V, Birmingham 1810. 2⅜in (6cm).

Plate 88 Queen Anne Scots silver-mounted horn snuff mull, engraved with 'diaper motif' on hinge and thumbpiece. Unmarked, *circa* 1710. 2¾in (7cm).

Plate 89 Early Victorian silver-mounted snuffbox formed as clog, the finely carved ivory container mounted with foliate silver lid. Hilliard & Thomason, Birmingham 1853. 3⅛in (7.9cm).

88

89

**90**          **91**

**Plate 90** Victorian semi-ovoid snuffbox with a domed hinged lid, engraved floral motifs and contemporary crest. John Tongue, Birmingham 1863. 1⅞in (4.6cm).

**Plate 91** Queen Anne oval snuffbox, the lid with Coronation bust of the Queen in full Garter Robes from a medal by John Obrisset, taken from the portrait by Sir Godfrey Kneller, shortly after the Queen's accession in 1702. With stand-away three-lugged hinge. Thomas Bevault, London 1712. 2⅝in (6.7cm).

**92**

**Plate 92** George III silver-mounted coconut shell formed as table snuffbox. The hinged lid engraved in centre with a horse driving a mill wheel, and debased 'egg and tongue' border. The scene perhaps a rebus on the owner's name, whose initials 'FHM' may have been 'Miller'. Unmarked, *circa* 1780. 5½in (14cm).

**93**          **94**

**Plate 93** William III lid from an oval snuffbox. The illustration is a miniature of a contemporary gallant who moves a black mask from his face, when a cornelian boss is operated by a concealed spring. It has a stand-away three-lugged hinge. Unmarked *circa* 1695. 3¾in (9.7cm).

**Plate 94** William III oval snuffbox, with a silver-gilt interior and stand-away hinge. The lid is mounted with a *verre églomisé* glass oval panel with a Charles I memorial plaque applied in gold on a black ground sandwiched between the back of a glass oval, and another glass panel. *Circa* 1700. 3in (7.6cm) by 2½in (6.3cm) by ⅜in (0.9cm).

When the King died in 1830, his valuable stock came on the market, but the high prices did not deter other clients. The eccentric Charles Stanhope, then Lord Petersham, 4th Earl Harrington, having already purchased 216 pounds of snuff in 1816 for £75, now obtained a further 101 pounds of several varieties of the King's snuffs for £80! He was one of the best known names in society during the Regency and the reign of George IV, figured frequently in contemporary prints, and was a compulsive snuff glutton, who invented the Petersham Snuff Mixture, and even

**Plate 95** *Left:* William III small shallow rectangular silver-mounted ivory snuffbox with three-lugged stand-away hinges. The yellowing ivory lid is carved with a 'Ceres and Cupid' motif and scallop shells in the corners. The hinges and the retaining clasp are of brass. Unmarked, *circa* 1695. 2¾in (7cm) by 2⅛in (5.4cm) by ¼in (6.35mm) deep.

*Right:* William III shallow rectangular silver-mounted ivory snuffbox with three-lugged stand-away hinges. The lid is carved with a basket of fruit and flowers motif, and scallop shells and a cherub in the corners and at the base. It has a simple shaped thumbpiece. Unmarked, *circa* 1695. 3in (7.62cm) by 2½in (6.3cm) by ¼in (6.35mm) deep.

wore a snuff-coloured overcoat. His room resembled a snuff-shop with snuff-jars labelled in gilt.

Many tobaccos had exotic names. Spanish Bran, popular from 1760 to 1815, was the most expensive among the King's snuffs, selling at £3 per pound. For moistening the powder, an aromatic rose-scented vinegar from Spain was sold in a phial.

Macouba, hailing from Martinique, was strongly scented with Otto of Rose. An oriental snuff from Masulipatam in India possessed such a powerful flavour that a quarter to half an ounce sufficed when added to a pound of snuff. Sabilla, a brick red powder, was popular as a tooth powder, and thought to keep away neuralgia.

Among other unusual names, Brazile was a slightly larger grained unscented powder, termed 'Fine', 'Demigros', and 'Gros' for the size of the grain, comprising fine, medium and coarse. Carotte was a coarsely grained tobacco roll before rasping. The familiar vegetable-shaped Carotte, which also translates as a 'plug', appears at top left of the fine 18th century Fribourg & Treyer Trade Label shown here.

The Carotte, also known as 'rapee' when made from a coarser leafed tobacco, was rolled from cured tobacco leaves from Brazil and Central America. It was rasped on silver or ivory-mounted pocket graters, ranging from 2in or 3in long (5.8cm to 7.6cm) to 12in (30.4cm) for household use.

A writer on snuffboxes added a wistful note. 'Expensive snuff-boxes are too well known to mention them, beyond that it is doubtful whether some of the very fine examples of the jeweller's art that are seen in museums, were often, if ever, in daily use'.

This is a fair point. As is well known, Kings, Czars and Ambassadors had full to overflowing drawers of spectacular bejewelled presentation snuffboxes to distribute for favours received and hoped for. These survive today as unblemished and unused *objets de vertu*. In fact, many of the heavy fine Georgian and Victorian boxes illustrated in this book are in quite pristine condition, and may have never seen even a speck of snuff!

**Plate 96** View of the hinges on the two ivory boxes opposite.

**Plate 97** A George III navette shaped double snuffbox. The lids and body are bright-cut with a guilloche border. Concealed jeweller's hinge, engraved with a laurel motif. The oval central aperture enabled the owner, by inserting his thumb, to offer snuff right and left. This feature is also seen on French boxes. George Cowdery, London 1784. Fully marked on the lids and with lions passant in both compartments. 3¾in (9.5cm) by 1¼in (3.2cm by 1½in (3.8cm) deep. Weight: 4oz (124.414g.).

**Plate 98 A-D** These exceptional pieces demonstrate the apotheosis of the English engraver's art. Both are unmarked, *circa* 1720-25.

A.

B.

**C.** The oval double-opening box is engraved with a party of knights approaching a castle. The sides illustrate interior scenes of knights with a King and a Philosopher. 3½ in (8.8cm).

*By courtesy of Brand Inglis, Esq.*

C.

The double snuffbox on page 46 displays a plasticity in the figures which is greatly reminiscent of the superbly conceived processing tricorned gentlemen encircling the Treby/Holdsworth Punchbowl by Paul de Lamerie, London 1723.

The highly important catalogue of the Paul de Lamerie Loan Exhibition, Goldsmiths' Hall 1990, contains a distinguished article by Mr Gerald Taylor, Keeper of the Ashmolean Museum, Oxford, which houses the Lamerie Punchbowl, with a learned discussion on the authorship of the ornament (p.52).

Mr Taylor implies that contrary to the widely held belief that William Hogarth executed the work, it could have come from the hand of his master, the noted silver-engraver Ellis Gamble. Mr Taylor adds: 'It has recently been discovered that Gamble was a partner with Paul de Lamerie in 1723, some three years after Hogarth had found the work "too limited in every respect".' Dismissing the claims of two other authorities whose ascriptions of early 18th century engraving tentatively suggested 'in the manner of Hogarth' and 'in exactly the style which Hogarth might be supposed to prefer', he says 'the engraving of the friezes around the Holdsworth punch bowl in no way accords with Hogarth's trade card, nor does it tally with any of his authenticated graphic work'.

In Mr Taylor's view Ellis Gamble and not William Hogarth executed the enrichment on the punchbowl, 'although Hogarth may have been employed by his recent master to provide drawings for the ambitious project. Nor can it be ruled out that Gamble took it upon himself to execute the engraving'. But, Mr Taylor cautiously adds: 'The names of the designer of the compositions of the Holdsworth punch bowl and the engraver therefore still remain undefined'.

The similarity to the engraving of the Lamerie Bowl, and the link with Ellis Gamble, must therefore surely apply also to this snuffbox, for it is stated to originate 'from the *atelier* of Ellis Gamble'.

**Plate 99** George IV rectangular oval cushion-shaped snuffbox. The lid has an integral-hinge, and the sides are engine-turned with alternating bands of barleycorn and wave motifs, the sides with cast hunting motifs. The thumbpiece is of the florally cast variety. John Jones III, London 1828. 3½in (8.9cm) by 2¼in (5.7cm) by ¾in (1.9cm) deep.

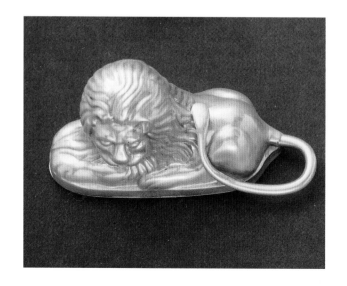

**Plate 100** George III lion-shaped snuff-box depicting a couchant lion of fierce countenance with a well modelled mane. Flat hinged base, the tail forming the handle. George Ashworth and Company, Sheffield 1812. 2½in (6.2cm) by 1⅜in (3.4cm).

# Vesta Cases

These attractive little boxes are now much in demand, after being spurned for many years. Of course, there were always isolated collectors who concentrated on British 'Vesta Cases' or American 'Match Safes', and from time to time choice specimens appeared in the saleroom and in antiques magazines.

The comparatively high prices now being paid for other types of box – vinaigrettes, snuffboxes, or nutmeg graters – led would-be collectors to this attractive, more reasonably priced type of container. Many hundreds of specimens exist, in a wide variety of materials, for example, gold, silver, enamels, treen, base metal, and niello.

Among the unusual British and American types are the 'advertising cases'. An interesting variation shows 'The Walk Over Shoe Company… America's Leading Boots and Shoes. Over 2,500,000 pairs made and sold in 1902'. One of the puzzle-lid boxes known as 'Ne Plus Ultra' – 'no more beyond' bears the legend 'How the devil do you open it, Charlie…have you got the rats?' There is a wide range of French 'Naughty Nineties' subjects, mainly seductively-clad beauties, and also 'figurals' displaying, among others, a series of boots and shoes (the sulphur-headed matches were struck on the soles), mailed fists, 'the man in the moon', a devil with red glass eyes, Mr Punch, violins, and many more.

Another quaint specimen was formed as an oval, ribbed fishing creel, the inner lid finely enamelled with a brace of salmon on a bed of tinted glass, 2¼ inches (5.7cm) wide. This was by the celebrated London novelties maker, Thomas Johnson, 1888.

The pieces illustrated have been selected for variety, rarity and quality of enrichment. The Victorian rectangular case, for instance, by Frederick Marson, Birmingham 1856, bears on the lid an engraving of a chimpanzee smoking a cheroot. The heavy box-type by Harris & Brownett, London 1853, possesses a 'go to bed' aperture. (The match was inserted in the tiny hole, and lit one's way in the dark.) Another unusual variation is the 'Camera Case', by George Unite, which illustrates a folding camera (the 'bellows type' was introduced in France in 1839).

In order to examine the type, how it evolved, and some of its early history, we must hark back to Roman and Neolithic times. The vesta case is a descendant of primitive firemaking implements, commencing with aboriginal wood-friction sticks, neolithic iron pyrites, nodules, 17th century flints, steels, and tinder boxes. 'Tinder' as the early kindling was known, comprised wicks made from twisted and charred rags, silk floss and a type of fungus found on trees, known as 'amadou', from *amadour,* the French for 'to wheedle' the spark into a flame.

Vesta cases arrived around 1832, with the advent of William Newton's patent wax taper match, containing a number of untwisted cotton threads covered in wax, and named for Vesta, the Roman goddess of hearth and household. They were retailed by Richard Bell of 22 Bread Street, London.

The 'vesta' was itself a development of the chemist John Walker, who in 1826 invented the 'Friction Match' which he sold from his shop at 59 Stockton High Street. The story of John Walker and his invention was told in 1909, by Michael Heavisides, the local printer and Stockton-on-Tees chronicler, in a tuppenny pamphlet, 'The true History of the Invention of the Friction Light by John Walker of Stockton-on-Tees April 1827'.

Walker's match was a three inch long splint, dipped in a paste of chlorate of potash, sulphide of antimony, gum arabic, and water. When dry, this mixture formed a hard head.

**Plate 101** Victorian vesta case-cum-travelling taperbox of severely plain form, engraved with a contemporary crest. It has a copper ridged striker forming a compartment for the vestas. One side is hinged to permit the taperstick (housed in lengthwise shallow groove) to drop down for use. Thomas Dexter, London 1846. 3in (7.6cm).

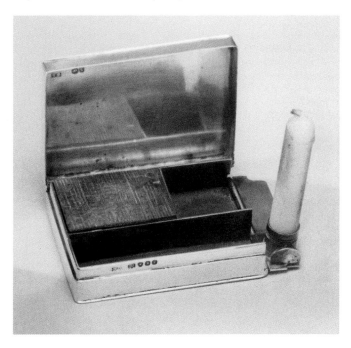

**Novelty vesta cases:**

**1.** Box-type, heavy gauge, engraved with scrolls, foliage and diapers, and a shaped central cartouche. With a 'Go to bed' aperture (the lighted match was placed in the tiny hole, and lit one's way in the dark). Harris & Brownett, London 1853.

**2.** Oval rectangular, striker on the back, with concentric engine-turning. William Neal, London 1859. 1¾in (4.4cm).

**3.** Rectangular with rounded ends, the lid enamelled with a blue Viscount's coronet and monogram. Double lidded, with striker on the side. Retailer: I Hudson, Oxford Street. Benjamin Barling, London 1849. 2¼in (5.7cm).

**4.** 'Roll-top lid', rectangular. Striker on the side. No maker's mark, Birmingham 1857. 2in (5.1cm).

**5.** Rectangular, double-lidded, with striker on the smaller lid. Foliate scrolling and engine-turning. William Phillips, Aylesbury Street, Clerkenwell, London 1844. 2⅛in (5.3cm).

**6.** Vinaigrette type, striker on the back and with tartan concentric engine-turning. Nathaniel Mills, Birmingham 1845. 1½in (3.8cm).

**7.** Small vertical rectangular, engraved on the lid with 'Chimpanzee smoking a cheroot'. Striker on side, with aperture for 'deadheading' the matches – to douse them. Frederick Marson, Birmingham 1856. 1¼in (3.2cm).

**8.** Large book, the striker is revealed when the lid slides forward. With arabesque ornament on a scored ground. Charles S Wallingford & Shirley Deakin, Birmingham 1858. 2¼in (5.7cm).

**9.** Smaller book, the spine serving as a striker. Engraved with foliate scrolls and a rococo cartouche. Nathaniel Mills, Birmingham 1848. 1¾in (4.4cm).

The famous 'Lucifer Match' appeared *circa* 1829, invented by another chemist, Samuel Jones of 'The Light House' 201 The Strand, London, who advertised 'S. Jones's Lucifer Matches that ignite by the friction produced by drawing the Match briskly through a piece of Sand Paper, and are warranted never to impair by keeping'.

Gradual and differing improvements, as well as colourful and permanent packaging improved the product. Around 1832, Jones introduced the 'Fusee Match', which substituted paper or amadou for a short length of smouldering fuse dipped in phosphoric inflaming composition.

From around 1860, vesta cases, cigarette boxes, for personal and table use, and gentlemen's travelling nécessaires sported a fuse of multi-coloured fabric, knotted at the end, for lighting cigars, pipes, etc. The use of such fuses permitted smokers to ignite their cigars in even the harshest gale. They were known as 'Alma Cords', probably from the 'Battle of the Alma', fought on the banks of the Russian river during the Crimean War of 1854. Fine Fabergé and other Russian and European boxes have also been noted.

The vesta case was equipped with a striker, either on the base, or a cog-wheel. Some boxes have a pierced aperture on one side of the lid, to sever the tip of a cigar. The 'striker' might be concealed as the spine of a book, or a ribbed integral lid. Ornament consisted of scrolling floral and diaper motifs, engine-turning, brightcutting and casting.

This small receptacle which many collectors find so attractive sadly lacks in-depth literature. Apart from a few pamphlets and collecting magazine articles, little appears in print.

**Novelty vesta cases:**

**1.** Lantern with hinged lid and glass reflector, with striker on the lid and 'Alma Cord'. Retailer: Asprey. H W Dee, London 1871. 1¼ in (3.1cm).

**2.** A bellows-type camera case, with 'Alma Cord' fuse in tube, engine-turning and diaper motifs, and suspensory chain. George Unite, Birmingham 1867. 2in (5.1cm).

**3.** Watch-type, with an 'Alma Cord'. This was probably named for the Battle of the Alma, in the Crimean War, scene of an important victory over the Russians on 20th September 1854. The cord, a slow-burning smouldering tinder, allowed the smoker to relight at will. Such fusees, with knotted ends, have been noted on Fabergé cheroot and cigarette cases; as these are usually in pristine condition, they were probably never used. Engraved with engine-turning and foliate motifs. Retailer: Carlin, 109 Regent Street. Benjamin Barling, London 1861. 2in (5.1cm) in diameter.

**4.** Larger watch-type, heavy gauge, and quite plain. Engraved with the coat-of-arms of the Earl of Bradford. With 'Alma Cord' and striker on the side of neck. Retailer: Bryant. Thomas William Dee, London 1864. 4½in (11.4cm) in diameter.

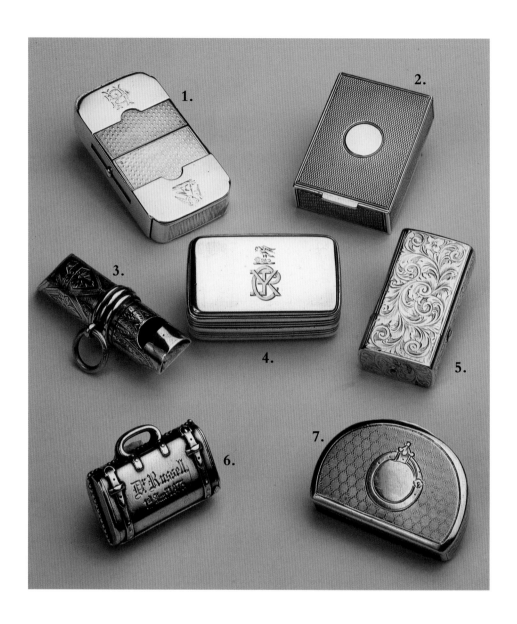

## Sundry shaped vesta cases:

**1.** Horizontal, rectangular: with double sliding lid and 'go to bed' aperture, striker on base, and floral scrolling. Alfred Taylor, Birmingham 1866. 2in (5.1cm).

**2.** Vertical rectangular with striker on the back. Engine-turned and with vacant plaque in centre. Henry William Dee, London 1866. 2in (5.1cm).

**3.** Whistle, the striker on the cut-away base. Florally bright-cut. Hilliard & Thomason, Birmingham 1874. 2½in (6.3cm).

**4.** Deep rectangular, with reeded sides. Striker on back, with hinged lid known as 'Ne Plus Ultra' ('No more beyond this') and with a contemporary crest. Retailer: Jenner & Newstub, 33 St James's Street. Thomas Johnson, London 1859. 2in (5.1cm).

**5.** Vertical rectangular, with 'go to bed' aperture in the lid, striker on the base, and with floral scrolling. Alfred Taylor, Birmingham 1866. 2in (5.1cm).

**6.** Gladstone bag, cast, with striker on the side and side opening. William Summers, London 1871. 1½ in (3.8cm).

**7.** Semi-oval, with striker on the back, diaper-type engine-turning and a buckled belt around a vacant circlet. Frederick Marson, Birmingham 1865. 1¾in (4.4cm).

**Vesta cases:**

1. Vertical rectangular, with push-piece on the lid, and a separate internal striker. Engine-turned and with floral motifs. Retailer: I Bryant, Oriol Street, Oxford. Benjamin Barling, London 1860. 2⅜in (6cm).

2. Oval, with slide action opening and striker on the base. H W Dee, London 1875. 2¼in (5.7cm).

3. Vertically opening lid, rounded ends and striker on the base. Engraved with two little bonneted girls – a 'Kate Greenaway' subject. Sampson Mordan, London 1881. 2in (5.1cm).

4. Sloping side rectangular, one side enamelled with a 'Swains Scene', probably based on music hall characters, and the motto 'Fly with me, sweet Gyurl', the other side with a study of 'saddled horse and two hounds'; the rims enamelled with scrolling foliage and yellow flowerheads. Joseph Hayes Taylor, London 1880. 2in (5.1cm).

5. Cushion-shaped, with striker on base. Henry Jones, Birmingham 1888. Jones entered his mark at the Birmingham Assay Office in December 1867, working to 1890, at 55 Great Hampton Street. 2in (5.1cm).

6. Queen Victoria's Golden Jubilee, vertical rectangular. Enamelled with the multi-coloured Arms of Great Britain, surmounted by the Imperial Crown and a white and blue enamel escutcheon, containing the Queen's intertwined monogram and 'Jubilee 1887'. Striker on the base. Sampson Mordan, London 1886. 2⅜in (6cm).

7. 'Pencil case', the sliding action lid set with studs and striker on the base. Floral and engine-turning. Edward & John Septimus Beresford, London 1879. 2in (5.1cm).

**Vesta cases:**

**1.** Couchant elephant, with striker on the side. Stokes & Ireland, Birmingham 1884. 1in (2.5cm).

**2.** Pen-knife, with pipe probe, twin pen-knife blades, and striker on the side. Retailer: Bryant. Louis Dee, London 1880. 3in (7.6cm).

**3.** Acorn shape, with striker on the base. Finely engraved. Gardner & Warr, Birmingham 1883. 1¾in (4.4cm).

**4.** Claret bottle, with striker on the base, inset with an enamel dog portrait. Thomas Johnson, London 1887. Opens at the base. 2¼in (5.7cm).

**5.** Mussel shell, with striker on the base. Hilliard & Thomason, Birmingham 1881. 2in (5.1cm).

**6.** Shoe, with striker on the lid. 'Here's the last' enamelled on the base. Jane Brownett & Alexander Jones, London 1877. 2¾in (6.9cm).

**7.** Carbide lamp, with red and clear glass reflectors, cowl-type hinged cover, and a suspensory ring. Striker on the base. William Osborn, Birmingham 1881. 2in (5.1cm).

**8.** Queen Victoria's Golden Jubilee, appliqué with 'Crown Imperial' and bust of the Queen on the other side. Florally engraved. Stokes & Ireland, Birmingham 1886. 1¼ in (3.1cm).

**9.** Vertical, with inset 'compass', sloping lid and striker on the base. Stokes & Ireland, Birmingham 1886. 1⅜in (3.4cm).

# The Victorian Scent Bottle

Among the many *objets-de-vertu* shown are a number of intriguing scent bottles, some of which double as vinaigrettes, mainly from the 1860-80s workshop of one of the more ingenious novelties makers, Henry William Dee.

Some of the finely conceived articles offered were a lady's fan, with a tiny circular vinaigrette on one of the delicately pierced 'sticks', dated 1877, another formed as a multi-coloured enamel horse-shoe, with the jockey-cap lid in alternating white and green racing colours, and white enamel 'nails', 1869, and a black enamelled tubular flask with white floral scrolls and foliate motifs, and the base with a superbly pierced quatrefoil grille behind a bevelled glass lid, 1872, and many more superb specimens.

The popular London stockist of these and other *bibelots* was the firm of Walter Thornhill of 144 New Bond Street. This famous retailer offered a wealth of unusual pieces.

In addition to toilet articles, the firm also stocked a series of silver-mounted glass claret jugs, formed as cockatoos, walruses, eagles, and lotus leaf motifs. Culme identifies the designer and silversmith Alexander Chrichton, the ingenious Edward H. Stockwell, and the modeller James Barclay Hennell as the creators of these attractive items. There were also cockatoo mustard pots.

No prices have been traced, but whatever their original cost, these are among today's highly sought-after 'wine related' antiques which command high figures in the auction houses and antiques shops. A magnificent silver-mounted olive-green glass cockatoo by Alexander Chrichton, 1882, was sold in 1993 for £10,500 in a London saleroom!

Although Walter Thornhill was primarily a stockist, the firm also produced its own novelties – pencils, chatelaines, cigar lighters, etuis, smokers' articles and pen-knives. The well-known 'fish pen knife' incorporating a knife blade, nail file, propelling pencil protruding from the mouth, and a 'cat-call' whistle in the tail first appeared in 1883, and bears the Patent Office Design Registry mark. It is 3½ inches (8.8cm) long. It may be added that the writer used such a fish penknife for many years without realising he could call his cat on its whistle!

### Victorian and Edwardian Smallwares

Very few illustrated price lists have survived. They must have been destroyed, or lost. Or perhaps they are in private libraries unavailable to researchers.

None the less some details do emerge. During an exhaustive search for the original cost of some of the beautiful scent bottles and other novelties from among the few illustrated trade journals, several interesting pieces surfaced, chiefly from the

**Plate 102** *Below left:* Victorian silver-mounted cannon-barrel vinaigrette-cum-scent bottle, the cannon mouth being the scent compartment, the breech containing the vinaigrette. The mounts repoussé with foliage and scrolls. Unmarked, but with Victorian Registration Marks for 1880. 3in (7.6cm).

**Plate 103** *Below centre:* Victorian fan-shaped silver-mounted scent bottle set with a circular vinaigrette, the end stick mounted with a small silver pencil. The ivory sides of the 'sticks' are arranged as 'dance cards'. Sampson Mordan, London 1870. 2⅞in (7.3cm).

**Plate 104** *Below:* Victorian silver-gilt scent bottle formed as a lady's fan. The florally pierced slide-away slide simulating the 'sticks' reveals ivory *aides-mémoirs*, either side. The hinged lid is opened by a 'push-piece', with suspensory chain and 'finger ring'. H W Dee, London 1877. 3¼in (8.3cm).

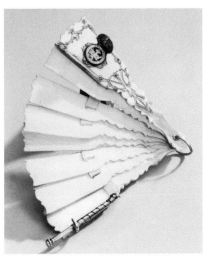

**Plate 105** Victorian scent bottle formed as a cast, silver-gilt and coloured enamel horse-shoe, the 'nails' in white enamel, the lid formed as a jockey's cap in alternating bands of black and green enamel. H W Dee, London 1869. 3in (7.6cm).

Sampson Mordan workshop. This firm, although specialising in pens and pencils, offered a range of novelty shaped pencils, but also made other *objets,* like bellows-shaped scent bottles, at 95/- (£4.75), shell portmanteau etuis for 5 guineas (£5.25), and 'Aladdin's Lamp spirit cigar lighters at 4 guineas, foiled champagne bottles at 30/-, 35/- and 40/- (£1.50, £1.75, and £2), and post-horn flasks at 17/6d (88p).

What, might one reflect, did the beautiful cast Rose, Carnation and Thistle, Balloon-vinaigrettes with suspensory baskets, the confections of the 1870s, by Thomas Johnson and Edward H Stockwell, cost originally?

### A Note on Some Popular Victorian Perfumes

The Jury which examined various wares submitted for the Great Exhibition in Hyde Park in 1851, showed a particular liking for an *Eau-de-Cologne* sent by an Austrian perfumier. It was not so much the fragrance of the toilet water that attracted notice, but the splendid fountain from which it was dispensed. Indeed, Joseph Farina's offering was so popular with the crowds that the supply ran out before the Jury could test the product. Eventually, an overlooked, unopened cask was found, and the Jury awarded the Cologne an 'honourable mention'.

Among its entries France sent some *vinaigrettes-de-toilet,* aromatic vinegars, with, of course, the usual attar of roses fragrance (which may still linger on a tiny dried-out sponge), and an attractive variant, 'Orange Flower Vinegar'. A book of contemporary recipes gives the ingredients:

> Fresh Orange Flowers 1½lbs.
> Distilled water     8 lbs
> Spirit of Orange Flowers 1 lb
> Macerate for 12 days, strain and filter.

### A Famous Ingredient

The well-known London perfumier Eugene Rimmel writing on 'The History of Perfumes' in 1868, learnedly discoursed on various topics connected with the craft. While discussing some ingredients, Rimmel rambled delightfully on Civet – a natural substance from the civet-cat, from whose glands this fragrance is made.

'An animal of the feline tribe, which is found in Africa and India. Formerly Dutch merchants kept some of these cats in long wooden cages, and had the perfume scraped from them two or three times a week with a wooden spatula. Civet, in the natural state, has a most disgusting appearance, and its smell is equally repulsive to the uninitiated, who would be tempted to cry out with William Cowper (*Conversation 1781*).

> I cannot talk with civet in the room
> A fine puss gentleman that's all perfume
> The sight's enough, no need to smell a beau
> Who thrusts his nose into a ★raree show.'
>
> ★*Raree Show: a peep show.*

Rimmel continues: 'Yet, when properly diluted and combined with other scents, it produces a very pleasing effect, and possesses a much more floral fragrance than musk. Its price varies from 20 shillings (£1) to 30 shillings (£1.50) per ounce, according to quality.'

Wood engraving of a civet cat, taken from *A General History of Quadrupeds* by Thomas Bewick, 1824.

**Plate 106** A shaped repoussé Victorian card case enriched with scrolls. The subject is the Gothic Kronborg Castle on the island of Zealand near Elsinore, the venue of Shakespeare's *Hamlet*. By legend the ghost appears on the flag battery, the platform before the castle. A famous *cause célèbre* took place in one of its apartments: Queen Matilda, daughter of Frederick, Prince of Wales, and sister of George III, the estranged wife of the deranged princeling Christian VII, was imprisoned there for her admitted infidelity with the adventurer Johann Frederick Struensee. Nathaniel Mills, Birmingham 1847. 3¼in (8.2cm) by 2⅛in (5.4cm).

Possibly this was a commissioned commemoration piece, as foreign subjects from the Mills' workshop are extremely uncommon.

## The Silver Card Case

Lovers of English silver, particularly from the William IV and Queen Victoria periods, are familiar with the shallow rectangular boxes known as 'card cases', the relics of a gracious age which flourished from the 1830s until about 1865. These attractively designed containers are die-struck, acid-etched or engraved with topographical views, and usually originate in Birmingham.

The ornament matches the ornament on other die-stamped or engraved snuffboxes and vinaigrettes, but because the surface was larger, the designers-cum-die-sinkers became more ambitious, drawing on the graphic arts, and introducing stylised floral and geometric designs based on Classical motifs. Examples might celebrate for instance, royal events and notable anniversaries, with the British emblems – Tudor roses, thistles, crowns or busts of Shakespeare, the Duke of Wellington and Queen Victoria.

Among some of the less common subjects were the Wellington memorial at Hyde Park Corner, Nelson's Column (sans the Landseer lions), St John's College, Cambridge; Christ Church, Oxford; the Tower of London from the Thames; Norwich Cathedral; Whitehall; Worcester Cathedral; Chatsworth House and Alnwick Castle, the Northumbrian ancestral home of the Percys.

An outstanding example of die-sinking and stamping from the Mills workshop, Birmingham 1847, depicts the Danish castle at Kronborg, near Elsinore. This is illustrated here by courtesy of an important silver box collector.

The practice of leaving calling cards had early beginnings. An XII Dynasty (1991-1786 BC) Egyptian nobleman, after attending a temple to worship, would leave behind a man-shaped figural glazed tile struck with his initials and titles. The Chinese too developed an intricate ceremonial. As recorded by two Jesuit missionaries in 1688 when a Chinese gentleman made a call on another, he first sent in a long scroll giving his titles and honours.

Members of high society, living at Versailles within the feudalism of Louis XIV's court, quit when the King aged and decamped to Paris to build themselves fine town houses, keeping contact by paying calls on one another. They welcomed the advent of the calling card, finding it simpler to leave a memento of their visit. The practice soon spread. A Florentine diarist recorded in 1731 that the custom had been brought from Spain by diplomats, and was widely popular.

Before the arrival of the printed or engraved card, playing cards were pressed into service, cut into segments and inscribed with the caller's name. A Parisian paper merchant advertised 'cartes pour visite' in 1760, engraved with elegant rococo scrolling and serpent motif frames.

In 1796 Lady Bessborough paid the famous Florentine painter Francesco Bartolozzi £20 to engrave her 'visiting card'. This noted engraver also produced visiting cards for Sir Joshua Reynolds and 'Mrs Parker, Sackville Street'. This fashionable Mayfair address was just off Piccadilly. Foreign cards were avidly collected and became sought-after souvenirs of the Grand Tour.

'Visiting' or calling cards arrived in England in the late 1780s, but continued well into the 19th century. In due course, the custom evolved of turning corners down. Messages could be left by using the stratagem of dog-earing one or all four corners, each of which bore an abbreviated code. Cards which were turned up at the corner meant that they had not 'been left by a lackey'.

An important collection of visiting cards contained sheets of calling cards with sets of frames, and landscapes. From the 1840s, embossed American cards were on glossy paper, and in Belgium they were printed in rainbow colours of gold, silver and bronze. There were cards from Spain, Germany, even Russia, illustrated with a variety of motifs – palaces, easels, cherubs and a coach and horses, all with a label for the name.

# The Box Hinge

Most box-hinges recorded, whether of ecclesiastical or secular function, were until the beginning of the 18th century of the 'knuckle and lug' variety. That is, the lid would have the 'lug' or ears, and the base would have the 'knuckles', which then united the top and bottom of the box by means of the traverse 'pintle' or bolt. Thus, most hinges would have three, five or even seven knuckles and lugs, which for brevity's sake will henceforth be referred to as 'lugged'.

The first signs that the hinge had become an important feature of 'fastening' arrived with the ivory Diptychs (folding Altar-pieces composed as two leaves) of the late 13th-early 14th centuries, which have base-metal 'three-lugged' hinges cut into the ivory and which, like their later descendants, the Netherlands boxes, stand-away from the edge, to permit the plates to open fully, yet also allow them to close fairly tightly.

This 'knuckle and lug' feature is not confined to French and Flemish work, but may be observed on Italian, Spanish and German Diptychs, Triptychs (three-fold panels) and Caskets. This 'three-lugged' method of fastening was, of course, carried to the hinges of vessels, and tankards, ewers, and even the mounts of coconut cups, shells and mazers all possessed them.

Most hinges of the 17th century are of the stand-away type, and possess three or five lugs and, very often, this feature alone can reveal an important clue to the age of the article, even in the absence of any marks. An interesting and curious example

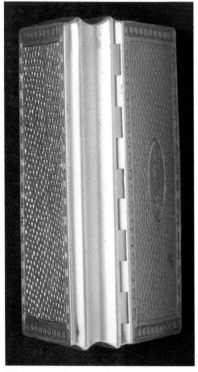

**Plate 107** Tenon and mortise hinge of the box shown on page 88

of the foreign stand-away hinge is to be found in William Hone's *Table Book*, dated London 1827. This illustrates (pp.527-9) an intriguing large heart-shaped silver box with stand-away three-lugged hinges at either side of the rims. The receptacle is engraved to simulate the human heart, and the story surrounding the article is macabre yet fascinating.

Lord Edward Bruce, son of Sir Edward, baron of Kinloss, was killed in a duel at Bergen-op-Zoom, a small Dutch town not far from the Flemish border. The date was 1613. Tradition had maintained that Bruce's heart was sent home and interred in the old abbey church of Culross in Perthshire. Bruce had been challenged by Sir Edward Sackville on what appears to be a 'trumped-up' charge. In 1808, a search was made and a silver box containing the embalmed heart was found. After a careful sketch had been made (which Hone illustrates) the relic was reinterred.

Here, then, is an unimpeachable Netherlands specimen of the stand-away type of hinge of early 17th century provenance, and when it is further recalled that the little oval spiceboxes are enriched with amatory motifs of early Dutch origin and that, furthermore, they almost invariably possess three or five-lugged stand-away hinges, this origin is thereby confirmed, although of course, the articles themselves were made in England.

The inference that because they are usually found in three subtly soldered sections does not preclude them from being purely English in origin. The clever English craftsmen, having already copied the enrichment and emblems from Dutch and other foreign influences, would hardly hesitate to employ foreign methods, though the normal type of English box would have been 'hand-raised'. The larger oval snuffboxes with the same type of stand-away hinge might thus also be originally of Netherlands influence.

**Plate 108** George III silver-mounted cowrie-shell of very small size, formed as snuffbox. The shell, which is of the genus *Cypraea Arabica*, or Arabian Cowrie, has a superbly fitted hinged lid. This is engraved with arabesques and the owner's monogram. Unmarked, *circa* 1770. 1¼in (3.2cm) by ⅝in (1.6cm). The hinge (illustrated below) is a miracle of the hinge-maker's craft, and is of the 'tenon and mortise' variety, that is, the five projecting lugs of the lid fit tightly into the corresponding apertures of the mount. When closed, the hinge is completely invisible.

### The Eighteenth Century Hinge

The advent of the 18th century brought one important development: the hinge was gradually moved away from the rim of the container towards the centre. Thus, an oval silver-mounted cowrie-shell snuffbox would have a band of delicate diaper engraving at both the apex and the nadir of the box, that is, there would be a disguised hinge within the top band of the diaper engraving, probably of the five-lugged variety, and no hinge at all in the bottom design, but both motifs would be exactly matching. The engraved ornament, of course, would be quite symmetrical both top and bottom. Sometimes, when it was not possible to engrave top and bottom bands of embellishment on the lid, attention would be drawn away from the hinge by means of a grotesque mask engraved within a cartouche of foliate motifs and, of course, in the case of the bright-cut specimens, where the quality of the engraving was such that the brilliant facets distracted the eye completely, it might not even be considered necessary to disguise the hinge at all.

### The Nineteenth Century Hinge

The 'integral hinge' so beloved of writers on snuffboxes, while a feature of French and German containers from the early 1730s, was quite well-known on other hinged articles – Dutch 'Marriage Caskets', Hispano-Moresque Caskets, Iberian Caskets, from the 15th to the mid-17th centuries – on any article, in fact, where fine workmanship was demanded. The traverse pin within the finely rolled hinged cylinder which was soldered to the very edge of the bezel eventually developed as an inexpensive type of hinge, and from the early 1820s, is found on almost all hinged lid receptacles. Sometimes, as in the work of the Birmingham craftsmen of the mid-1840s, the hinge was so successfully disguised that it may be deduced that a specialist hinge-maker might have spent days (at a time when labour was all too cheap) on one superlative article. It has been endeavoured, in this present work, to illustrate the virtuosity of the various schools of hinge-makers, as this minor art is so frequently taken for granted.

# CHAPTER 2

# Boxes with Royal Associations

## *The Barber Surgeons' Case*

The detailed inventories of the instrument cases in the preceding chapter have a particular bearing on the first item in this chapter on 'Royal Relics'. It is a most curious phenomenon that many articles which appear gruesome and frightening if they belong to ordinary people, suddenly take on a new and compelling interest if they have belonged at any time in their long history to a Royal personage.

Thus, by courtesy of the Worshipful Company of Barbers, appears a most exciting early 16th century receptacle with elaborate and fascinating Royal associations. This, is, of course, the famous 'Barber-Surgeons' Case' given by King Henry VIII to the Barbers *circa* 1512. Quite apart from the interest of its patron, the article itself is a most superlatively constructed 'box' possessing, on the one hand, most elaborate enrichment and, on the other, a primitiveness which betokens its great age.

The peculiar fascination which surrounds this beautiful instrument case is all the more heightened by the fact that, until the mid-1930s, its very existence was unknown and, indeed, no mention is made of it in the official History of the Company of Barber-Surgeons. To quote the account relating to the Case issued by the Worshipful Company of Barbers: 'There is every evidence that it was made to the order of Henry VIII, for presentation to the Barbers' Company, who practised minor surgery as well as the craft of "Barbery", an important body in Henry's day, and of whom he became patron on granting them a charter in 1512. It may have been on the occasion of his Coronation, the tradition being that the City Livery Companies were represented in the Coronation procession and that the official appointed to this duty carried an emblem representative of his trade or guild. Whatever the event or the reason of the gift it was undoubtedly given before 1525 as the Greyhound supporter to the Arms was only used by Henry VIII until that year, when it was replaced by the lion.

The presence on the Case of the enamelled Arms of the Barbers and, below that, separately, the cognizance of the Surgeons' Company, establishes the fact that it was given to these bodies before the granting of the combined Arms in 1540.'

The Account continues: 'This silver Case is in the form of an upright standing box 7¼ inches high, is of oblong section 2¼ inches by 2 inches at the top and slightly tapering towards the base, from which projects, for a few inches lower, a smaller piece of similar section. The cover is loose but is retained in position by the wood and leather interior which finishes above the lip of the body, thus forming a bezel over which the cover fits. A length of chain fastened at each end to a ring held in the mouth of a lion's mask on both sides of the body passes through rings, attached similarly to the cover, and so further secures the cover in position whilst allowing it to be raised. The corded and moulded borders that outline the case are gilt, leaving the flat surfaces of silver.

On the front of the body of the Box, which has a recess each side, in which are niched and canopied figures of Saints Cosmo and Damian, the Patron Saints of the Barbers' Company, are enamelled the Arms of the Company, viz: Sable a chevron between 3 fleams [a kind of ancient lancet] argent, which were granted to them by Edward IV, in 1462.

On the front of the cover, also enamelled in colour, are the Royal Arms of Henry VIII. Applied in relief are the Greyhound and Dragon Supporters used by Henry VII, and until 1525 by his successor; the whole being surmounted by the Royal Crown. Below the Arms of the Company on the body of the box, and also in relief,

**Plate 109** Henry VIII instrument case known as the 'Barber-Surgeons' Case'. Parcel-gilt, that is, partially gilt. All sides, the top and base, front and back of the case are illustrated, and the article is fully described in the text. Unmarked, *circa* 1512. 7¼in (18.4cm). Top section 2¼in (5.7cm) by 2in (5.1cm).

*Courtesy of the Worshipful Company of Barbers*

is a "spatula surmounted by a rose crowned", a cognizance [device in heraldry borne for distinction by all the retainers of a noble house, whether they bore 'Arms' or not] granted to the Surgeons' Guild by Henry VII in 1492. Being a cognizance, not a coat-of-arms, the device is shown thus, instead of in a shield. Under Henry VIII, the Company of Surgeons was incorporated with the Barbers' Company and the Arms of the two united. The Companies were again dissolved by an Act of George II, but the Arms of the Barbers' Company still retain the charges which properly belong to the Company of Surgeons.

The back of the body is engraved (in a panel) with a subject representative of the Martyrdom of Thomas a Becket (the choice of subject being strange, for the memory of the Saint was unpopular with the autocratic monarch. Becket had maintained the primacy of spiritual power against the temporal power of the monarchy, whereas Henry had maintained opposite principles when he proclaimed himself supreme head of the English church; it has to be remembered, of course, that this gift was given long before the King's involvement with the Pope over his Divorce with Queen Catherine of Aragon). On the cover portion is an engraved panel depicting St. George slaying the Dragon.

On the right side it is enriched by engraving in foliate scrolls, and a mask and a figure of Cupid. Below this, in its niche, rests a beautifully modelled figure of St. Catherine, the Saint of Healing. Turning to the left side, a similar style of engraving will be seen, introducing grotesque masks, while below, opposite to St Catherine, and similarly placed, is a figure of St John. On the cover section on the same side, around the gilt lion's mask through which the chain passes, are mermen and dolphins.

In red enamel, silver and gilt on the top of the cover, is the Tudor Rose, supported again, as in the case of the Arms, by the Greyhound and Dragon, the whole being surmounted by the Royal Crown. On removing the cover, is revealed a wood and leather fitment with divisions for surgical instruments, which latter unfortunately have not survived.'

It will now be apparent why so much emphasis was placed earlier on the surgical instruments in shagreen cases. Medicine, especially surgical instruments, did not alter very much between the 16th and 17th centuries, and while the instruments contained in the magnificent Barber-Surgeons' Case would probably have been enriched with glowing enamels and inlaid with damascened precious metals, their

form and functions would probably have differed little from the silver instruments made almost a century and a half later.

In his wonderful appraisal of *English and Scottish Silver Spoons*, written in collaboration with Mrs Jane Penrice How, the late Commander G. E. P. How, RN, in dealing with the identities of the Apostles appearing on the 'Barber-Surgeons' Case' said the following: 'This quite lovely Mediaeval object is fully described in the

*Catalogue of Silver-Work Bronzes Etc – Lee Collection*, by W. W. Watts, as follows: "On the front are figures of SS Cosmo and Damian, patron saints of doctors, whilst between the figures is an enamelled shield of the Arms of the Company granted by Edward IV in 1462. Below the Company's arms is a Spatula surmounted by a crown and a Tudor rose – a cognizance granted by Henry VII to the Surgeons' Guild in 1492. On the front also appear the enamelled arms of Henry VII; the royal supporters, a greyhound and dragon, being those in use before 1525 when they were replaced by the lion and unicorn".

Although unmarked, this case can thus be dated with certainty to between the years 1492 (when Henry VII granted the crown and Tudor Rose to the Guild) and 1509, the end of the reign of Henry VII.★

We are only concerned with the figures on this case, which, as can be seen from the illustration, could easily be adapted as spoon finials, even to the pediments on which they stand. Those here illustrated on the front are the brothers, SS Damian and Cosmo, Patron Saints of medicine. Both these figures are represented as young unshaven men, one, to dexter, carrying the water bottle in his left hand, and an object not clear, possibly a book, in his right; the other, to sinister, carries the Pot of Ointment in his left hand, his right hand being held across the body, but apparently with intent to hold the draperies rather than in blessing (see St John on side of the case). No spoons topped with the figures of these Saints are known to exist, or to be mentioned in records, but they may well have been made to special order for members of the Barber Surgeons' fraternity. On the dexter side of the instrument case is the figure of the clean-shaven St John, the Cup held in his left hand, the right hand held across the body. Here, as with SS Damian and Cosmo on the front of the case, the figure could easily be adapted as a spoon finial, and in all probability the model is one used for the purpose in the late 15th-early 16th century... On the sinister side of the case is the figure of St Catherine, known from wills and inventories to have been employed as a finial on spoons though no genuine English examples so topped are at present recorded.

Here the beautifully modelled Saint carries her emblem of the Sword, apparently sheathed, in her right hand; one of the quillons (the arms forming the cross-guard of the sword) would seem to have been broken off. At her feet is the Wheel, the emblem of her martyrdom, and in her left hand she carries a book. This model may well have been one of those used as spoon finials in the early 16th century'.

This excellent analysis of the figures on the Case could hardly have been bettered; coming from the greatest authority on Apostle Terminals, it must be considered the final word on the identity of the Saints and their Emblems.

Something ought to be said about the Barber-Surgeons themselves. Until quite recently, it was widely believed that the Barbers were merely itinerant mendicants, practising 'quack' medicine, while at the same time pursuing their normal trade, but modern research has established that many of these 'Barber-Surgeons' were, in fact, educated men of medicine, who studied and spoke Latin, and, within the limits of their day, knew as much about primitive surgery as many accredited surgeons. Their vocation has always attracted much attention and thus a 'tradition' has sprung up around them of haphazard 'surgery'. It has to be remembered that some of the accepted methods in use in the late 16th century were of equal barbarism but people who had little to lose underwent 'operations' from which, surprisingly, quite a few survived.

★*Note*
Commander How's assertion that the Case can be dated 'with certainty' to between 1492 and 1509 (which would make it of Henry VII provenance) and the official text issued by the Worshipful Company of Barbers ascribing it to *circa* 1512 (which would date it as of Henry VIII origin) are not, in reality, greatly contradictory: the former is based on the Commander's great scholarship in relation to the types of terminals on spoons, the latter on the type of 'cognizance' applied on the front of the case. Either way, there is a divergence of three years, which period does not materially alter the approximate dating.

# The King's Hair

On 30 January 1649 (1648 according to the contemporary reckoning) King Charles I suffered the supreme penalty. With his death, this sad and often macabre tale begins.

The embalmed remains were privately interred without much delay, having been brought on a disguised boat up an icy River Thames, repeatedly hindered by ice floes. The boat contained the decapitated body of Charles I, who had just been beheaded for treason. At Chertsey the party had to be 'poled off' by local fishermen, it avoided Parliamentarians at Datchet and finally managed to reach the Castle at Windsor. The Puritans, fearing that were the exact site of the tomb known, it might become a martyr's shrine, insisted on a secret interment, unattended by burial rites or other ceremonies. The King's courtiers were eventually granted grudging permission to bury him in St George's Chapel, Windsor, in a vault already occupied by King Henry VIII and his third wife, Queen Jane Seymour.

After the Restoration, Charles II would have liked to re-inter his Royal Father in a place more befitting the martyred King, but it was found, inexplicably, that the exact site of the tomb had been forgotten: whether as a result of the mutilations which the Puritans had made to the Chapel, or because in their haste the courtiers had failed to mark the spot, is not known. There the matter languished for another 160 years.

It was not an altogether unhappy accident, therefore, that during reconstruction work in St George's Chapel in the year 1813, workmen engaged in the task of building a mausoleum in the Tomb-house, accidentally breached one of the walls of a vault. They found therein not only the coffins of King Henry VIII and his Queen, but also a third, covered in a black velvet pall, and bearing a leaden plate inscribed 'King Charles 1648'.

### Sir Henry Halford

At this juncture, the name of Sir Henry Halford makes its appearance, and as it is one which will recur constantly in this account, it is necessary to cite something of its pedigree and associations with the Martyr King.

### Of Royal Descent and Royalist Ancestry

In addition to being the Physician to King George III, and President of the Royal College of Physicians (and thus eminently suited to preside at a Royal exhumation) Halford (1766-1844) was also a scion of a noble Royalist family which, furthermore, bore a direct lineal descent from King Henry III (1216-1272), his own position being 18th in succession. His ancestor, Sir Richard Halford, had been a loyal supporter of King Charles, who knighted him in 1641. During his campaign at Naseby, Charles slept at Wistow, Halford's Leicestershire estate for a few days before the Battle, and would have returned there after his defeat had he not been 'so closely pursued that he did not dare to stay to have his saddle changed'. The King's saddle and that of Prince Rupert, who accompanied him, were left at Wistow.

It will accordingly be apparent that Henry Halford was considered no mere medical practitioner, but a staunch Royalist in his own right. The invitation to attend that historic exhumation on the first Thursday of April, 1813 was spontaneously extended, but might have been less enthusiastic had there been a premonition that Halford would take advantage of an unhappy and distressing accident to despoil the remains of Charles I.

### The Exhumation

Halford himself published an innocuous account of the opening of the King's casket, which described in detail the similarity of the features with those in Van Dyck's famous portrait of Charles I – thus proving beyond all possible doubt that at long last his remains had been discovered. He also described the burial vault, and listed those present at the opening: The Prince Regent, The Duke of Cumberland, the Dean of Windsor (in

**Plate 110** William IV oval elliptical snuffbox with a delicate foliate rim and reeded sides, and a gold rim to the original bevelled glass lid with 'stand-away' hinge. Under the glass is a lock of King Charles I's hair (fully described in *The King's Hair*) on a faded blue velvet pad. James Scott, Dublin 1831. 3⅜in (8.6cm) by 2¼in (5.7cm) by 1⅛in (2.9cm) deep.

whose care the remains reposed), Count Munster, Benjamin Charles Stevenson, Esq., and Halford himself. Stevenson was also a descendant of a loyal Royalist family.

Fortunately for the sake of historical accuracy, an anonymous contemporary account described what actually took place. The exhumation, contrary to popular belief, was not the result of a carefully planned arrangement, but one made on the spur of the moment. When the Prince Regent was informed that a casket bearing King Charles's name had been discovered in St George's Chapel, he immediately adjourned to the vault together with such gentlemen as were in his company (pausing only to summon Halford and the Dean). The only persons available to open the casket were a plumber and his lad, who happened to be working in the precincts at the time, and to these unskilled artisans fell the task of removing the King's cere-cloth, and exposing the Royal visage. This delicate operation was accomplished with a chisel! The plumber, poor man, was undoubtedly extremely nervous. Obeying the Prince's instructions to lift out the head, he did so, and promptly dropped it on the floor, whereupon the Prince swore at him and left the chamber in disgust. Halford's subsequent claim that a piece of bone had remained unnoticed when the casket was closed up again, and that the Prince Regent, rather than disturb the remains, presented him with the relic, is thus manifestly shown to be untrue.

### Halford's Relic-Snatching

Henry Halford, who was disliked by many for his hauteur to inferiors and subservience to superiors, and known accordingly as the 'Eel-backed Baronet', had one failing above all others: he was an inveterate gossip and loved to indulge in anecdote. The opportunity thus offered to him by the absence of the Prince was too tempting, and he led a general 'relic-snatching'. He removed the King's fourth cervical vertebra, and portions of the hair of the beard and head. Stevenson went even further and desecrated Henry VIII's casket (which was much decayed) removing a tooth of the mighty Tudor.

Oddly enough, the Prince Regent, who must have known that something unethical had occurred after he left the vault, as he himself had obtained a lock of King Charles' hair to give to his daughter Princess Charlotte, said nothing to Halford; in fact, he gave him his 'Certificate of Authenticity' when the account was published. Apparently Halford was not despised by his contemporaries for removing portions of the Royal hair, as this practice was quite widespread during the preceding centuries – in 1784, for instance, the body of Mary Tudor was disturbed, and two feet lengths of her hair were annexed. These were subsequently sold at the

Duke of Buckingham's sale at Stowe in 1848. Similarly in 1786, the remains of Queen Catherine Parr were disturbed and various relics removed.

What really enraged the Royal Family and indeed all decent citizens, was Halford's deplorable practice of wearing the King's vertebra on a fob-chain and displaying it to all and sundry. He was particularly fond of shocking his guests at dinner by showing them the relic and saying 'Here is a piece of Charles the First'.

### The Return of the Relic

To the consternation of his friends, Halford made no attempt to deny the allegations that he had behaved unethically. In fact, he continued to flaunt the relic, and even had a gold-lined box made for it, with a suitable Latin inscription. It was only many years after his death that his grandson, Sir Henry St John Halford, deciding that it was time for the relic to be returned to its original source, offered it back to the Queen. Sir Henry was summoned to Marlborough House, where the Prince of Wales received it from him on behalf of the Queen and, 'by saying no word of thanks and turning his back, made it plain, to the great distress of the dear old man, that he supposed the relic to have been improperly come by'.

The final chapter of this sorry tale was written in a brief statement in *The Times*, 17 December, 1888:'The Prince of Wales on Thursday visited St George's Chapel, Windsor, and replaced in the vault containing the coffin of Charles I certain relics of that monarch which had been removed during some investigations more than seventy years ago. These relics having ultimately come into the possession of the Prince of Wales, he decided, with the sanction of the Queen, to replace them in the vault from which they had been taken, but not to disturb the coffin of the King. The Dean of Windsor was present.'

In 1964, an Irish snuffbox made in Dublin in 1831 came to hand. The lid was formed as a glassed-in compartment containing a lock of greying-auburn hair resting on a blue velvet pad. Inside the box, written on a small piece of card, and stuck into the bottom with mucilage, was the following inscription: 'The hair beneath the glass lid of this box is that of King Charles the First. It was obtained when the coffin of the King was opened in 1813: after a search had been made for it in St George's Chapel, Windsor, and was given to my father J. H. Cochrane by a relative of one who was present at the time. HLC.' (It is obvious that the aforesaid gentleman had the Snuffbox specially made to accommodate the Relic.)

The ascription was extremely interesting, but was it conclusive? After all, the Victorians were notorious for their fondness of ascribing relics to various mythical celebrities, and this specimen could have been purely apocryphal. It was therefore decided to submit a minute sample to modern chemical analysis. After much difficulty (no-one felt sufficiently competent to undertake such a delicate task) the services of Dr Richard Spearman, a distinguished dermatologist from University College Hospital (who had made a study of this very subject, namely, the analysis of ancient, even pre-historic human hair) were obtained.

Having found him, what properties was he to look for? Well, firstly, the approximate age of the hair, and secondly, the presence on the hair of any embalming fluids. It was known, from contemporary records, that the King had been embalmed by the 'Chirurgeon Trapham' in 1649, and it was possible to discount the possibility that the hair was not that of the King, it being quite unthinkable to disinter an ordinary embalmed body and remove from it any portion of the hair. After massive research in the Reading Room of the British Museum, it was discovered that the contemporary methods of embalming would have involved the use of certain resins and waxes, and upon receiving this information, the analyst was able to proceed. No more than three hairs were removed from the lock, and upon these, the fascinating modern scientific processes were performed.

### The Analyst's Report

*'A Report on a sample of Human Hair said to have come from Charles the First*

The hairs were examined microscopically to determine possible chemical alteration as a result of ageing and the use of embalming preparations. The hairs were also examined to find out whether they were from the scalp or the beard. The possibility that they had been dyed was also investigated.

### Appearance by Fluorescence Microscopy

The hairs when examined microscopically under ultra-violet light had a brighter self fluorescence than modern human hair. This bright fluorescence was reduced in hairs soaked overnight in an organic solvent, xylene, to remove embalming substances. Some resins, such as canada balsam, have a similar blue self fluorescence, and this suggests that the hairs were treated with some resinous substance, possibly rosin. I have not, however, examined the fluorescence of rosin.

Air bubbles are found in the centre of old hairs, but none were seen in this sample. Air normally enters through the damaged hair cuticle; this may, however, have been prevented in this instance by substances applied to the hair during embalming.

### Fluorescence of Hair stained in 0.1% Acridine Orange

Hairs stained in this fluorescent dye and then examined microscopically under ultra-violet light showed a patchy orange fluorescence. This indicates damage to the chemical structure of the hair mainly confined to the hair cuticle. The effect was very similar to the changes we have found in hair from dynastic Egyptian mummies.

### Hair Colour

The hair is lighter brown than the scalp hair shown in portraits of Charles the First in the National Portrait Gallery although the beard is shown as a lighter reddish brown. Since, however, the present specimen appears to be scalp hair, it must have faded if it came from Charles the First. [Note: The learned Doctor has obviously overlooked that these old portraits in the Gallery are uncleaned, and that the colour thus shown to be darker than the specimen of hair, was originally much lighter in life.]

Some fading sometimes occurs in old hair, and we have found that modern dark hair became slightly darker in colour after being buried for eighteen months in soil.

If at any time in its history this sample had been exposed to light, as in a show case, this could cause fading from a darker to a somewhat lighter brown colour.

I soaked some hairs overnight in warm dilute hydrochloric acid which should remove henna. As the colour of the hair was unchanged after this treatment, the hair was probably not dyed.

### Conclusion

These findings are consistent with the view that the hair sample is old and that it has in the past been treated in some embalming preparation. It appears to be scalp hair and is not dyed. The only inconsistent feature is its light colour, but this could have resulted from fading. Therefore, I believe that this hair sample could have come from Charles the First.'

### Stuart Relics

Not surprisingly, there are few fully authenticated Stuart Relics. The important Stuart Exhibition held in London at the New Gallery in 1889 contained many genuine relics, among them the pitiful possessions given by King Charles to his faithful Groom of the Bedchamber, John Ashburnham, on the day of execution, including the King's watch and shirt. Other relics included the blue silk vest in which the King met his death and more impersonal relics, such as books, ribbons, medallions and portraits.

Of the pieces of hair known to have been annexed by Halford, four are traceable: Lord Ashburnham and Sir Benjamin Stevenson both had specimens, as had William Barclay Squire, Esq., and Sir Walter Scott, who begged a piece from Halford through the eminent physician Matthew Baillie, and wore it in a gold ring for some years.

# A Jacobite Relic

It is entirely natural, perhaps, for every researcher, to dream of the one outstanding item which will make all the back-breaking work worthwhile. Frequently, after months of deep and massive searching very little emerges; sometimes, as in this present work, there are 'untapped' subjects galore! While it would be quite impossible for the writer to select any one item as his favourite (they are all of his own selection, although he was greatly assisted by the many owners), his very strong Royalist sympathies have attracted him to the oval engraved snuffbox which is the subject of this analysis.

This is made all the more attractive by the fact that the hard work has already been done: an opinion on the superb 'emblemata' on the lid was sought from a leading Cambridge scholar, who is *the* authority on the Stuart Period.

*A tentative Opinion from Prof. J H Plumb, Litt. D, FSA, Life Fellow of Christ's College, Cambridge, who writes:*

'I have spent a fascinating weekend on the box. It is obviously engraved with emblems which relate directly to the Stuarts. Presumably, the intention, if the box can be dated on stylistic grounds to about 1700, is to imply that what happened to Charles II would probably apply to James II. So, probably, the box belonged to an ardent Jacobite. I read the emblems in the following way:

The son (pun on the 'sun') of Charles I is clearly the central figure at the top of

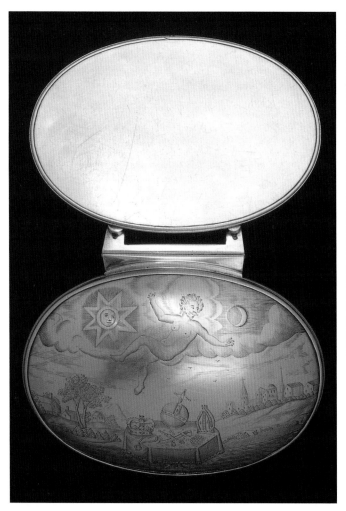

**Plate 111** William III oval elliptical snuffbox with stand-away hinge, the domed lid exceptionally engraved with symbolic Royalist subjects. The disguised 'inner lid' depicts a 'Dogs gnawing bones' motif in partially cast high relief. Lawrence Coles, London 1697. 3in (7.6cm) by 2in (5.1cm) by ½in (1.3cm) deep.

the box. The fact that he is unclothed shows that he is in heaven (and, of course, a martyr) will return or emerge (as the moon is doing from the eclipse) from the Boscobel Oak (the oak tree with the Welsh mountains behind, which was commonly used as a symbol for Charles II at the time of the Commonwealth) to his kingdom (indicated by the engraved city on the right) or this might read from Breda (I have not seen an engraving of this city, but it might be related to a city with twin spires) and restore the succession (the crown), royal authority (orb), the church (mitre), bring peace (the sceptre laid across the sword) restore the coinage (the bits of gold on the table), and hang (the halter) his enemies.

And the rest of the story is told on the chased (inner) lid. There is the picture of a peaceful and plentiful countryside and obviously the dogs are gnawing the bones of the king's enemies. The fact of the guineas on the table, suggests, I think, that the box can be dated just after 1696 when the re-coinage by the government of William III created great difficulty for most people and brought about a chronic shortage of cash. Also I think that this emblematic description of restoration of the Stuarts is cast in an historic form so that it could not be regarded as treasonable. It could be argued that it only depicted what had happened in 1660, although the implication, of course, is clear enough: what happened once might happen again'.

In Chapter 1, page 58, the Dutch type of 'wide flange' hinge is discussed. This oval box with the 'Jacobite Emblems' is of a very similar type, and this fact, in addition to Dr Plumb's reference to Breda as a 'city with twin spires', (Breda was a fortified town in Holland from which, in 1660, Charles II stated his conditions for his return to the English Monarchy) a careful comparison with Plate liii, No. 3 in the *Medallic Illustrations* which shows a beautifully struck silver medal commemorating the Peace of Breda, 1667, depicts this city almost exactly as it appears on the lid of the box, with the exception, of course, of the primitiveness of the latter and the elaborate conception of the former.

This apparent Dutch provenance could relieve several puzzling factors. First, the type of engraving: who was there in England at the turn of the 17th century who could have undertaken such clear 'emblemata' with impunity but an artist of the Dutch School? Further, in view of Dr Plumb's carefully implied suggestion of 'the treasonable implications' of producing such a box in England, perhaps the article was made in Holland to an English commission? Secondly, the un-English type of hinge, and thirdly, and perhaps most important of all, the vagueness of the London hallmarks struck inside the base of the container. The maker's mark is barely discernible, and the date-letter, while it is unquestionably there, can hardly be seen at all.

Yet another enigma lies within the clandestine or hidden inner lid of the box, which has a high domed outer lid to accommodate this. The work, although resembling 'casting', is not completely solid, but is wrought as a partially-cast plaque in high relief, somewhat reminiscent of Benjamin Pyne's 'religious subjects'; this plaque is unmarked, but one thing is quite apparent; whoever made this outstanding receptacle was a Master Boxmaker, and to any lover of the House of Stuart, it is a wonderful relic indeed.

# A Counter Box Showing Charles II

Counter boxes have received careful attention in Chapter 1, and Simon van de Passe's method of die-stamping was also included in the survey. The pierced-top counter box illustrated is but one of the many such 'British Worthies' series, but differs in one important respect: it has, as *its* subject, a hitherto untraced portrait of the youthful Charles II. The disc which enriches the circularly pierced box depicts a young man with a large nose and flowing locks (in profile it is not unlike Samuel Cooper's famous miniature of 'Charles II when young' which is figure 23 in the *Illustrated Handlist of Miniature Portraits and Silhouettes* of the Victoria & Albert Museum). Deeply penetrating research has revealed no other source for this portrait: certainly, it does not appear in *Medallic Illustrations*, and other similar publications.

The term 'unique' is a very dangerous expression, and it may well be, in spite of the many learned opinions which were sought and obtained, all of negative form, that there may be hundreds of these 'unknown portraits'. Suffice it to say that of the many leading authorities who were consulted, only one very senior member of a famous numismatical house was able, at the very first glance, to exclaim 'Without a doubt, this is the young Charles II'. Perhaps there will be dissenters, but such is the price of knowledge; without contradiction, there can be no learning!

The die-struck counters contained in the box are of the common variety, and of the five specimens shown, four are clearly identifiable: reading from left to right: Queen Elizabeth of Bohemia, the daughter of King James I of England, King John (the reversed counter is that of King Edward III), King Edward IV, and King Henry II.

**Plate 112** Charles II pierced circular counter box, the repoussé lid with a bust of the King, the sides pierced with foliate motifs, engraved on the base with a tulip motif and contemporary initials. Containing contemporary game-counters by Simon van de Passe. Unmarked, *circa* 1660. 1in (2.5cm) in diameter by 1½in (3.8cm) deep.

**Plate 113** A Charles II variant of the Coronation Medal, by an unknown hand, formed as a small counter box. The body is die-stamped with floral motifs, the lid with a rare uniface cliché of King Charles, crowned, holding the Sovereign's Sceptre. Circa 1661. ¾in (1.9cm) in diameter.

**Plate 114** William III 'Boscobel Oak' oval snuffbox, with a reeded rim and stand-away hinge. The lid is inset with an oaken panel upon which is pinned a 'cut-out' depicting the scene in Boscobel Wood, with Charles II sitting in the oak tree, while armed riders prowl below. A cherub offers the King three crowns, symbolic of the Three Kingdoms. The 'Motto ribbon' is empty. Unmarked, *circa* 1700, probably engraved by a Netherlands artist. 3¾in (9.5cm) by 2½in (6.3cm).

# The Boscobel Oak Boxes

A great deal has already been written about these finely engraved, somewhat mournful relics of the tribulations of the young King Charles II following the martyrdom of his Royal father. The present specimen was selected for the beautiful clarity of the engraving (which follows the traditional iconography) and, once again, in pursuance of the theory that 'stand-away' hinges betoken Dutch or Low Countries influence. Moreover, the motto-ribbon at the base of the lid is empty, and this could suggest that the engraver was ignorant of the subject matter and was merely copying the portrait from another version. An interesting example of this 'ignorance' occurs on one of the oval 'spiceboxes' illustrated elsewhere, where the obviously English engraver, copying a French motto 'Vn Sevl Me Blesse' – 'One alone injures me' – has heavily incised the 'l' in 'Blesse' to make the word read 'Beesse', which makes no sense at all…

The story of the Boscobel Oak has been retold often enough, but perhaps not in the words of the original biography by Thomas Blount (1618-1679), published 1660: 'About three of the clock on Saturday morning [6 September, 1651], being come near the house [Boscobel], Richard [Penderel] left his Majesty in the wood, whilst he went in to see if no souldiers were there or other danger; where he found Col. William Carliss (who had seen, not the last man born, but the last man kild, at Worcester, and) who, having with much difficulty, made his escape from thence; was got into his own neighbor-hood, and for some time concealing himself in Boscobel Wood, was come that morning to the house to get some relief of William Penderel, his old acquaintance.

Richard having acquainted the Col. that the king was in the wood, the Col. with William and Richard goe presently thither to give their attendance, where they found his Majesty sitting on the root of a tree, who was glad to see the Col. and came with them into the house, and did there eat bread and cheese heartily, and (as an extraordinary) William Penderels wife made his Majesty a posset, of thin milk and small beer, and got ready some warm water to wash his feet, not onely extreme dirty, but much galled with travail.

The Col. pull'd off his Majesties shoos, which were full of gravel, and stockens which were very wet, and there being no other shoos in the house, that would fit his Majesty, the good wife put some hot embers in those to dry them, whilst his Majesties feet were washing and his stockens shifted.

Being thus a little refreshed, the Col. perswaded his Majesty to go back into the wood (supposing it safer than the house) where the Colonel made choice of a thick leafed oak, into which both William and Richard hel'd both the King and the Col. and brought them such provision as they could get, with a cushion for his Majesty to sit on; in this oak they continued most part of that day, and the Col. humbly desired his Majesty (who had taken little or no rest the two preceding nights) to seat himself as easily as he could in the tree, and rest his head on the Colonels lap, who was watchfull that his Majesty might not fall; and in this posture his Majesty slumber'd away some part of the day, and bore all these hardships and afflictions with incomparable patience.'

Blount epitomised Colonel Carliss (sometimes called 'Careless' by later biographers) thus: 'This Col. William Carlis was born at Bromhall in Staffordshire, within two miles of Boscobel, of good parentage, is a person of approved valor, and was engag'd all along in the first war for his late Majesty of happy memory, and since his death has been no less active for his Majesty that now is; for which and his particular service and fidelity before mentioned, his Majesty has been pleased by letters patent under the great seal of England to give him, by the name of *William Carlos* (which in Spanish signifies *Charls*), this very honorable coat of armes (illustrated, and analysed thus: "He bears vpon an Oake proper, in a Feild Or, a Fesse Gules, charged with 3 Regal Crowns of ye second: by the name of Carlos. And for his Creast a Civic Crown, or Oaken Garland, with a Sword and Scepter crossed through it Saltierwise") *in perpetuam rei memoriam*, as 'tis expressed in the letters patent.'

In conclusion, there is a very touching little verse engraved on a copper-gilt oval pendant in the Victoria & Albert Museum, one side of which bears the Arms described above, the other a finely engraved portrait showing both the King and Carlos in the Oak, and engraved inside, the following verse:

> 'Renowned Carlos! thou hast won the day
> (loyalty lost) by helping Charles away
> From Kings' blood-thirsty rebels jn a night
> Made black with rage of thieves & hell's dispight,
> Live! King-loved Sowle thy fame by euer spoke,
> By all whilst England beares a Royall Oake.'

# Royal Portrait Pomanders

There is no attempt, here, to accord any direct Royal provenance with the rare 'globular pomanders' which bear finely engraved portraits of English Kings and Queens on the 'loculi' or segments. This specimen is of the six-segment variety, and shows six English monarchs: one each from the Houses of Lancaster and York, and four from the House of the Tudors. These are, in chronological order:

| | |
|---|---|
| Henry IV | 1367–1413 |
| Edward IV | 1442–1483 |
| Henry VII | 1457–1509 |
| Henry VIII | 1491–1547 |
| Edward VI | 1537–1553 |
| Elizabeth I | 1533–1603 |

**Plate 115** Elizabethan pomander of sexagonal 'apple' type, engraved on all the segments with fine portraits of the Kings and Queen of England. On a circular collet foot with a cast trefoil terminal. Engraved inside on each loculus or segment with contemporary 16th century ornament in 'moresque' floral motifs. The *loculi* have no 'slide-lids'. Unmarked, *circa* 1600. 2in (5.1cm) by 1½in (3.8cm). *Courtesy of the Wellcome Medical Historical Museum*

It is not thought that there was anything particularly special about these 'Royal Portrait' pomanders – they were probably wrought as 'patriotic Mementoes', in much the same manner as portraits of The Evangelists appeared on German specimens – but what is of interest is that of the six monarchs depicted on the English example, three, at least, are known to have been particularly interested in perfumes, namely, Henry VIII (whose recipe for a pomander containing ambergris is among the Ashmolean MSS), Edward VI, who liked rose perfume, and Queen Elizabeth, who likewise had a special fondness for the rose, which would seem to have been the favourite perfume of the Tudors.

Some 'Portrait Pomanders' are very finely engraved, others quite coarsely, and it is

**Plate 116** James I pomander, formed as a small book. The 'covers', with clasps, are engraved with mice. The spine is engraved with a diaper motif. The interior has three divisions for perfumes or spices. With a suspensory chain. Engraved in the lid with contemporary initials. Unmarked, *circa* 1610. 1¼in (3.2cm) by 1in (2.5cm) by ⅜in (1cm) deep.

highly probable that *émigré* Dutch engravers were busily turning out these new 'novelties'. As one contemporary 20th century expert has remarked: 'Dutch engravers were ten a penny in the late 16th-early 17th centuries!'

The subject of pomanders having been treated extensively (vide *Investing in Silver* pp.105-107) it is not proposed to repeat published material, but there are some aspects which have come to notice, and are therefore included here. The late Director of the Wellcome Medical Museum, Dr E Ashworth Underwood, stated that 'a pomander with six sections enabled six substances to be inhaled simultaneously'. This would certainly explain the absence of 'slides' on the present example, and why many pomanders appear never to have had these 'slides' or covers, or any provision for these, to enclose the segments.

The very early prototype of the pomander would seem to be the German *Bisamapfel*, or 'musk-ball' which Hugh Tait mentions in another learned article in the November 1963 issue of *The Connoisseur*, dealing with 'an anonymous loan to the British Museum of Renaissance Jewellery'. Mr Tait specifies that 'one of the earliest mediaeval pomanders of this segmental type is preserved in the Bayerisches Nationalmuseum in Munich…made in the Rhineland 1470', but John Timb's *Nooks and Corners of English Life*, published in 1867, refers to an inventory of Henry V, dated 1423, which enumerated a 'musk-ball of gold, weighing *eleven pounds*, and another of silver-gilt. Finally, Giles Merton, writing in *Argentor* 1948, stated his opinion that 'pomanders were not always used for the purpose of holding perfume. Many of the Renaissance pomanders were pearshaped and *held cosmetics* in their division'.

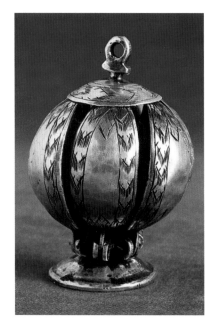

**Plate 117** Charles I pomander: of sexagonal 'apple' variety, parcel-gilt on a central column and with a screw-down lid. Scratched all over with 'debased laurel' motifs. On a cast collet foot and with a suspensory loop on the closing screw. Unmarked, *circa* 1630. 2½in (6.3cm) by 1⅛in (2.9cm).
*Courtesy of the Wellcome Medical Historical Museum*

# Queen Charlotte's Casket

Perhaps the most essential requisite which the researcher into the historic past should possess is that combination of healthy curiosity and passion to dot all the 'i's, and cross all the 't's – which can become both the bane and salvation of his work – and the intelligent use of which can lead him into all sorts of fascinating adventures.

The present writer's great obsession is the identification, as far as is humanly possible, of the many themes appearing within these pages, and thus he found himself intrigued by the historical background to the cast oval plaque set within the lid of the silver-gilt casket bearing Queen Charlotte's Royal Cypher. Expert opinion was sought, but the scene remained obstinately obscure; famous battles of the period were scrutinised (the subject appears to contain warriors as well as the three central mounted figures), prints and drawings involving famous historical *causes célèbre* cast no light on the enigma. It seemed that Thomas Heming, the maker of the casket, had invented an ornamental theme without any factual basis.

Having exhausted the normal sources of enquiry, it became necessary to delve deeper into the matter; the first and most pressing problem was how a Royal relic had left its original surroundings and passed into lay possession.

It became expedient to search Exhibition Catalogues and learned articles, and one fact of passing interest did emerge: the casket had been shown in May 1939 at an Exhibition entitled 'The Age of Queen Charlotte', held at the Luton Museum. Various works of art, including ceramics, furniture and silver, were exhibited by several world-famous firms, and beyond the customary description and a brief note on the rococo style in which the article was wrought, nothing more was added.

The enigma was finally solved through an article by the scholarly expert on antique porcelain, Dr Bellamy Gardner, who, in the July 1939 issue of *The Connoisseur*, wrote of 'Rare Souvenirs of King George III and Queen Charlotte', and cited several rare items of Chelsea Porcelain which had been '*sold among Her Majesty's effects by Messrs Christie in the year 1819*'. Armed with this information it was possible to trace the rare early catalogue (a slim volume, labelled simply 'Queen Charlotte's Catalogue, 1819') and to track down the 'Superb Service of silver-gilt Plate' (sic), which comprised thirty articles of a Toilet Service in a red leather case, lined with green velvet.

Among the more important pieces were a mirror, a ewer and basin, several circular boxes and salvers on 'small feet', and a '*pair of large scalloped Toilet Boxes and Covers with roses and flowers in high relief, on four feet*'. In accordance with contemporary practice, neither the name of the maker nor the date of manufacture was given. Now, the backbone of research is comparative correlation with other published works, and in an article in the July 1965 issue of *Apollo Magazine*, A V B Norman, writing of 'An Augsburg Travelling Service', stated (*inter alia*) that the 'Zoffany Portrait of Queen Charlotte at her dressing table', in the Royal Collections at Windsor '*shows five boxes in use*'. Again, it was a simple matter to trace Zoffany's portrait (and hope, incidentally, alas, in vain, that the cataloguer might say something about the plaques), but from a close examination of the portrait showing the Queen at a draped dressing-table, in the company of the Prince of Wales and the Duke of York, painted at Old Buckingham House, *circa* 1766, it becomes obvious that the toilet articles which she was using were not of the same rococo style as the present casket, but from another service, also mentioned in the Christie Catalogue of 1819, which was more in keeping with a German oval style.

As is well known, the Court Goldsmith to George III in the third quarter of the 18th century was Thomas Heming, and A G Grimwade, FSA, writing on 'Royal Toilet Services in Scandinavia', published in the April 1956 issue of *The Connoisseur*, described and illustrated an almost identical casket which was part of a toilet service made by Heming for the Queen of Denmark, Caroline Matilda, posthumous daughter of Frederick, Prince of Wales and sister of George III, in 1766. On close examination, the caskets greatly resemble the present specimen, with the exception, perhaps, that the former are somewhat longer and shallower, and that instead of the cast plaque inset on the lid, have cast floral motifs.

In writing of yet another Heming service made for a nobleman in 1768, Mr Grimwade made the point that 'Heming obviously used the mouldings of the Royal Service (belonging to Queen Caroline Matilda) when the Williams-Wynne service was ordered two years later… since he must have been aware that the earlier service was across the seas, he would have felt safe from incurring any suggestion that he had tarnished the lustre of the Royal prototype by producing what is virtually a copy. The use of the existing mouldings must, of course, have made the production of the second service both speedier and cheaper. Heming's profit on this may well have been larger in consequence'. Judging by the almost exact duplication which appears on Queen Charlotte's casket, dated 1771, it would be safe to assert that Heming used the same mouldings yet again and, what is more, having already used them in the production, only three years earlier, of a service for a noble *English* family (not one beyond the seas), did not hesitate to reproduce them once more, but this time for his chief Patroness, the Queen of England herself!

Within this apparent duplicity may lie the answer to the original question: 'what is the subject of the cast plaque on the lid of the casket?' For a clearer explanation,

**Plate 118** George III silver-gilt rectangular toilet casket. This Royal relic belonged to Queen Charlotte, consort of King George III and is engraved with her personal cypher inside the lid. The rococo body is enriched with repoussé floral sprays and 'scroll and beaded foliate' motifs on the four scroll-terminal feet. The lid is embellished with shell, foliate and gadroon motifs, and set in the centre with a cast pictorial plaque within an oval laurel wreath cartouche. The lid is of the 'rising domical' variety, and has a concealed integral hinge. Thomas Heming, the Royal Goldsmith, London, 1771. 8in (20.3cm) by 5in (12.7cm) by 4in (10.2cm) deep.

it becomes necessary to know something of the background of Queen Charlotte herself. Writing in 1899, Percy Fitzgerald, in a wholly masterful and interesting account of the life of 'The Good Queen Charlotte', cited a very important incident in the future Queen of England's early life, and one which must have made a great impression on her, as indeed, it made an impression on the English court, and probably eventually led to her marriage with King George III.

Sophia Charlotte had been born in May, 1744 in the North German Duchy of Mecklenburg-Strelitz. She was the niece of the fourth Duke, Adolphus Frederick and, says Fitzgerald, 'was carefully educated, was fond of botany and natural history, devoted to music: she was a good housewife, and skilful and laborious at her needle. Above all, she was reared in principles of the strictest piety and morality'.

Fitzgerald continues: 'The almost pastoral happiness of the little court at Strelitz had been rudely disturbed by the wars between the Great Frederick (Frederick the

Great) and the Empress Maria Theresa, which was to prove disastrous for the small German territories, which he overran with his armies and pillaged and laid waste. His excuse was that they would not join him in the contest. The little Duchy of Mecklenburg-Strelitz suffered cruelly: contributions were levied, the young men were forced into the king's army, furniture and property plundered; even the churches were despoiled. After the great defeat of Daun (Field Marshal – 1705-66) at Torgau in 1760 the whole of Germany seemed to be at the conqueror's mercy: so desperate was the outlook, that an extraordinary step was taken by the second of the young princesses then at Strelitz, which was to determine her future destiny. As the victory seemed to portend a new series of horrors and despoilings, *she addressed an earnest letter to Frederick, describing the sufferings of her country and appealing to his mercy and forbearance.'* This was, continues Fitzgerald, 'an exceptional step in one so young, she was then only sixteen – and was as timely as it was efficacious'.

The letter is too long to quote in full, but contains such imploring visions as: 'It was but a few years ago that this territory wore the most pleasing appearance. The country was cultivated, the peasant looked cheerful, and the towns abounded with riches and festivity. What an alteration at present from such a charming scene. I am not expert at description, nor can my fancy add any horrors to the picture; but surely even conquerors themselves would weep at the hideous prospects now before me'. The viciousness of the soldiery and the confusion and the horrors are emphasised. ''It was noted' says Fitzgerald, 'that almost immediately after this letter was dispatched, a complete change took place in the Prussian king's system. A missive to General de Ziethen (1699-1786) enjoined order and regularity in the conduct of the army. The king, indeed, was so pleased with the young princess and her appeal, that the letter was shown and handed about; a copy found its way to the English court and to the Princess of Wales, by whom it was shown to the king, who was greatly struck by it'.

It has now to be clearly emphasised that the preceding material was based on biographical and historical fact: what follows now is purely conjectural, but wholly logical and, in the absence of positive identification, it is perfectly feasible that Thomas Heming, the Court Goldsmith to the Royal Household, should wish to please his Royal Mistress by reviving happy memories for her of her own 'little victory' over Frederick the Great. It is even conceivable that the Queen herself commissioned the subject of the plaque, namely, a group portrait of Frederick the Great and his officers at the scene of one of his many victories in the 'Seven Years War'. One of the foremost German-Polish painters of the time, Daniel Nicholas Chodowiecki (1726-1801), who painted Frederick many times, might have executed the original painting from which Heming drew inspiration.

It is indeed a far cry from an unidentified portrait plaque on a silver casket to a detailed and unusually inspiring vignette in the life of a beloved monarch. To the devoted researcher, however, this linking of fact and history with fiction and conjecture is part of the absorbing nature of his work: the most fascinating aspect of this, is that an inanimate object can also, on occasion, 'tell its own story'.

CHAPTER 3

# Applied Ornament

In order to facilitate a more complete understanding of the techniques involved in 'Applied Ornament', it may be of some benefit to indulge in a comparative survey, although, at first glance, this does not appear to have any connection with the matter under discussion.

The simple truth is that 'ornament' is a much subtler device than it appears to be: it is not only an enrichment, designed to cover bare surfaces or hide imperfections, it is also the silversmith's answer to the painter's art of chiaroscuro, literally 'light and shade', the device attributed to Leonardo da Vinci which provides depth and perspective to an otherwise flat surface, in other words, the much coveted 'Third Dimension'. Thus a box enriched with 'ornament' not only possesses absorbing embellishment, but also imparts a feeling of spaciousness and continuity, as if, were it possible, the owner could 'step inside' the frame of the lid and share the experiences of the figures or subjects placed on it.

It may well be that Leonardo initiated the trend, but earlier examples, if the more crudely applied, remain extant to show that man has long been preoccupied with the craft of perspective; a plate in the Hermitage Museum at St Petersburg, made *circa* AD 527-567 in the reign of the Emperor Justinian I, illustrates early Byzantine trends towards perspective. The relief is not high, but the impression of depth is achieved by the positions of the various figures portrayed. The subject is 'A shepherd with his flock', and a goat appears to be nibbling the branches of a tree in the far background (actually the top left of the picture), while another goat is centrally placed, to the right of the main subject, and a dog with its paw raised is in the extreme foreground. These devices have the effect of placing the shepherd in the centre of the composition, which is, in fact, on a perfectly plain surface.

Following Leonardo's invention it is significant that the use of perspective appears

**Plate 119** William III oval tobacco box with a stand-away hinge of the five-lugged variety. The stepped lid is superbly engraved with a contemporary 'smoking and drinking' scene, symbolic of 'the good life', depicting a lighted octagonal candlestick or taperstick enriched with its own coat-of-arms, two crossed churchwarden pipes on a paper containing tobacco, a baluster wine glass and a straw-bound wine bottle on a finely engraved pedestal table. Overall flies a bird, holding a motto ribbon in its beak which bears the Latin motto: *Ne Quid Nimis* or 'Nothing in Excess'. Maker's mark obscured, London 1700. 4in (10.2cm) by 3½in (8.9cm) by 1in (2.5cm) deep.

on plate (as well as in paintings) from the third quarter of the 16th century. Two forms were employed: cast and engraved ornament, and both seem to have been parallel with each other, but whereas the former technique was used by the Swiss and German silversmiths, who were particularly skilled in its application, the latter belonged mainly to the Netherlands, primarily Holland.

The great Nuremberg craftsman, Christoph Jamnitzer (1563-1618) was a master of perspective in silver. His famous series of 'Phaeton Kredentzschalen', that is, standing dishes made partly for show but also for offering wine to an honoured guest, are splendid manifestations of his craft. They are illustrated in Rosenberg's *Der Goldschmiede Merkzeichen*, plates 84-5. One of the tazzae depicts the sisters of Phaeton, son of Helios (who was slain by Zeus for driving the chariot of the sun to earth, thus endangering the world), bewailing his death. In keeping with the mythological legend, which states that they were turned into poplar trees for doing so, the figures sprout leaves and branches from their heads; two of the figures are in front of, and two behind, a magnificently sculptured sarcophagus, which is shown in full perspective, thus achieving a bewildering effect of 'depth'.

The German engravers, too, produced beautiful perspective effects, and one, the Liège-born, German domiciled artist Johann Theodor de Bry (1561-1623) was able to refine the process even further by the use of a yet simpler device: he also produced a series of standing dishes, of much the same form as Jamnitzer's 'Kredentzschalen', except that his tazzae were of deeper concave form, so that the outside figures in the engraving appeared to look inward towards the centrally placed figures. The effect was further heightened by the introduction of architecture at either side of the composition and in the background, creating the illusion of chiaroscuro yet once again. The eminent specialist on ornament, the late John F Hayward, wrote an important article on this subject for *Apollo Miscellany* in 1950.

Several series of engraved dessert and dinner plates of English provenance but by foreign artists are extant. These include the two sets, dated 1567 and 1569, allegedly engraved by Pieter Maas of Cologne. The latter illustrates the story of the Prodigal Son, and the former (set of twelve) 'The Labours of Hercules'. Again, by the use of architecture and masonry, an illusion of perspective has been created. The famous 'Strawberry Hill Sale' of the effects of Horace Walpole, held in April, 1842, contained a set of twelve dessert plates engraved by Simon van de Passe comprising the story of the Prodigal Son. Its date was not given in the catalogue.

So much for engraved ornament which sets out to create a deliberate illusion of perspective. The ornamentation of silver boxes was often so cunningly effected that the owner was quite unaware of the deception being practiced upon him, while at the same time he experienced a feeling of well-being on beholding the box. For, and there seems little doubt about it, people like boxes for their own sake, not for the purpose or the contents. Where the article is quite unadorned, the simplicity of 'line' or the 'feel' of the patination satisfy the senses, but where there is clever enrichment, this gratification can be overwhelming.

A fleeting review of some of the methods embodying chiaroscuro of one kind or another may serve to emphasise this point. Casting and engraving having been already summarily dealt with (they are examined at greater length later in this chapter), there remain other media where most subtle use of the device may be observed. Of these, 'piqué-work', which was popular in the late 17th-early 18th centuries, is a good example. Three superb specimens in the medium are illustrated on page 115. Basically, the technique consisted of a tortoiseshell or mother-of-pearl ground inlaid with silver patterns or motifs. Examine the specimen, *circa* 1730, which depicts a *Commedia dell' arte* group (one of whom is a bagpiper) engaged in some sort of dance. The costumes are traditional and there are plumes of mother-of-pearl in their hats. One of the characters (at bottom left) seems to have his leg supported in a mother-of-pearl crutch. The 'stomping' back-view of the figure at top centre is a most beautifully judged vignette of a peasant at play. This particular

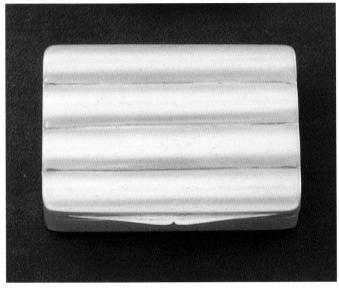

**Plate 120** George III heavy gauge snuffbox, the lid and base enriched with ridged corrugations, and with a simple thumbpiece. William Pugh, Birmingham, 1810. 2⅜in (6cm) by 1½in (3.8cm).

**Plate 121** George III oval snuffbox, the lid formed as a raised ellipse on a shallow bezel, and with heavy encircling rib around the body. John Robertson, Newcastle, *circa* 1800. 2⅝in (6.7cm) by 2in (5.1cm).

John Robertson I. 21 Dean Street, Newcastle – appears in trade directories from 1801. Dr Margaret M V A Gill in her excellent *Directory of Newcastle Goldsmiths*, 1980, cites a full schedule of items which Robertson sent to assay between 11th November 1796 and 31st July 1801. She lists two types of box: a snuffbox, a tobacco box and a 'snuffbox cover'. She adds that Robertson was an important customer of Thomas Bewick for a wide range of engraving, his account 'To 1 years engraving' rising to £29.19.8 in 1800. The box is engraved with the contemporary owner's name.

box was part of the famous Berney Collection of Piqué, and was sold in June, 1927, when it was ascribed in the catalogue to the 17th century and as of English origin.

Further examples of perspective in ornament may be observed in many of the boxes illustrated: these include the marvellously conceived 'Jacobite Relic' (Plate 111), which depicts Charles I descending from Heaven; here, the domed lid lends depth to the subject. It is, in fact, the very antithesis of the German 'Kredenzschalen', in that it is of convex form, whereas the latter was concave, but the effect is almost the same. The chequered foreground extends to the very rim of the box, and thus serves effectively to create a 'natural horizon', or the dividing line between the ground and the sky, so that the countryside with the rolling hills and church spires, houses and trees, recedes into the background. Of course, the medium which so beautifully achieves this separation is the centrally placed table which appears to be hexagonal in shape: the major portion of this protrudes into the foreground, thereby increasing the perspective.

The William III oval tobacco box illustrated on page 81 was the subject of a close analysis in the first edition. There, it was conjectured that the coat-of-arms in a shield, at the base of the octagonal candlestick, might yield clues on the original ownership. Furthermore, two crossed churchwarden pipes reposed on a scrolling paper holding tobacco; to the right was a wine glass and a straw-covered wine bottle, and on the left, an octagonal candlestick with a lighted candle. Overhead flew a bird bearing the motto ribbon in its beak. All rested on a pedestal table, and the motto was 'Ne Quid Nimis' (Nothing in excess). One of the pipes was engraved on the heel with the letters 'T.K.'. It was tentatively suggested that these might be the owner's initials, and there the matter rested. The devices used by the craftsmen to obtain perspective were also discussed, to no great result.

In 1976, the Wadsworth Athenaeum at Hartford, Connecticut, published a

**Plate 122** George IV rectangular silver-gilt snuffbox, the sides and base engine-turned with basketweave motifs and with cast foliate borders. The lid is cast with mythological representation of the story of Aeneas, taken from Virgil's *Aeneid*: Aeneas fleeing from the flames of Troy, with his father, Anchises, who holds the household gods (the Penates) and leads his boy Ascanius. The whole set in a scrolling baroque frame. Joseph Taylor, Birmingham 1821. 3½in (8.9cm) by 2¾in (7cm) by ⅞in (2.2cm).
This box is fully analysed and discussed on page 85.

catalogue of the silver presented by Mrs Elizabeth B Miles, a generous benefactress. This illustrated (page 131) a very similar box, although it was dated '*circa* 1680'.

The caption stated that it was 'an unusual still life engraved in perspective'. The applied ornament, however, differed from the William III example illustrated here. Instead of a scrolling sheet of paper supporting crossed pipes, they rested on a circular plate. The catalogue further states '…the plate (is engraved) with the crest of the Austin family of Shalford House, Surrey. On the heel of one of the pipes are the clearly legible initials "I.C.", perhaps the engraver'. With the exception of the absence of the bird bearing the motto ribbon, this earlier box is identical.

The ornament on this second box merited a closer examination, and an inconsistency was found. The pedestals supporting the consoles or tables differed in design, and did not really resemble any known British furniture style. An authority in the Woodwork Department at the Victoria & Albert Museum stated emphatically that it was not English, and that he had never seen the type in any furniture of any period. Such a statement obviously merited seeking another opinion. The expert on genre subjects at the National Gallery confirmed that he had never seen a subject like it. It has to be concluded, therefore, that this engraving is an invented genre. The armorials were presumably applied to please the owner, the engraver varying the various motifs to suit. The fact that the mottoes agree could simply imply 'good food and gracious living', as is suggested by the gentleman at the Victoria & Albert Museum. It will be interesting to note further variations, should these surface.

The 'Topers' scene Edinburgh box, page 85, is a finely conceived repoussé subject in the manner of Teniers. The device of perspective is divided between the rectangular bench which one figure bestraddles and the centrally placed circular table around which the card-players sit. The angle at which the bench is placed serves to emphasise the depth of the room. The lusty players (one has obviously been dealt a 'bad hand') engage their feet beneath the circular table, and yet again, a feeling of perspective has been attained.

It was presumably inevitable that the passion for 'Baroque-type' extravaganza which assailed Europe during the 18th century should spread to enrichment on boxes, and many fine specimens of this trend remain extant, but more curiously, there was an apparent revival of these themes in England in the second decade of the 19th century, and Birmingham craftsmen in particular, Joseph Taylor and John Bettridge are but two, worked in this medium. Seeking about for suitable subjects where 'depth' existed, they settled on a series of mythological subjects, and, from

**Plate 123** William IV shallow oval snuffbox, the lid with 'stand-away' hinge and enriched with a repoussé chiaroscuro subject of a 'Tavern Scene' in the manner of Teniers the Younger. By an unascribed maker, Edinburgh 1831. 3in (7.6cm) by 2⅜in (6cm) by ½in (1.3cm) deep.

**Plate 124** George IV snuffbox with cast lid portraying Diogenes' dialogue with Alexander the Great. Maker: Thomas Shaw, Birmingham 1825.                    *Courtesy of the Birmingham Assay Office*
This maker is sometimes confused with Thomas Spicer but, in fact, Spicer was a watch-case maker, who did not make vinaigrettes or snuffboxes. He worked between 1816-42.

very careful research, which has failed to locate the exact sources of their genre, it would seem that the casters and modellers created an amalgam of themes. Thus, in analysing the superb silver-gilt snuff box by Taylor dated 1821, it is possible to discern the subject as 'Aeneas fleeing from Troy with his father Anchises who carries the household gods (or Penates)', but quite impossible to locate the source. Of course, it is possible that the actual painting does exist, but an examination of A. Pigler's *Barockthemen*, published in Budapest 1956, which lists thousands of paintings, reveals that it could be from Tintoretto's school, or from the hand of twenty other artists, or from none, and where does the search begin?

The feeling of perspective in this case is created by two illusions: the heavy scrolling 'baroque border' and the receding figures of soldiery in the background, a splendidly-prowed rowing boat at bottom left, from which the central figure, presumably Aeneas, is stepping, and a fallen column in the centre of the group. There is a turreted and castellated castle in the far background.

Not quite so subtle, perhaps, but still possessing a certain 'depth', is the group which can be easily identified as 'Diogenes' dialogue with Alexander the Great'. It will be recalled that the King, on asking which boon the great Greek philosopher and cynic would most crave, received the reply that his desire was that 'the king would not stand between him and the sun!' The illusion of perspective is here achieved by placing the famous 'tub' in which Diogenes is said to have lived amidst a mass of trees and foliage, so the figure of Diogenes appears 'to stand out'. Furthermore, the latter's arm, pointing towards the King, obscures the uniform of the soldier in the centre, thus creating an 'artificial horizon'. The figure of Alexander, to the right, is, in turn, emphasised by placing it in front of the group of warriors in the background.

Yet once again, it has not been possible to trace the source of this subject, but it might have been executed by any painter of the Classical Period, and could have been taken directly from a contemporary engraving, of the same period as the box. The English engraver Richard Earlom (1742-1822) was particularly active in these historical and mythological themes.

# Bright-Cutting

Asurprising medium for chiaroscuro, and one which would seem most unsuited to the illusion, is the technique of 'bright-cutting'. A brief definition of the method can be of service here: it is 'engraving in free style, without the limitations of drawing-in the pattern'. This requires elaboration: in most other types of engraving, the artist either worked from imagination (as on many later Birmingham-made boxes, where contemporary trends in fashion and commerce were mirrored, without recourse to pre-conceived designs, with a few notable exceptions) or traced the motif on a gamboge-coating, that is, a yellow resinous substance which darkened the surface of the silver and thus facilitated the engraving. In bright-cutting, the engraver used specially prepared tools, primarily the 'square graver' – a type of 'scorper' or 'scooper' – which were kept in a state of sharpness by an emery-stick, and by placing the full weight of his body behind every 'cut', produced the effect of 'depth'.

This very special technique appears to have arisen in the mid-1760s, although specimens of this very early period are rare. It involved (and still does, but for very few craftsmen, as the art of bright-cutting by hand is a dying craft) absolute confidence on the part of the engraver. Working, with very few exceptions (these being the famous 'Adam Motifs') entirely freehand, he proceeded to build up the feeling of perspective by a series of different devices. The ground, that is the actual surface of the metal, was 'scored in' by the 'threading-tool', giving, as the term implies, a series of thin parallel lines, Even this conventional background was made to appear deeper by lighter and heavier strokes, giving the effect, yet again, of chiaroscuro. The illusion was further accentuated by 'optical deception', namely, slanting lines working away from the central motif, which might be a floral or foliate

**Plate 125** George III rectangular cut-corner toothpick case, superbly bright-cut with three octagonal panels containing floral sprays and a contemporary monogram in a festooned escutcheon on a 'double-dot' scored ground. With a fine hidden-integral hinge, the sides enriched with swags of foliate bright-cutting. Phipps and Robinson, London 1789. 3½in (8.9cm) by 1in (2.5cm) by ¼in (6.3mm) deep.

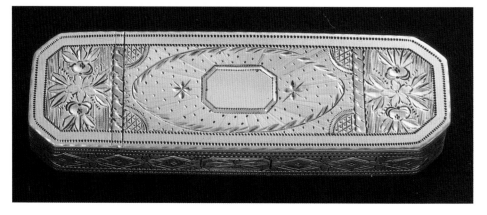

**Plate 126** George III finely bright-cut rectangular cut-corner toothpick case, with 'raying bright-cut' enrichment and an octagonal rectangular escutcheon in the centre of the lid for a monogram, and foliate bright-cut motifs at either end of the lid, and formed as 'diapers' on the sides. With a finely constructed hidden-integral hinge, velvet lining and a mirror inside the lid. Samuel Pemberton VI, Birmingham 1791. 3½in (8.9cm) by 1in (2.5cm) by ¼in (6.3mm) deep.

**Plate 127** George III large rectangular snuffbox, the lid engraved with 'raying bright-cut' enrichment, and embellished with an appliqué bust of George III in gold. The border is engraved with 'double-dot' scoring. The hinge is of the sunken-integral type. The thumbpiece is scalloped. Joseph Willmore, Birmingham 1817. 3⅞in (9.9cm) by 2¾in (7cm) by 1in (2.5cm).
Engraved with the following presentation inscription: 'A Token of Respect from the Noncommissioned Officers and Privates of the Holne Pierrepoint Troup of Volunteer Cavelry To Capt Bettison, August 12th, 1817.' *Courtesy of the Birmingham Assay Office*

**Plate 128** George III deep vertical oval snuffbox: enriched all over the lid (which has a hidden-integral hinge) with bright-cut floral and cornucopia motifs on a scored threaded ground, and on the side with alternating bands of 'double-dot' scoring, foliate scrolls, and 'guilloche', that is, interlacing bands, with quatrefoils in the centre. Engraved in the centre of the lid is a contemporary monogram surmounted with a basket of fruit. Phipps and Robinson, London 1813. 3½in (8.9cm) by 1¼in (3.2cm) by 2½in (6.3cm) deep.

design or a mantled cartouche containing a coat-of-arms. The centrally placed design thus attained a 'three-dimensional' appearance.

A favourite method used by London bright-cutters (the Phipps and Robinson partnership was particularly successful in this medium) was to employ a 'double-dot' scorper, that is, a tool with a cutting-face so incised, and engrave an ellipse which seemed to consist of hundreds of dots. It was actually a type of cross-hatching, namely, engraving in parallel lines in two series, crossing each other, and using 'straights and curves'. The design was then further enriched by a centrally placed cartouche and the effect was complete. For brevity's sake, this effect is often known as 'raying bright-cut' ornament.

The double-dot method was also employed in 'diaper' or 'diamond-shape' designs and the 'threading-tool' was used to engrave the outside 'lozenge' or to provide a 'ground' for the foliage. Nowhere is the use of 'thread' motifs so successfully illustrated as on the superb rectangular snuffbox bearing a gold portrait bust of George III. The bust is also cast in relief, so that the figure appears to emerge from the very centre of the lid (see above).

It must be emphasised that the wear and tear of centuries, the patination, has contributed to the charm of bright-cutting, as a piece of new plate with newly

**Plate 129** George III oval elliptical snuffbox with a superlative 'slant-integral' hinge set in the centre of the twin lids which open at right-angles to each other. Most beautifully bright-cut with 'diaper and quatrefoil' motifs on a 'scored threaded' ground on the lids, and with similar enrichment on the sides. Phipps and Robinson, London 1787. 3in (7.6cm) by 2¼in (5.7cm) by ¾in (1.9cm) deep.

applied ornament (in spite of polishing) is quite rough to the touch. It is recalled with amusement that a perfectly genuine George III tea-tray was condemned by several 'specialists' as 'modern engraving', because the bright-cutting was sharp to the touch. Of course, in that particular case, the explanation was quite simple: the article was in absolutely 'brilliant state', and the engraving had never been polished! On close examination, under a glass, the process, like so many others, becomes nonsensical: it appears to consist, as on a pair of sugar-tongs, for instance, of a series of 'nicks and wriggles'; it is only when the object is viewed in perspective that the effect is realised to be light and shade. Douglas Bennett, in a pamphlet on Irish silver in the 'Irish Heritage Series', 1976, gives a fascinating gloss: 'The four gilt horses of San Marco, Venice, believed to be by Roman artists from the 3rd century AD, have deep scratches or cuts that run full length on the figures. The unknown artist who

**Plate 130** George III rectangular snuffbox engraved with scale-motif bright-cutting, and the contemporary inscription 'Arctic Regions' (the subject is not known, but it could possibly refer to a racehorse). William Wardell and Peter Kempston, Birmingham, 1817.
The tenon and mortise hinge is shown on page 58.
*Courtesy of the Birmingham Assay Office*

88

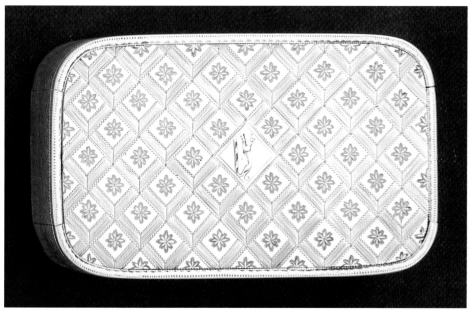

**Plate 131** George III 'trick' snuffbox, rectangular with rounded corners. Superbly bright-cut with 'diaper and foliate' motifs and engraved in the centre diaper with a contemporary 'Greyhound' crest. The opening mechanism exactly matches the later William IV specimen by Edward Edwards (shown on page 120). Phipps and Robinson, London, 1806. 3in (7.6cm) by 2½in (6.3cm).

modelled the animals had a knowledge of light refraction.

These cuts are almost identical but on a much larger scale to bright-cut engraving and serve the same purpose because if these large heavily gilt copper animals had not been systematically cut, they would have shown no contours in sunlight. The engravers of the neo-classical period were very conscious of this problem of light reflection on contours and were constantly striving to improve and accentuate the delicate decoration on vessels.' It should, of course, be emphasised that Irish bright-cut ornament is exceptionally fine.

Finally, before passing to other methods of illusion, it is necessary to examine a very common motif which appears on many articles of English plate from the early 17th century: the Acanthus-leaf design. Of course, the very name is derived from the Greek, in which language it is the term for 'spike', which is as good a description

**Plate 132** George III rectangular cut-corner snuffbox, engraved with raying bright-cut enrichment in the centre of the lid, and with a superbly masked 'sunken-integral' hinge, and foliate bright-cut ornament around the rim. Samuel Pemberton VI, Birmingham 1788.

This is an early specimen of bright-cutting.

*Courtesy of the Birmingham Assay Office*

**Plate 133** George III silver-gilt circular patchbox, bright-cut with foliate motifs and an oval cartouche containing a contemporary monogram. Bright-cut around the bezel with a foliate motif. Joseph Taylor, Birmingham 1798. 1⅝in (4.1cm) in diameter by ½in (1.3cm) deep. Fully marked inside base, maker's mark only in the lid.

**Plate 135** George III silver-gilt egg-shaped vinaigrette possessing the finest bright-cut embellishment possible, the ovoid lid with a finely concealed integral hinge. The engraver first gilt the box, then bright-cut the floral and geometric motifs, and finally scored the background with the 'threading tool'. The apex of the lid is bright-cut with a snowdrop motif. The grille is a simply pierced lift-out specimen. Samuel Meriton II, London *circa* 1790. (Maker's mark only). 1½in (3.8cm) by 1⅝in (4.1cm) in diameter.

**Plate 134** *Top* George III rectangular snuffbox, the lid beautifully bright-cut with 'diaper' motifs and the centre rectangular panel containing elliptical 'cross hatching' on a double-dot scored ground. The sides are similarly enriched, with contemporary monograms in oval escutcheons on the lid and sides. Phipps and Robinson, London 1798. 2¾in (7cm) by 2½in (6.3cm) by ¾in (1.9cm) deep.

*Bottom* George III rectangular cut-corner snuffbox, the surfaces superlatively bright-cut with foliate sprays and swags on a scored threaded ground, with a 'fans' and 'musical theme' motif on the lid and a finely constructed hidden-integral hinge.
Phipps and Robinson, London 1791. 3in (7.6cm) by 2½in (6.3cm) by ¾in (1.9cm) deep.

as any for its elegant but spiky leaves. The best-known species today is *Acanthus mollis* (bear's breech), but the ancients favoured *Acanthus spinosus*, which had more finely divided leaves, and stylised the natural plant into an elegant art-form. As an enrichment on silver it is particularly effective because the leaves are deeply incised and spiky-edged to make them 'project' into the foreground, attaining once again a feeling of 'dimension'. Jackson's *History of English Plate*, in the introduction to Chapter VIII (page 204) mentions the use of acanthus foliage as an ornamental design on Elizabethan plate but, of course, the motif is seen at its best on Roman Corinthian Capitals in ornament on architecture. Owen Jones' great work *The Grammar of Ornament,* published and superlatively illustrated in colour in 1856, devotes a chapter to this form of enrichment, but Jones believed the motif, used by the Romans as 'a scroll within a scroll' to be ineffective until 'the principle of one leaf growing out of another in a continuous line was abandoned for the adoption of a continuous stem throwing off ornaments on either side', in other words, the spreading of the motif lent perspective to the whole.

# Methods of Enrichment

In all, there are nine distinct methods of 'Applied Ornament' used on silver boxes. Of these one, bright-cutting, has already been examined. The other eight are Casting, Engraving, Hand-carving, Piqué inlay, Engine-turning, Repoussé and Embossing, Die-stamping and Acid-etching.

It should be explained that the last two methods have been the subject of intensive research and were not previously identified with box-lid enrichment, not, that is to say, by the general public, although certain sections of the Trade might have known of their existence. In order that all these categories should be clearly understood, a short résumé of all the techniques involved is appended, but the full research material is revealed in dealing with the latter methods.

It must be emphasised that the revelation that such important makers as Nathaniel Mills, Matthew Linwood and Joseph Willmore resorted to 'mechanical methods' in their enrichment, does not in itself indicate either impatience or contempt for the medium, but merely echoes the contemporary trend for competitive trading; there could be a vast difference between the price which a London shopkeeper might ask for a richly engraved snuffbox, and the price he would be prepared to pay to the manufacturer. It is surely to the credit of these craftsmen that their articles lost nothing of their beauty, and actually gained some, in spite of this early form of 'mass production'.

**Plate 136** George III cartouche-shaped snuffbox, silver-gilt, the lid with a cast 'Topers' Scene' in the manner of Teniers the Younger or Ostade. Of superb quality and in the finest chiaroscuro effect. T J and N Creswick, Sheffield 1812. 4in (10.2cm) by 3in (7.6cm) by ⅞in (2.2cm) deep.
This box is engraved on the base with the following inscription: 'James Creswick, Crookes Moor, Sheffield'. This, therefore, is the maker's own snuffbox, and is suitably magnificent; it is in absolutely mint condition.

**Plate 137** Victorian cast-top snuffbox with a vertical portrait of the Watt Memorial in Handsworth Church, erected 1824, by Chantrey. Nathaniel Mills, Birmingham, 1838. Weight: 7 oz. 3 dwts.
(This box is fully discussed on page 141).
*Courtesy of the Birmingham Assay Office*

**Plate 138** George III silver-gilt cast-top snuffbox, the lid cast with a baroque scrolling motif and 'Fortuna or Ceres in her Temple, holding a cornucopia' and vine motifs on the sides. Matthew Linwood V, Birmingham 1816. *Courtesy of the Birmingham Assay Office*

**Plate 139** Victorian heavy silver-gilt snuffbox, the lid enriched with engraved floral motifs and a cast floral cartouche enclosing a pair of swans. It has a cast floral thumbpiece. Gervase Wheeler, Birmingham 1837. 2¾in (7cm) by 1⅜in (3.5cm) by ¾in (1.9cm) deep.

**Plate 141** George IV small rectangular silver-gilt snuffbox, with a finely modelled cast butterfly on the lid, and a projecting thumbpiece. John Bridge, London 1825. 1¾in (4.4cm) by 1in (2.5cm) by ¾in (1.9cm) deep.
This insect has been identified as a butterfly by the Natural History Museum.

**Plate 140** George III silver-gilt rectangular cast-top snuffbox with a tavern scene in the 'Teniers' manner, set in a scrolling foliate cartouche. The sides and base are finely engine-turned with the 'basketweave' motif. Joseph Fearn, London, 1818 (AGG 1816). 3½in (8.9cm) by 2⅜in (6cm) by ¾in (1.9cm) deep.

## Casting

This is one of the oldest of all methods of enrichment on metalwork: all the Classical sources used it: the Greeks, the Romans and Egyptians. Basically, the method has remained unchanged for thousands of years. Even in Egyptian Dynastic times the *cire perdue*, 'lost wax', method was used and was still in use when the 17th, 18th and 19th century boxes were made. Both the monk Theophilus, who wrote his famous treatise on metalworking, *Diversarum Artium Schedula* in the 12th century, and Benvenuto Cellini, the great Florentine artist of the 16th century in his *Trattato della Scultura*, described the process in detail.

Cellini's is the more concise, and is devoted to a description of the method of casting a statue. With the use of a little imagination, however, the process is much the same as that employed in casting 'plaquettes' or box-lids, and although it is somewhat lengthy in context, the description is well worth repetition, as it is still valid today. In order to cut unnecessary detail, only an abstract is given.

**Plate 142** Large George IV rectangular snuffbox, heavily cast all over with acanthus motifs. Lawrence & Co., Birmingham, 1826. 4in (10.2cm) by 1¾in (4.4cm) by 1¾in (4.4cm) deep.
*Courtesy of the Birmingham Assay Office*

**Plate 143** George III silver-gilt cast-top snuffbox, the lid cast with flowerheads on a matt-chased ground, the motif repeated on the base. Appliqué herringbone motifs on the side. No maker's mark, London 1807. 3½in (8.9cm) by 2¼in (5.7cm).

**Plate 144** George IV silver-gilt cast-top snuffbox depicting 'Pointer in a field'. The rim is heavily cast with foliate motifs and the sides and base with engine-turned basketweave motifs. Ledsam, Vale & Wheeler, Birmingham 1828. 3½in (8.9cm) by 2¼in (5.7cm).

**Plate 145** George III vinaigrette of 'cushion-shape', with a slightly projecting thumbpiece. Matthew Linwood V, Birmingham 1811. 1in (2.5cm) by ¾in (1.9cm).

**Plate 146** George III shaped vinaigrette formed as a 'raying shell', with a slightly projecting thumbpiece. Matthew Linwood V, Birmingham 1806. 1in (2.5cm) by ¾in (1.9cm)

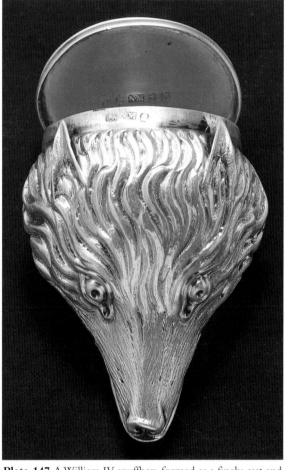

**Plate 147** A William IV snuffbox, formed as a finely cast and chased fox's mask. Nathaniel Mills, Birmingham 1830. 3⅛in (7.9cm) by 2½in (6.3cm).
Note: This is a rare subject; one of the few specimens noted dated 1826, also by Mills, was sold at Christie's in 1910.
*Courtesy of the Birmingham Assay Office*

**Plate 148** Victorian shaped vinaigrette formed as a mussel shell, of cast form and with an integral-hinge and suspensory loop. Sampson Mordan, London 1876. 1¾in (4.4cm) by ¾in (1.9cm).

**Plate 149** George IV circular vinaigrette formed as a watch, the lid with a cast 'forget-me-not' motif set with turquoises, and cast foliate border. With a similarly enriched suspensory loop handle. Thomas Newbold, Birmingham 1820. 1in (2.5cm) in diameter by ¼in (0.63mm) deep.

*Cellini's Method*

The figure was first modelled in clay over which a coating of wax was laid; a mixture of pounded clay, ashes and brick was then applied, till a second skin formed over the wax. Soft clay was then laid on to strengthen the mould, and the whole was thoroughly dried and placed in a hot oven, which baked the clay, both the core and the outside mould, and melted the wax which ran out from small holes made for the purpose (hence, the term 'lost wax'). A hollow was then left corresponding to the skin of the wax between the core and the mould, the various relations of which were preserved by small rods of bronze which had been previously driven through from the outer mould to the rough core (in order to prevent the model from slipping). The mould was now ready, and the molten bronze poured in until the whole space between the core and the outer mould was full. After slowly cooling, the outer mould was broken away from outside the statue and the inner core as much as possible broken up and raked out through a hole in the foot. The projecting rods of bronze were then cut away, and the

**Plate 150** George IV large rectangular silver-gilt vinaigrette, the lid enriched with cast foliate scrolls and with a foliate border, the sides incurving, and the base with similar cast motifs. Edward Smith, Birmingham 1827. 1½in (3.8cm) by 1in (2.5cm).

**Plate 151** George IV large oval silver-gilt elliptical vinaigrette, with a cast-top showing 'A Pair of Wading Birds', the base concentrically engine-turned with 'barleycorn' motifs, and with a cast foliate border. Ledsam, Vale & Wheeler, Birmingham 1829. 2in (5.1cm) by 1⅜in (3.5cm). Georgian cast-top subjects are uncommon.

**Plate 152**

*Left.* Victorian rectangular vinaigrette, the lid with a cast-top subject – 'First past the post', showing two jockeys racing past the post, one leading by a head. The tents in the background are engraved on a matted ground. With a cast foliate rim. Nathaniel Mills, Birmingham 1839. 1¾in (4.4cm) by 1¼in (3.2cm).

Engraved on the base is the following inscription: 'Won by Miss Powell's Laura at Aberdovy Races, Sept. 1839. Presented as a prize by Mr. Lionel Lemon'.

*Right.* Victorian large rectangular vinaigrette, the lid with a cast-top subject – 'The Family Music Session', the rim of the cast foliate type. There is a hint of 'barleycorn' engine-turning on the base. Edward Edwards, London 1842. 2⅛in (5.4cm) by 1⅜in (3.5cm).

This family group subject may be based on the well-known painting by the Huguenot painter Philippe Mercier (1689-1760) which shows 'Prince Frederick and his sisters making music', the Prince being the cellist. The scene is placed in a baroque scrolling cartouche.

whole finished by rubbing down and polishing over any roughness or defective places.

On the cast 'plaquettes' intended for box-lid enrichment, the surface was afterwards touched up by hand to remove any traces of the mould, and to give further depth to the subject. This finishing off process also disguised the method of manufacture. Many cast boxes have similar enrichment on the sides and on the base. These were cast in

**Plate 153**
William III rectangular cut-corner snuffbox, the lid finely engraved with scrolling acanthus foliage and with 'debased laurel' motif borders. With a stand-away nine-lugged hinge and projecting thumbpiece.
Maker's mark not clear:    I–
                                M–
                                ME
But the engraving might be of Dutch origin, styles of ornament at this period being almost identical. *Circa* 1700. 2⅛in (6.4cm) by 2in (5.1cm) by ½in (1.3cm) deep.

sections and later soldered together, and the inside and outside of the receptacles were then covered by fire-gilding to cover all traces of the solder-marks, as well as, of course, to protect the inside from corrosion by the acidity of the snuff or aromatic vinegar contents. There are nevertheless many ungilt boxes extant, but it must be admitted that silver-gilding tends to heighten the effect of the chiaroscuro.

*Fire-Gilding*
Since this term is inevitably encountered in references to 'Applied Ornament', a description and definition of the process might, at this point, prove of interest. Technically speaking, the method involved the application of an amalgam, that is to say, a mass of gold formed into a pulp by chemical manipulation with mercury. Frederick Bradbury's important work on *A History of Old Sheffield Plate* clearly defines the process, but since it is, of course, intended for use on copper, the distinction has to be made between precious metals and base metals, otherwise, the method is basically the same.

'An amalgam was made by boiling the gold in about five times its weight of mercury in an iron ladle which had been coated with whitening and water and then dried. The amalgam, having been poured into cold water and brought to a semi-fluid condition, was put into a leather bag and squeezed to get rid of the mercury. This operation forced the mercury through the pores of the leather and left the gold in the bag. The proper consistency of the gold was about that of stiff clay, and it was divided into portions sufficient to cover the article which it was designed to gild... (there follows a recipe for application on copper where another amalgam of nitrate of mercury was involved)... then the vessels with the gold side up were placed in open pans and set over a coke fire, the heat of which caused the mercury to

**Plate 154** George IV small rectangular vinaigrette with a cast-top subject – 'A lakeland view with buildings in the background'. William Simpson, Birmingham 1828. 1in (2.5cm) by ¾in (1.9cm).
The location of this scene cannot be traced.

97

evaporate and leave the gold only. This process was known as fire-gilding, and is practically the same as that described in Benvenuto Cellini's treatise on Goldsmithing'. (It is interesting that Bradbury, too, made use of the same sort of comparative analysis as in the present work.)

### Engraving

This subject has already been investigated *inter alia* in relation to the work of the German, Dutch and English silversmiths, but since the method has to be included in any attempt at complete classification, a definition and historical survey is indicated.

Sir Charles Jackson's definition of 'engraving' is concise and will do as well as any, especially as he also firstly defines 'flat-chasing' (vide: *Illustrated History of English Plate*, page 208): '(It (flat-chasing) consists of surface decoration, composed of flat lines incised, or rather, depressed, with a mallet and chisel without a cutting-edge; and differs from engraving, in that the latter is executed with a sharp-edge graver which, in being used, actually cuts away a part of the metal worked upon'. The early use of engraving in England appears to stem from the 12th and 13th centuries, and, as always with very early plate, can be seen to best advantage on church silver. Both chalices and patens of these periods survive which bear simple 'Gothic' foliate ornament or the 'Agnus Dei' motif. On Tudor and Elizabethan plate, engraved ornament became more elaborate and consisted mainly of foliate scrolls in the Renaissance manner, with a leaning towards grotesque monsters and birds.

Much material has been sifted by various writers, not least by the author of this present work, in attempts to determine beyond conjecture the provenance of various articles with such eminent engravers as Simon Gribelin, William Hogarth and a few others, with little or no result. It might, therefore, be of interest, at this point, to introduce another aspect connected with 'Applied Ornament' on boxes which could supply a possible key to the identity of some of the later engravers, and which is based on critical observation and research.

**Plate 155** Charles II sideways oval tobacco box, the lid engraved with a manteled shield containing a stag's head. With light cable gadroon borders on lid and base.
'LS Crowned', London 1675. 3¾in (9.6cm) by 3in (7.6cm) by ⅞in (2.2cm) deep.

*Courtesy of the Worshipful Company of Goldsmiths*

**Plate 156** Charles II large oval tobacco box with cable gadroon rims top and bottom. Engraved on the lid with an elaborately manteled coat-of-arms incorporating a grated helmet in profile surmounting and surmounted by eaglets. RS in Heart, London 1682. 4in (10.2cm) by 3¼in (8.3cm) by 1¼in (3.2cm) deep.

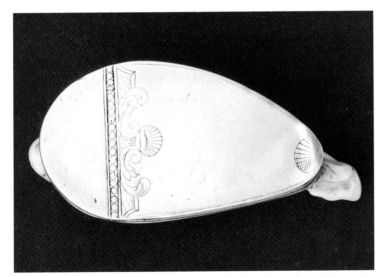

**Plate 157** George II silver-mounted cowrie-shell snuffbox, formed from the 'teeth' of the mollusc. Engraved with 'architectural scroll and shell' motifs and with a well-disguised integral hinge, and reeded mounts. Unmarked, *circa* 1730. 2¼in (5.7cm) by 1¼in (3.2cm).

**Plate 158** George III large rectangular vinaigrette of very shallow form, hand-engraved on the lid with a 'Hare in Den' subject (after Thomas Bewick). Samuel Pemberton VI, Birmingham 1809. 1¾in (4.4cm) by 1¼in (3.2cm)

With the possible exception of Fabergé (who instituted the 'workmasters' punch, and thus identified them) and some of the latter day artist-goldsmiths, whose practice of insisting that their engravers' signature appears on finely enriched plate ensures that their identity will be remembered, few of the workshops of the preceding centuries subscribed to the belief that the craftsmanship of individual workers should be thus recognised, including also the Matthew Boulton manufactory where workmen's punches – a fleur-de-lys, and odd letters – were struck in inconspicuous places. The same has, perhaps, always been true of most firms: enrichment, like most other fine work, has been taken too much for granted. It is only when it is realised that such anomalies will hamper the historian in years to come, that steps may be taken to avoid them.

In researching for possible sources of the engraved subjects on silver boxes of the late 18th and early 19th centuries, it was inevitable that the name of Thomas Bewick (1753-1828) should make an appearance. This great master-engraver lived and worked on Tyneside, and in comparing most snuffboxes and vinaigrettes of these periods, particularly of Birmingham origins, a certain 'Bewickian' atmosphere was noted about many of them. As most of Bewick's subjects were taken either from nature – his *History of Quadrupeds* and the *History of British Birds* are masterpieces in the art of the woodcut – or from contemporary life, many of the engraved scenes on the box-lids resemble these. Furthermore, Bewick had, in addition to his brother, John, a number of first-rate pupils, and altogether this 'School' turned out many thousands of superb 'cuts' or wood-cut engravings.

**Plate 159** Queen Anne oval tobacco box, the lid embossed with a heavy slant gadroon circlet embracing scalloped matted ground enriched with foliate motifs. With light twisted wire rims and a reeded collet on the base, and engraved with contemporary cyphers on the lid. Benjamin Bentley, London 1705. 3¾in (9.5cm) by 3⅛in (7.9cm) by 1in (2.5cm) deep.
Currently in use by the Goldsmiths' Company as a toothpick box.
*Courtesy of the Worshipful Company of Goldsmiths*

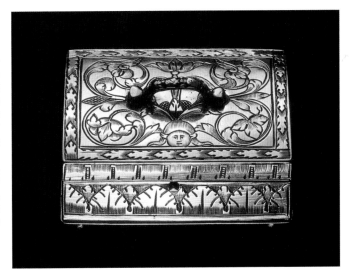

**Plate 160** William and Mary rectangular spice-casket, the slightly domed lid superlatively engraved with chinoiserie motifs comprising a 'debased laurel wreath' around the rim, palm leaves vertically engraved around the sides and foliate scrolling motifs and a Chinaman wearing a head-dress, on the lid. With a small hinged 'bracket' handle and on four ball feet. The hinge (not shown) is of the stand-away type. 'TT Crowned', London, *circa* 1690. 1⅞in (4.8cm) by 1¼in (3.2cm) by ⅝in (1.6cm) deep.
Mr Timothy A Kent in his scholarly work *London Silver Spoonmakers*, The Silver Society 1981, tentatively attributes 'TT Crowned' to Thomas Tysoe, Gracechurch Street, who appears to have been a smallworker, apprenticed to the Haberdashers' Company. Mr Kent summarises the ascription with 'attributions to Thomas Townley or Thomas Tucker would appear to have nothing to support them'.

As has been the case, however, with the majority of the scenes noted, only a very few are directly ascribable to Bewick: the others, while in the idiom of this artist, were obviously either blatantly plagiarised, or else drew inspiration from his themes. Such few scenes as were identifiable were the Matthew Linwood subject (illustrated on page 113 of *Investing in Silver*) 'The man and his dog' (the dog watches while his master is having his dinner) stated by Thomas Hugo in his *The Bewick Collector*, London, 1866, to appear as a tail-piece in the first edition of *History of Quadrupeds*, and the Pemberton 'Hare in the reeds', a cast version of which by Thomas Newbold, Birmingham 1820, also appears on page 138.

One concrete conclusion which emerged from a close examination of all the thousands of Bewick woodcuts in the British Museum was the fact that both he and some of his pupils also engraved trade cards, letter-headings and invoice heads for various Newcastle personalities. Bewick himself engraved the silversmith John Robertson's trade card in 1814, and, as he is known to have engraved at least one salver (it is now in the Victoria & Albert Museum) and had been first the apprentice and then the partner of Ralph Beilby, who was a gifted engraver on silver, it is possible that he produced work for other silversmiths also, possibly John Robertson.

Taking this coincidence as a possible key to the identity of other copper-plate engravers who might have worked in silver, the Birmingham Trade Directories were perused, and a few more names isolated:

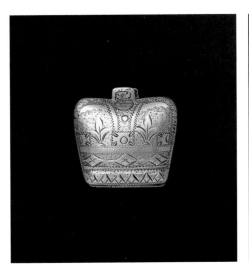

**Plate 161** George III shaped vinaigrette formed as a crown, bright-cut with 'double-dot scoring' and foliate and diaper motifs and with a stand-away hinge. Simpson and Son, Birmingham 1819. ¾in (1.9cm) by ⅝in (1.6cm).
This is a variation of the more common Willmore 'Crown' made to commemorate the Coronation of George IV in 1820.
**Plate 162** George III shaped vinaigrette formed as a 'horseshoe'. The lid is engraved with three bands of foliate motifs. It has a slightly projecting thumbpiece. Cocks and Bettridge, Birmingham 1811. 1in (2.5cm) by ¾in (1.9cm).

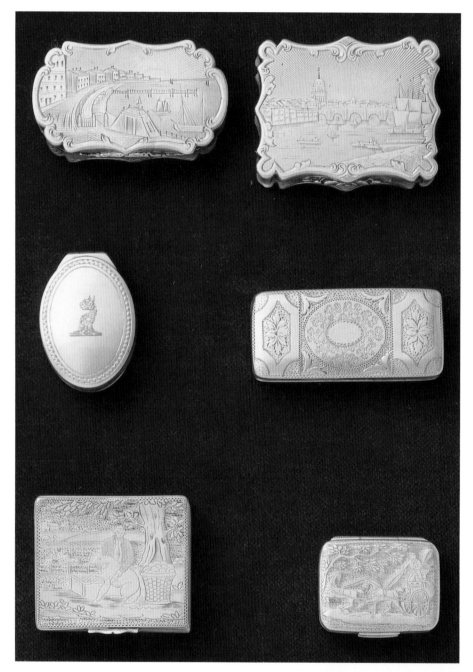

**Plate 163**

*Top left*. Victorian shaped rectangular vinaigrette, the lid hand-engraved with view of 'Brighthelmstone' (Brighton) showing the Old Chain Pier. On an engine-turned radial ground, with projecting foliate thumbpiece. Nathaniel Mills, Birmingham 1847. 1½in (3.8cm) by 1in (2.5cm).

The little 'pedestal-shaped' building in the foreground was the box-office where tickets were obtained for access to the pier. One then entered the gate on the left and proceeded to the pier, which was quite a way from the entrance, along the Marine Parade.

*Top right*. Victorian rectangular vinaigrette, hand-engraved with a view of 'London Bridge seen from the South Bank of the Thames' on the lid, on an engine-turned radial background. Nathaniel Mills, Birmingham 1846. Size 1⅜in (3.5cm) by 1in (2.5cm).

There is a smaller version below, also by Mills, dated 1847.

*Centre left*. George III vertical oval vinaigrette with a stand-away three-lugged hinge, the lid with a bright-cut 'wriggle' motif and an engraved contemporary crest in the centre. It has a florally pierced grille. Richard Lockwood, London 1800. 1in (2.5cm) by ¾in (1.9cm).

*Centre right*. George III shallow rectangular vinaigrette, the lid engraved with a central elliptical escutcheon containing an 'abstract' motif, the side panels containing bright-cut foliate motifs. Joseph Willmore, Birmingham 1810. 1¾in (4.4cm) by ¾in (1.9cm).

Note: the 'abstract' motif has been noted on French 'gold piqué-inlay' boxes of *circa* 1780.

*Lower left*. George III large rectangular vinaigrette: the lid superbly hand-engraved with a 'Shearing Scene' on a 'double-dot' ground. With a projecting thumbpiece and a fine shell and filigree stamped grille. Thropp and Taylor, Birmingham 1812. 1½in (3.8cm) by 1¼in (3.2cm).

*Lower right*. George III small rectangular vinaigrette, the lid hand-engraved with a 'Man in gig' motif on a 'double-dot' scored ground, with a stand-away hinge and projecting thumbpieces. Samuel Pemberton VI, Birmingham 1811. 1in (2.5cm) by ¾in (1.9cm).

**Plate 164**

*Left*. Small rectangular Victorian vinaigrette with incused sides, the lid hand-engraved with 'London Bridge, viewed from the South Bank of the Thames' (see above for a larger version), on an engine-turned radial ground. Nathaniel Mills, Birmingham 1847. 1in (2.5cm) by ¾in (1.9cm).

*Right*. George III vertically engraved vinaigrette depicting 'The Lavender Seller', hand-engraved in imitation of a 'Cries of London' subject. Matthew Linwood V, Birmingham 1813. 1in (2.5cm) by ¾in (1.9cm).

There are many versions of this subject by many artists.

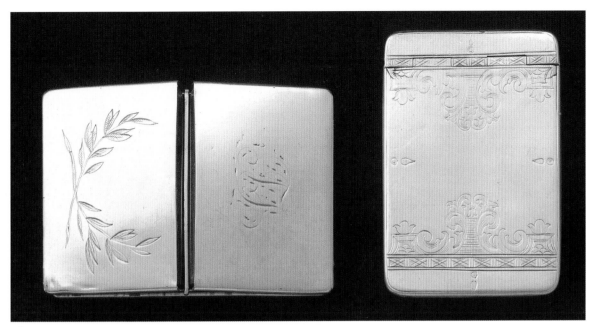

**Plate 165**

*Left.* George III shallow rectangular snuffbox with twin lids, opening away from each other. Engraved on one lid with a 'laurel wreath' and on the other with a contemporary monogram. Hester Bateman, London 1788. 3in (7.6cm) by 2¼in (5.7cm) by ½in (1.3cm) deep.

*Right.* George I flat vertical snuffbox, the lid engraved with 'architectural' motifs – scrolls and scales – interspersed with floral terminals. The hidden-integral hinge is masked by 'band-motives' in a straight line, repeated at the other end, near the projecting thumbpiece. Starling Wilford, London *circa* 1720. (Maker's mark and lion passant only). 3¾in (9.5cm) by 2⅛in (5.4cm) by ¼in (6.3mm) deep.

**Plate 166** Victorian tobacco-cum-pipecase of rectangular shape and finely hand-engraved overall with scrolling foliate motifs, and with a heavily cast foliate border. The rectangular lid protects the tobacco compartment, the side lid protects the pipecase, and the base has a compartment for vestas. This receptacle would also accommodate a medium-sized clay-pipe. It has a well disguised integral hinge.

W R Smiley, London, 1855. 5in (12.7cm) by 2½in (6.3cm) by 1¼in (3.2cm) deep.

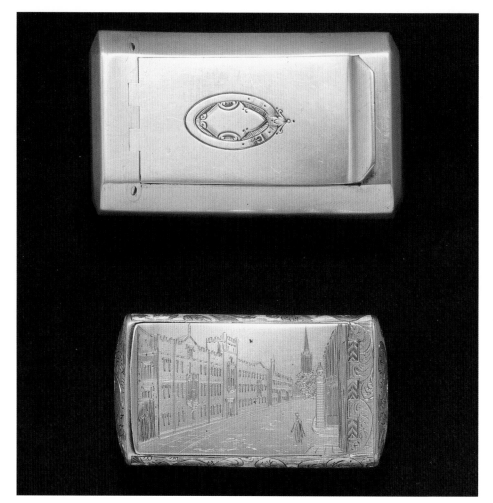

Plate 167 *Top.* George III small plain octagonal snuffbox with a sunken-integral hinge and plain up-bending thumbpiece. Engraved with a 'Garter' motif on the lid. Simpson & Son, Birmingham, 1812.

*Bottom.* George IV small engraved-top snuffbox, hand-engraved with 'University College, Oxford' on the lid, and 'chevron' motifs to mask the sunken-integral hinge. William Postans & George Tye, Birmingham, 1823.

*Courtesy of the Birmingham Assay Office*

Plate 168 William IV silver-gilt vinaigrette, the lid finely hand-engraved with a 'Griffin amidst foliate scrolls' motif, and with a fine integral hinge and cast foliate thumbpiece. Rawlings and Summers, London 1830. 1⅝in (4.1cm) by 1¼in (3.2cm).

1) FRANCIS EGINTON, *circa* 1770, who engraved Joseph Taylor's trade card and also that of Taylor and Perry (the artist who worked for the latter might have been a son of the former, with the same Christian name, as the card was necessarily later: Taylor and Perry did not enter their mark until 1829).

2) THE TYE FAMILY, *circa* 1815-30. These were all associated in some manner with silversmithing: Edward Tye was a gilt-toy (probably silverware) and pearl-bead manufacturer, George Tye and William Postans (better known as Postans & Tye) made the charming little 'engraved scene' snuffbox which depicts University College, Oxford in 1823 (see above), and the conclusion that the scene was engraved by yet another Tye – John – who worked as an engraver and copperplate printer at 12 Cherry Street, becomes irresistible, especially in view of the fact that he also engraved an advertisement for T. Hampton, Gun and Pistol Manufacturer of Livery Street, which shows the usual mid-1820-30 'Hunting Scene' subject, with mounted huntsmen, pointers and countryside motifs.

3) JOHN REYNOLDS, *circa* 1800-30, who engraved Samuel Pemberton's advertisements.

4) THOMAS COCKS, *circa* 1805-30, who appeared in the Birmingham Trade Directories as an engraver and copperplate printer. It is quite possible that he was the partner of John Bettridge who was also active about this time. This would explain the excellence of this partnership's work, namely, the fact that for once, work did not have to be sent to an 'outworker' but that the engraver worked on the premises, thus permitting a far closer relationship between maker and engraver, who could consult each other on various important points arising.

**Plate 169** Large Victorian vertical cheroot case, the sides, lid and base finely hand-engraved with contemporary coaching and sailing themes and other like motifs. Engraved overall with scrolling acanthus foliage. John Tongue, Birmingham 1844. 5½in (14cm) by 4½in (11.4cm) by 1½ (3.8cm) deep. Stella Margetson, in her interesting account of the old days of coaching, *Journey by Stages* (published by Cassell in 1967), recalls something of the splendour of the 'Red Rover' Coach depicted on the side of this finely engraved box. 'The "Red Rover" to Manchester, besides being painted scarlet, was decked out with red harness for the horses and red coats for the guard and coachman, and when Sherman of the Bull and Mouth (Edward Sherman, who ran a rival service) succeeded in running the "Red Rover" off the road, Robert Nelson promptly started a new fast coach called the "Beehive", with superior accommodation for comfort and safety to any coach in Europe. Edward Sherman had married three elderly widows in quick succession and, with the money they bequeathed him, he acquired the old Bull and Mouth inn in St Martin's-le-Grand, originally called the Boulogne Mouth in honour of Henry VIII's capture of Boulogne Harbour.' It is not known what the 'Old Salopian' refers to, nor the 'Glasgow & Ajax', but this may have been a tea-clipper.

**Plate 170** Victorian vertical rectangular cardcase, hand-engraved with a view of Sir Walter Scott's home 'Abbotsford House', on a concentric engine-turned ground. Set in a scrolling floral cartouche and with castellated and plain towers in all four corners, enriched with further concentric engine-turning. Nathaniel Mills, Birmingham 1840. 4in (10.2cm) by 3in (7.6cm).

**Plate 171** Superbly hand-engraved Victorian silver-gilt vinaigrette designed as a book, the lid and base forming the 'covers'. The lid is engraved with a vertical panel depicting a floral arrangement in a vase, around which two birds fly, the whole supported on a console. The perimeter of the panel is engraved with scrolling acanthus foliage. The back-cover is similarly embellished with a panel containing a 'tulip and butterfly' motif. Engraved along the back to simulate a book-spine with 'souvenir' on a label. With a finely hand-pierced grille. Rawlings and Summers, London, 1840. 1½in (3.8cm) by 1in (2.5cm) by ¼in (6.3mm) deep.

## Hand-Carved Allied Materials

*Treen*

This group includes all the 'allied materials', namely, treen, and its sub-divisions, natural products – ivory, mother-of-pearl, tortoiseshell (both the opaque type and thinly sliced finely figured), cameos, striated and moss agate, aventurine, and semi-precious stones such as cornelian – and man-made patterns such as mosaics.

The divisions of treen are as follows:

*Boxwood*: this wood possesses a smooth texture which commended itself as a natural medium for hand-carving, and many fine religious items as well as secular articles were both carved and engraved. A mid-19th century definition is specific: 'Box is a very valuable wood. It is of a yellowish colour, close grained, very hard and heavy'. Certainly, the silver-mounted specimen illustrated below is an excellent example of its versatility.

*Walnut*: this is an uncommon wood in use for snuffboxes, although hollowed-out walnut-bole (the gnarled sucker on the trunk of the tree) tobacco boxes of very large size have been observed, which were lead-lined and richly ornamented on the

**Plate 172** William and Mary silver-mounted oval tobacco box, the lid and base composed of finely carved boxwood plaques. The lid, set in a scalloped rim which is pinned into position, is carved with the arms of the Worshipful Company of Plumbers, and the owner's initials 'FH'. Unmarked *circa* 1690. 4¾in (12.1cm) by 3½in (8.9cm) by 1in (2.5cm) deep.

Before becoming a Member of the Guild, this owner would have to be apprenticed. The original documents relating to the Plumbers' Company are in the custody of the Guildhall Library, London, and during the period recording apprenticeships between 1660 to 1720, two apprentices with the initials 'FH' appear, namely Francis Heild, apprenticed 2nd March 1662 and Francis Hoad, apprenticed 29th June 1667.

**Plate 173**

*Above.* George III silver-mounted elliptical snuffbox, the lid with a well constructed integral-hinge and of slightly domical form, the container of 'Pontypool Japanware', originally of a dark green colour, with a band of gold around the rim. The lid is inscribed: 'John Evans Born 25 March 1772', and is fully hallmarked inside. Phipps and Robinson, London 1805. 3in (7.6cm) by 1⅝in (4.1cm) by ¾in (1.9cm) deep.

'Pontypool Japanware' was invented *circa* 1728 by Thomas Allgood, the manager of the Pontypool Ironworks, owned by the Hanbury family. Allgood also invented a method of tinning iron sheets, and this led to the perfection of the method of lacquering on the tinned plates. Soon, the Pontypool Japan factory was opened as a separate works by Edward Allgood. The first building to be chosen was at the bottom of Trosnant, a suburb of Pontypool, and here Edward Allgood and his sons, with their wives and children, worked together keeping the process a family secret. This snuffbox was made during the life of Billy Allgood, one of the sons, who died in 1813, and the business finally closed in 1822. Many fine articles were made in this pleasant medium, and included beautifully painted trays, baskets, teapots and coffee-pots. Billy Allgood claimed that many of his best pieces were 'stoved' that is, baked in an oven, for as many as twelve to sixteen times, rubbed down with pumice powder, and re-lacquered until the iron plate and the lacquer had become as one, almost like Battersea Enamel but without its fragility. Various colours, too, were introduced, a rare shade of blue, for instance, as well as shades of red, ranging from sealing-wax red to deep crimson or ruby.

*Below.* George III silver-mounted leather snuffbox of the vertical cut-corner rectangular variety. The lid is mounted with a silver cut-corner escutcheon engraved with the owner's monogram and 'Rockhampton'. It has a three-lugged silver applied hinge. Unmarked, *circa* 1770. 4in (10.2cm) by 2½in (6.3cm) by ¾in (1.9cm) deep. Leather was used for decorative and practical purposes from very early days. As John Waterer explains in *Leather,* issued by the Museum of Leathercraft in 1956: 'It is interesting that leather has always been used primarily because it was the best – and in some instances the only suitable – material for a given purpose… at an early date, for example, it was employed in sling seats, as in the "X" chair, and for backs, Spanish leather being sometimes so employed. Leather "carpets", that is to say, covers for furniture such as beds and tables, are mentioned as early as 1423 in an inventory of the wardrobe of Henry VI, being made of Spanish leather… large numbers… of containers still exist. The finest were individual cases into which the objects for which they were specifically made fitted snugly… they were made to hold precious books, reliquaries, jewels, knives and scissors, daggers, clocks, astronomical instruments and Church Plate.'

**Plate 174** George III rectangular silver-mounted snuffbox in hand-carved walnut, with twin sideways opening lids, inset with silver plates bearing the armorial crests of the Puleston family of Flintshire. The top is carved with bosses in Renaissance style, upon a matted ground, the body with the British national emblems: the Rose, Shamrock and Thistle, and on each corner with the head of King George III. The base has similar enrichment to the top. Unmarked *circa* 1813. 5in (12.7cm) by 2⅜in (7cm) by 2⅜in (6cm) deep.

The Puleston line began *circa* 1220 and was originally written 'De Pyveleston'. It was then seated at Emral, County Flint. The baronetcy of which this box was probably a commemorative relic, was granted in 1813, and the Prince of Wales Feathers on the Arms were in commemoration of Sir Richard Puleston's having had the honour of introducing the Prince of Wales into the principality on the 9th September, 1806. Sir Richard Price, born in 1765, who inherited the estates of his maternal family, assumed in 1812 the surname of Puleston, and was created a baronet in November 1813. The baronetcy became extinct in 1898.

lids with armorial bearings. The walnut tree as a species is mentioned in the earliest British botanical writings and it is supposed to have been introduced by the Romans. An inventory of 1587 lists *A bedsteed of wallnuttry, in Ladies chamber.*

### Ivory

This natural material (from the tusks of elephant, rhinoceros, walrus) has very ancient origins. The Golden Age of the ivory carver was at its height in the 13th century, but the craft went on well into the 17th. Most boxes made in this medium stem from the late 1680s, but a very finely carved-lid specimen, fully lined with silver, and thus fully hallmarked, has been noted. It was made (or at least put together) by John Leach, London, 1716.

### Tortoiseshell

As may be discerned from the mid-18th century comment of Edward Holdsworth in his *Remarks and Dissertations upon Virgil,* 1746, the medium is very old: 'Some of the Romans were so extravagant as to cover their doors and door-cases (the inner lining of the doorway) with Indian Tortoiseshell'. With the advent, in the late 17th century, of the craftsman John Obrisset (for fuller details *vide Investing in Silver,* p.101) a series of moulded designs and portrait busts were pressed in this material, and some, very few, were engraved, as in the specimen illustrated on page 110.

### Mother-of-Pearl

This is a by-product of certain bivalvular molluscs, primarily the *Pinna,* from which the majority of *nacre* – a smooth, shining, iridescent substance forming the inner layer of the shell – is derived. The use of mother-of-pearl in ornament on boxes is frequent, but hand-carved specimens are uncommon, especially from the hands of English craftsmen – the work is more reminiscent of the next category.

**Plate 175** William III oval silver-mounted tortoiseshell tobacco box, the panels set in scalloped rims, top and bottom, and with encircling rib around the body. The lift-off lid is engraved with a 'debased laurel wreath' border and the owner's initials in cyphered form and intertwining scrolls. The base is engraved with the owner's name 'John Collier' and the name of his home-town 'Bristol', both in scrolling characters, the latter in cyphered characters. Unmarked, *circa* 1700. 4½in (11.4cm) by 3¼in (8.3cm) by 1in (2.5cm) deep.

John Collier, son of John Collier, of Blagdon, Somerset, yeoman, was apprenticed to Robert Godfrey, barber-surgeon, on 8th April 1689. He was made a Burgess of Bristol in December 1698 and was living in the parish of St Michael in that city as late as 1722.

Illustrated are views of the top and base of the box, as well as one exhibiting the fine translucent tortoiseshell panel which constitutes the base.

*Cameos*

A very few boxes, chiefly vinaigrettes, and, very occasionally, a snuffbox have been observed with a hand-carved cameo (see page 112) set in a silver frame into the lid.

As most of these are of Italian origin, the subject selected for the enrichment is normally of a classical nature – the specimen illustrated depicts Venus and Cupid – finely carved. Margaret Flower in her excellent work on *Victorian Jewellery* published in 1951, states that 'The manufacture of shell cameos, the *Art Journal* of 1854 tells us, is said to be of Sicilian origin, and has been carried on at Rome since about 1805. However in about 1830 an Italian began the carving of shell cameos in Paris, "and at the present time (1854) a much larger number of shell cameos are made in Paris than in Italy. The Roman artists have attained perfection in this beautiful art".' The writer continues: 'The shells chiefly used are the red and white Bull's Mouth, the pink and white Queen's Conch, and the brown and white Black Helmet.'

*Agate*

The term 'agate' embraces a semi-precious stone which occurs, in the natural state, either in eruptive rocks, such as ancient lava, or in veins, as found in the German region of Saxony. There were also enormous deposits of the mineral in another German district, around the town of Oberstein, and a great trading centre sprang up which produced superlative examples in this most attractive medium. At the Great Exhibition of 1851, for example, several articles made in various types of agate were exhibited, and, to quote the *Report of the Juries* (all items to be exhibited were first examined for standards of merit): 'The manufacture of articles in onyx and agate, in their natural state or coloured of various hues by artificial processes [the art of "staining" was mentioned by Pliny and was a closely guarded secret for centuries; primarily red staining is obtained by means of ferric oxide, blue by salt of iron and a solution of ferro-cyanide, green by salts of nickel or chromium, and yellow by hydrochloric acid] has become a large branch of industry at Oberstein.'

When sliced in section, the mineral revealed beautiful markings; the 'moss-agate', which was always believed to arise from vegetable infiltration into the chalcedony, is in reality due to the infiltration of various oxides.

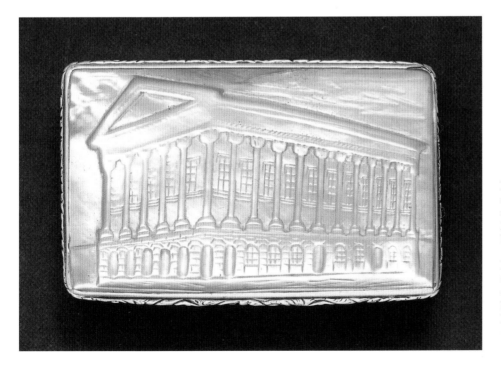

**Plate 176** Victorian snuffbox, the base and sides engine-turned, the lid carved in mother-of-pearl with a view of Birmingham Town Hall. This fine building was designed by Joseph Hansom (who also invented the cab named after him) and is modelled on the Temple of Castor and Pollux in Rome. It was completed in 1850, so this box must have been made to celebrate its foundation. Francis Clark, Birmingham, 1839. 3½in (8.9cm) by 2¼in (5.7cm).
*Courtesy of the Birmingham Assay Office*

111

**Plate 177**

*Upper left.* William IV oval vinaigrette. The lid has an inserted carved cameo 'Venus and Cupid' plaque with a cast foliate border, the sides enriched with cast diaper motifs. Nathaniel Mills, Birmingham 1836. 1⅝in (4.1cm) by 1¼in (3.2cm).

Carved cameo subjects are mentioned on page 111.

*Upper right.* Victorian oval vinaigrette, the shaped lid set with an agate plaque. The border and base are enriched with engraved 'wriggle' and foliate motifs, and with a suspensory loop. Frederick Marson, Birmingham 1875. 1½in (3.8cm) by 1in (2.5cm).

Marson entered his mark at Birmingham in 1845 and was working until 1896.

*Lower left.* George III silver-mounted cowrie-shell vinaigrette of the genus *Cypraea Arabica*, with a finely pierced 'quatrefoil and diaper' grille. The shaped oval elliptical lid is plain. Joseph Willmore II, Birmingham 1809. 1in (2.5cm) by ¾in (1.9cm).

As has been stated in the Willmore Genealogy, Joseph II entered his mark at the Birmingham Assay Office *circa* 1808. This article, therefore, must be one of his earliest pieces, and, indeed, none earlier has been noted.

*Lower right.* William IV rectangular silver-gilt vinaigrette, hand-engraved with scrolling foliate motifs, the lid set with a 'blister-pearl' mounted as a papillon dog, the sides slightly incurving. James Beebe, London 1836. 1½in (3.8cm) by 1⅛in (2.9cm).

Barry Clifford, writing in *The Book of the Dog*, states: 'It would appear that… the breed…was one of the first essentially European races to be taken to the Americas by the early Spanish settlers, and may well have been part ancestors of the Mexican chihuahuas'. A very rare specimen. A vinaigrette dated 1824, by the same maker, inset with a mounted 'blister-pearl' in the shape of a slumbering cat has also been noted.


*Aventurine*

This is a variety of quartz containing spangles of mica or scales of iron-oxide, which lend brilliancy to the mineral. It is mostly of Russian origin, and was mined in the Ural Mountains. Mostly reddish-brown or yellow in colour, it is also found in green, but an artificial form was discovered by chance when a workman at a glassworks near Venice accidentally let some copper filings fall into the molten 'metal', and thus the name, which also means 'accident' in Italian, was originated. The blue and gold spangled variety noted on several box-lids is of this artificial type. Oddly enough, the medium was also extensively used on Old Sheffield Plate boxes of the early 1740 period, possibly in imitation of the more expensive agate panels which appeared on silver boxes.

Plate 178 George III rectangular oval snuffbox: the lid and sides cast overall with floral enrichment and with a small 'shell' terminal and thumbpiece. The centre of the lid is inset with an oval portrait bust of William Shakespeare in a gold frame under glass, the sides have beaded rims. Frederick Hentsche (AGG 685), London 1819. 3¾in (9.5cm) by 2½in (6.3cm) by ¾in (1.9cm) deep.

## Cornelian

This, like agate, is another variety of chalcedony, but has a deep reddish colour, and is transparent if cut thinly; it is mostly encountered as an embellishment on late 17th century spice-boxes, but early 18th century snuffboxes, too, have cornelian bosses, or knobs. In late 18th century boxes, the panels might form the sides, but this type is uncommon.

## Mosaics

The widening facilities for continental travel in the 1840s and '50s permitted souvenir-hunters to sample European art-forms, and many travellers returned to England with mosaic inlays which were then applied to box-lid ornamentation. This, in turn, persuaded the ever-adventurous craftsmen to introduce this newly popular motif into their embellishment. It should be stated, however, that the Phipps and Robinson partnership (ever pioneering) was producing similar effects at the beginning of the 19th century, but with larger stones – the Victorian effect was obtained by the use of small multi-coloured chips set in a circle or a rectangle and outlined with further, but longer chips – and it is possible that other Georgian craftsmen also used the motif.

Various Italian views were popular subjects for mosaic inlay: scenic panoramas, the Ruins of Pompeii, The Colosseum at Rome, and groups involving domestic animals – sheep, dogs and horses – as well as specially commissioned subjects, such as favourite pets or a few portraits, have also been noted. From the historical point of view, mosaic enrichment is very ancient, and is found on Greek, Roman and Byzantine ornament. The Italian craftsmen of the mid-19th century excelled in this craft and sent several superb specimens to the Great Exhibition.

Plate 179 An unmarked mid-18th century bombe-shaped bonbonnière with stand-away hinge. The lid is set with a micromosaic architectural view, the base with a fine circular plaque of a kingfisher holding the reins of a pair of ducks pulling a small chariot, by the noted Roman mosaicist, Giacomo Raffaelli (1743-1836). 3in (7.6cm) diameter by 1½in (3.8cm) deep.

**Plate 180** George IV silver-gilt engine-turned vinaigrette, mounted with a micromosaic plaque showing a pair of mallards and a family of ducklings on a pond. With cast scolling border and a cast scroll thumbpiece. Thomas Newbold, Birmingham 1824. 3⅛in (7.9cm).

**Plate 181** George IV vinaigrette mounted with a micromosaic plaque showing a perspective view of the Roman Forum, in a gold mount with reeded sides and base and a floral thumbpiece. John Blades, London 1829. 3⅛in (7.9cm).

**Plate 182** George II piqué-inlay snuffbox of oval form, the lid enriched with 'masks and arabesques' motifs and two parrots pulling at a basket of flowers. The inner scrolling cartouche lends form and shape to the outer foliate scrolls. Unmarked, *circa* 1730. 3in (7.6cm) by 2¼in (5.7cm).

The mask at the top of the cartouche is in pure Pompeiian style, but the parrots are of French taste of the period of Louis XV. It is probable, however, that this box is of English origin, being influenced by the French designs in the same manner as the silver of the Huguenot craftsmen in the late 17th and early 18th centuries.

## Piqué Inlay

This group is difficult to ascribe to any one origin, as both English and French craftsmen worked in the medium from about 1675 to 1730. The type probably originated in France (there is still some controversy over the identity of the inventor) but, as with many other art-forms, the English workers were quick to follow the fashion. As was stated in relation to the *Commedia dell' arte* box the types of the figures used drew inspiration from Old Master paintings, but it is interesting to note that the third example illustrated (see above), while it is decorated in the French manner, with 'masks and arabesques', drew *its* inspiration, not from French, but ancient Pompeiian ornament, with the exception, of course, of the parrots!

**Plate 183** George II piqué-inlay snuffbox of oval shape, with a 'stand-away' hinge pinned to the lid. The lid is superlatively inlaid with silver foliate motifs in an ellipse and an inner cartouche of similar type. Tortoiseshell ground and base. The hinge is of the 11-lugged variety. Unmarked, *circa* 1730. 3½in (8.9cm) by 2¼in (5.7cm) by ½in (1.3cm) deep.

**Plate 184** Charles II piqué-inlay snuffbox, the tortoiseshell ground delightfully inlaid with 'Breughelesque' motifs – a Commedia dell'arte group – in silver and mother-of-pearl inlay. The whole is contained in a 'debased laurel' frame, also of silver. Unmarked, *circa* 1680-90. 3⅞in (9.8cm) by 2⅜in (6.3cm).

This box was sold in the Berney Sale of Piqué-work at Sotheby's, on the 22nd June, 1927, where it was described as being of the 'piqué-posé' variety, that is, the pattern was pressed into a pattern previously embossed.

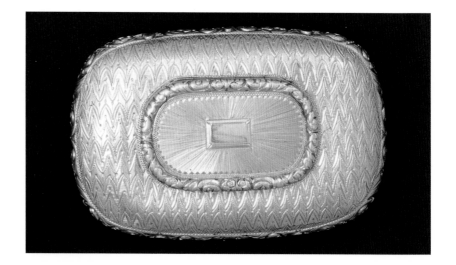

**Plate 185** George IV rectangular oval snuffbox, the lid of the oval 'flap' variety is placed in the centre of the top surface, and has a florally enriched cast border and a 'hidden-integral' hinge. The enrichment takes the form of 'eccentric engine-turning', by means of which a 'Gothic' effect is attained. Joseph Willmore, Birmingham 1820. 3½in (8.9cm) by 2½in (6.3cm) by 1in (2.5cm) deep.

## Engine-turning

This subject has received little or no careful study, and yet is one of the oldest techniques employed in 'Applied Ornament'. Most writers ascribe the craft to the middle of the 18th century and speak of it in passing. In fact, it is one of the most significant methods of enrichment, capable of subtle effects, and useful for more than one purpose. The main function of engine-turning, or 'Rose-engine Turning' as it ought to be designated (this is the name of the lathe on which the embellishment was done), was to provide a feeling of 'texture' to the metal, perhaps yet another form of chiaroscuro, but it is not generally realised that its secondary function was to protect the actual surface of the metal from excessive wear. The 'ridges and corrugations' resulting from 'turning' were not exceptionally deeply incised, but they did provide a 'ground' which prevented loving fingers from damaging the box by continual smoothing.

The method known as 'engine-turning' is very old: probably dating from the late Renaissance, but it was not used for metalwork until the end of the 17th century; its primary use as a form of enrichment was on ivory and boxwood. The catalogue of the

**Plate 186** Victorian 'table-size' snuffbox of rectangular shape, silver-gilt, the border cast with National Emblems, comprising Rose, Thistle and Shamrock motifs, the centre panel engine-turned with a 'basketweave' motif, and containing a cartouche bearing a contemporary monogram. The sides and base are similarly engine-turned. Edward Edwards, London, 1843. 5in (12.7cm) by 4in (10.2cm) by 1¾in (4.4cm) deep.

**Plate 187** George III silver-gilt rectangular cast-top snuffbox, the lid with cast 'coursing and foxhunting' subjects, and foliate sprays at each corner. Set in the centre with an engine-turned panel of the basketweave motif. Daniel Hockley, London 1813 (AGG 470). 3¾in (95.2cm) by 2½in (6.3cm).

Franks Bequest in the British Museum illustrates an ivory tankard mounted in silver-gilt of South German provenance, dated *circa* 1680, on which the whole of the ivory portion is 'turned on the lathe in a series of horizontal bands of several designs, two of them being wavy'. An illuminating footnote informs the reader that 'Nuremberg was a fruitful centre for the production of the wildest vagaries in the art of turning on the lathe, and a number of examples are to be seen in the museum Collection of Ivories. The Zick family, father (died 1632) and sons (one died 1666) were especially famous for such *tours de force* of misplaced ingenuity'. This last information would certainly support the claim, made by a senior Birmingham craftsman (whose workshop continues to produce hand-turned silver articles of the most superlative quality), that engine-turning was 'at least three hundred and fifty years old'.

The earliest method for turning metalwork on a lathe to produce decorative patterns was probably of French origin, although this is by no means certain.

Perhaps the first manual on the subject was written by Charles Plumier under the title *L'Art de Tourner* and published at Lyons in 1701. The work informs the reader in its subtitle on the frontispiece that it deals not only with turning in treen and ivory, but also iron and *other metals*, and goes on to list all the geometric shapes and effects obtainable with various tools.

The earliest ornamental turning lathe traceable is in the Science Museum, London, and is dated 'late 17th century'. It is of the 'treadle' type, and beautifully preserved. The following is an extract from the catalogue of *Machine Tools Collection* at the Museum: 'The nose end of the mandrel (the axis to which the work is secured) runs in a cylindrical collar and the pointed back end is supported in a hollowed adjustable

**Plate 188** George IV snuffbox of large size, with reeded lid and base and foliate thumbpiece. The base has cast 'self-legs', so that the box is lifted off the surface of the table. Joseph Taylor, Birmingham 1823. 4in (10.2cm) by 2¼in (5.7cm) by 1in (2.5cm) deep.

*Courtesy of the Birmingham Assay Office*

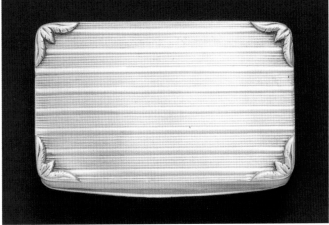

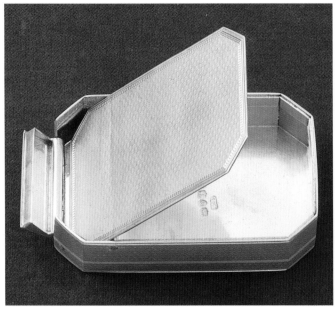

**Plate 189** William IV rectangular cut-corner 'trick snuffbox', enriched overall with engine-turning, and with 'simulated hinges' to deceive the eye. The mechanism of the masked lid is on a hinged pivot which is placed about ¾in (1.9cm) away from the drop-down hinged flange forming the false end of the rectangle. When the lid is closed and the flange replaced, little can be seen of the method of opening. Edward Edwards, London, 1831. 3½in (8.9cm) by 1⅞in (4.8cm) by ¾in (1.9cm) deep.

**Plate 190** William IV silver-mounted cowrie-shell of large size, formed as a snuffbox. The lid is finely engine-turned in alternating bands of barleycorn and wave motifs, with a plain escutcheon in the centre containing a crest. The thumbpiece is of the shaped scrolling variety. George Reid, London 1833. 3½in (8.9cm) by 2¼in (5.7cm).

This maker is not recorded in Jackson, but is in the Register at Goldsmiths' Hall, where his address is given as '18 Cross Street, Hatton Garden'. He entered his 9th mark in 1830.

centre. When rose-turning, the collar is released by removing a locking screw so that it is free to swing about a pivot in the headstock (the support for revolving parts). The mandrel carries a group of ten rosettes (these are the pattern discs, so called because they resemble a floral motif), any one of which may be made to press against a rubber (the implement used for smoothing the surface of the metal) which may be fixed anywhere along a bar running parallel with the mandrel… for rose-turning the mandrel is rotated slowly by means of a winch-driven pulley attached to the front of the lathe bed. A rosette fitted at the nose end of the mandrel has waves on the face in addition to those on the edge… (speaking of another later German lathe)… The mandrel headstock is hinged below and provided with a strong spring to keep any one of the several cams or rosettes in contact with a fixed rubber. The motion thus imparted to the mandrel caused a stationary cutting tool to produce on the work a wavy line or rosette instead of a true circle. By this means patterns suitable for decorating watch cases and snuffboxes could be produced'.

There were (and still are, as the methods are still in use which produced engine-turned patterns centuries ago) three main types of motifs as used in engine-turning:
(a) The 'Barleycorn' motif, which simulates an ear of barley, and produces the pattern over and over again.
(b) The 'Basketweave' motif, still the most popular of all, which is self-explanatory.
(c) The 'Fox's Head' motif, which depicted a group of three 'heads' or motifs arranged in the form of an 'arrow-head'. This motif was repeated over and over, to produce a satisfying pattern.

These three motifs were used to produce a wide variety of effects, either by eccentric or concentric cutting, resulting in geometrically accurate or distorted patterns, or by simple 'turning' resulting in alternating bands of 'wavy lines' and 'barleycorn' motifs, or 'wavy lines' alone, or various permutations. The most interesting use of engine-turning can best be seen on the Birmingham vinaigrettes which have architectural scene engravings on the lids. The very effective chiaroscuro device is simply radial engine-turning, and the engraving was applied on top of this. The early machines could do rotary, straight and oval work.

Four engine-turners working in Clerkenwell have been traced, and all were operative in the second decade of the 19th century, but the craft, of course, was at its height during the mid-Victorian period, in the 1840s and '50s. Not only the lids, but the sides and bases were engine-turned; the 'Fox's Head' motif is more common in French work than English and is dated *circa* 1830-70. Birmingham 'engine-cutters' as they were known in that illustrious city, were also few in number, but presumably they had large establishments which were able to keep pace with the mass of work.

## Repoussé and Embossing

The suspicion which immediately comes to mind on beholding a box-lid enriched with an inserted plaquette, as on most 'repoussé-subject' boxes, is that this might have been mass-produced by the use of a die-struck motif, and, indeed, there appears to be no reason to doubt this belief. The fact that only a few specimens of a certain subject survive, while many hundreds of another subject remain extant, merely indicates the popularity of the latter, and the intervention of such factors as emigration, accident, and hoarding, which restrict the availability of the former. Furthermore, as was the case with most small articles, little value was placed upon these, and it is only nowadays, when values have appreciated beyond imagination,

**Plate 191** Large Victorian rectangular silver-gilt vinaigrette, with an inserted repoussé plaque of York Minster from the south-east, struck in high relief. The lid is enriched with a cast foliate rim and with engine-turning of the basketweave motif on sides and base. Nathaniel Mills, Birmingham 1841. 1⅞in (4.8cm) by 1¼in (3.2cm).

**Plate 192** Victorian shaped rectangular silver-gilt vinaigrette, with an inserted repoussé plaque showing St Paul's Cathedral from the south-west, struck in high relief, the sides and base engraved with scrolling foliate motifs. Nathaniel Mills, Birmingham 1852. 1¾in (4.4cm) by 1¼in (3.2cm).
Mills retired from silversmithing *circa* 1855, but articles bearing his maker's mark for as late as 1866 have been noted. It is probable that the workshop was carried on in his absence, using the Mills's goodwill, until it passed officially to George Unite (see 'The Birmingham Boxmakers').

**Plate 193** Victorian large rectangular vinaigrette, the lid with an inserted repoussé plaque, showing St George's Hall, Liverpool, struck in high relief, and with a cast foliate border. Edward Smith, Birmingham 1854. 1½in (3.8cm) by 1⅜in (3.5cm).
St George's Hall, Liverpool was designed by Harvey Lonsdale Elmes (1815-1847), and according to Sir Banister Fletcher's *magnum opus*: *History of Architecture on the Comparative Method*, is 'the most perfect design of the Classic School, the great hall based on the tepidarium of the Thermae of Caracalla, Rome, while externally a colonnade design is handled with great effect. Professor Cockerell (Charles Robert Cockerell, 1788-1863) completed the decoration of the interior (A.D 1854)'. This view of St George's Hall is uncommon. Very few provincial public buildings were die-struck. Another edifice designed by Lonsdale Elmes, the Liverpool Collegiate High School by Nathaniel Mills III 1849, is illustrated on page 151.

**Plate 194** Victorian deep repoussé rectangular vinaigrette of the North, or Bar Gate at Southampton, part of the old fortification of the town, emblazoned with heraldry, and with a statue of George III in Roman robes. Nathaniel Mills, Birmingham, 1842. 1⅞in (4.5cm) by 1⅜in (3.4cm).

**Plate 195** Victorian vertical shaped rectangular card-case, the centre with a repoussé view of the Crystal Palace in high relief, and with repoussé foliate motifs around the rim. William Dudley, 1850. Dudley entered his mark at Birmingham in 1848 and was working until 1868. 4in (10.2cm) by 3in (7.6cm).

that many hitherto unknown subjects have been brought to light.

The early distinction has to be drawn between repoussé and embossed work, which could be done by hand (as described below in citing Theophilus' method, but which, in relation to most 19th century boxes, were struck in a die), and hand-chasing, which appears to be a type of repoussé, but which is, in reality, a hand-raised enrichment, effected by careful hammerwork struck on the top surface of the metal, to depress the surrounding silver, and thus heighten the motif. All three forms are listed here, as they are very often mistaken for each other. In repoussé-work and embossing, the plaquette was 'punched-out' so that the 'high places' appeared to stand away from the background, again providing some feeling of depth. The two terms are here applied to 'deep perspective' (the former), and 'shallow perspective' (the latter), although both were supplied by mechanical means.

*Masonic Boxes*

The text here is interrupted briefly for the inclusion of an analysis of the enrichment on the finely hand-chased silver-gilt snuffbox bearing Masonic emblems. It is placed under the general subject heading for two reasons: firstly, that the method of hand-chasing for the chiaroscuro effect is about to be examined, and secondly, because the subject of 'Freemasonry' is of interest to a wide section of people. The insertion of snuff and other boxes illustrated here bearing Masonic emblems, has been made, not because the containers are directly connected with the Masonic rites, but because they are ordinary boxes with unusual 'Applied Ornament' – yet another essay into the craft of box-lid enrichment – and, furthermore, are of fine workmanship. In order not to offend the susceptibilities of readers who might be Freemasons, and thus resent the revelation of some of their esoteric rites, the details and meanings of the symbols have been kept to a minimum, and the vagueness is therefore deliberate.

The silver-gilt snuffbox (below) is doubly uncommon. Firstly, it is the result of a 'marriage' between an English box, by James Phipps I, who entered his mark at Goldsmiths' Hall in 1754, and a French plaquette by the last surviving member of a famous French family of sculptors and copyists, Guillaume Coustos (1716–1777), and, secondly, the lid, being by a foreign artist, is signed. The item itself is a masterpiece of perspective 'on the flat', in which the central motif – a Masonic Temple – is supported on a 'stepped approach' with columns at either side and on a moulded plinth. The interior of the Temple is given depth by the use of a half-crescent device, which suggests a cupola, to which even further 'depth' is imparted by the suspended five-pointed Star of David incorporating the letter G for geometry (which symbolises one of the seven 'Liberal Arts', the remaining six being: grammar, dialect, rhetoric, music, astronomy and arithmetic) and which has other Masonic connotations.

The design is given further form by the introduction of a baroque scrolling cartouche, which wanders in and out of the motifs and finally forms part of the 'stepped approach'. In addition to the other Masonic symbols – the plumb-rule on the left, which forms part of the Jewel of the Junior Grand Warden, and the level on the right, which is part of the Jewel of the Senior Grand Warden – the whole is surmounted by the 'All-seeing Eye', which, to quote Bernard E. Jones's *Freemason's Guide and Compendium,* is 'a symbol of very great antiquity representing the ever-watchful and omnipresent Deity and, as a Christian symbol, supported by a host of Biblical references. Even in its Masonic form of an open eye within a triangle, it has been used as a Church emblem, but it came to freemasonry much more probably from alchemy than from Christian symbolism'.

The resourceful craftsman who hand-chased this box-lid, finished his work by giving the background a liberal 'matt-chased' effect, by the use of a special punch, which strikes tiny 'dots' all over the surface. The letters 'M.M', in the bottom right-hand corner are not part of the signature, but refer to the original owner, who was

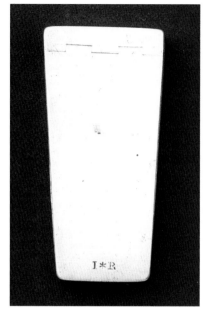

**Plate 196** George III 'keystone' shallow form snuffbox, with a finely constructed 'hidden-integral' hinge. Unmarked, *circa* 1770, engraved with the contemporary owner's initials. 2⅛in (5.4cm) by 1in (2.5cm) by ¼in (6.3mm) deep.
This box is probably of Masonic origin, the 'keystone' being one of the symbols of the 'Mark Masons'.

**Plate 197** George III rectangular silver-gilt snuffbox, the lid with an inserted hand-chased plaque enriched with Masonic subjects. with 'integral hinge' and simple scrolling thumbpiece. James Phipps I, London *circa* 1770 (box) Guillaume Coustos, Paris *circa* 1770 (plaque). 3⅜in (8.6cm) by 2⅝in (6.7cm) by ⅞in (2.2cm) deep.
*Courtesy the Board of General Purposes, Freemasons' Hall*

**Plate 198**

*Above*. Victorian shaped rectangular snuffbox, the lid partially gilt and enriched with the appliqué enamel insignia of the Masonic Order of the Knights Templar on crossed swords, and surmounted by a knight's helm. With scrolling foliage enrichment around the rim. George Unite, Birmingham, 1894. 2½in (6.3cm) by 2⅜in (6cm) by ¾in (1.9cm) deep.

*Courtesy the Board of General Purposes, Freemasons' Hall*

George Unite was apprenticed to Joseph Willmore in 1810 for a period of eight years. He entered his 'GU' in a rectangular punch at Birmingham in 1830 and again in 1839. The shape of the punch was changed in 1861, when it appeared in a shield. The business was to continue well into the 1930s.

*Below*. Large Victorian rectangular snuffbox with cast foliate borders, and enriched with engine-turning of the 'basketweave' motif on the lid, sides and base. Engraved in the centre of the lid with a presentation inscription and Masonic subjects: 'compasses and squares' in all four corners. Edward Edwards, London 1843. 4in (10.2cm) by 2⅝in (6.7cm) by ¾in (1.9cm) deep.

*Courtesy the Board of General Purposes, Freemasons' Hall*

a Master Mason.

To return to the original discussion on the subject of repoussé and embossed work, as has been stated, most 19th century box-lids were struck in machine dies. This mechanisation would explain the 'sameness' or uniformity of so many box-lid subjects, where the self-same scene appears on every box; thus, a shallow relief of one of the commonest subjects – Abbotsford House, the home of Sir Walter Scott (mostly struck to mark the occasion of his death in 1832) – will have the same Gothic turrets, chimneys, flag-tower and gardens as almost every other box enriched with this theme. A few specimens might bear some additional details such as the Gothic arched wall, looking south-west, or trees to the left, but overall, the subject was faithfully copied by various makers.

**Plate 199** George III large circular toilet-box with a pull-off lid, the perimeter bright-cut with foliate motifs, the interior of the lid with swags and festoons of foliage and a coat-of-arms in a shield, the base engraved with a Masonic theme – level, square and compasses and rule – and the date '1784'. Phipps and Robinson, London 1784. 5¼in (13.3cm) in diameter by 1in (2.5cm) deep.

This box has no Masonic purpose and is regarded as a 'Presentation Piece' probably given to the recipient, William Craswell, in token of some service to his lodge.

*Courtesy the Board of General Purposes, Freemasons' Hall*

123

The distinguished Birmingham elder-craftsman (whose views on the mechanisation of ornament appear below, and form an important contribution to current knowledge), on being asked about the possible identity of the Birmingham diemakers, replied that his father had told him, that in *his* youth (the firm goes back to the 1880s) 'there were individuals who were extremely clever in copying the work of others, in the early days'. This statement, of course, implies that there were original inventors and adaptors (full details of these and their patents appear below) but, in essence, it is the age-old story of the piracy of one man's work by twenty others.

*Theophilus' Method of Die-Stamping*
Of course, die-making for repoussé work is by no means a modern invention; quite apart from the Simon van de Passe counters which were struck in an intaglio die (as stated above), the great 12th century Benedictine monk, Theophilus, in his famous Treatise (also mentioned above) set forth his detailed instructions for this device. Translations from the original Latin text are twelve in number. The first English translation was by Robert Hendrie, published in 1847 by John Murray, but this, and subsequent versions, have been superseded by an admirably researched work *On Divers Arts* by John G Hawthorne and Cyril Stanley Smith, published by the University of Chicago Press in 1963. This finely balanced analysis, in addition to the actual translation, traces Theophilus' origins, by comparative methods, using the work of the earlier translators, to the 12th century German monk, Roger of Helmarshausen. The work, they believe, was written between 1110-40, and Roger used the pseudonym 'Theophilus' because it had a Byzantine sound, to identify himself with the Byzantine methods he admired and described.

In their footnote to Theophilus' method of *De Opere Quod Sigillis Imprimitur* or *Of work which is Impressed with Stamps* (here dealing with embossing or repoussé-work by primitive mechanical means) they say the following: 'This process of putting repetitive designs on thin sheet metal by pressing it against a carved form of a harder metal or stone is of great antiquity and ubiquity. It has been employed particularly to make small decorations out of extremely thin gold, and such objects may be seen among artefacts from ancient Mesopotamia, Egypt, Mycenae, and Etruria, as well as from the pre-Columbian New World. The product, though sparing of the precious metal and labour, looks flashy but cheap and is easily subject to damage'.

In passing, it is ironic that Hendrie in the footnote of his translation on the same topic, also comments on this, and continues that he had seen designs executed in Paris, in thin gilt copper, where the method of die-stamping was 'a simple lever, fitted upon a tall upright post, with a weight attached at one end; the other extremity of the lever was pulled by a rope. Our Birmingham and Sheffield manufacturers, could, were proper designs procured from our artists, defy all attempts at competition, and re-establish a neglected source of profit and industry'. Hendrie was thus obviously unaware that this very method, much mechanised, was in contemporary use by many Birmingham *and* Sheffield craftsmen, and had been for at least a decade!

In order to return to Theophilus' own description of repoussé-work, it is first necessary to point out that the technique, as seen by him, referred to hand-ornament raised by hammering from the back of the sheet of metal, and must be distinguished from his technique of 'striking in a die' as described by Hawthorne and Smith. It is included in this survey because of its unique medieval origin. In order to preserve the feeling of 'antiquity', Hendrie's version is used, although Hawthorne and Smith's translation is much smoother, and probably the more correct. The parentheses are the present writer's.

Theophilus begins: *'Percute tabulam auream sive argenteam quantae longitudinis et latitudinis velis ad elevandas imagines'* – Beat a gold or silver plate as long and wide as

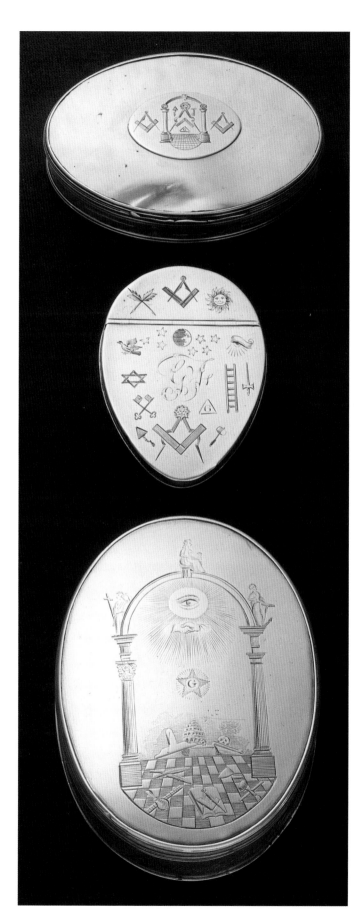

**Plate 200** George III circular silver-gilt snuffbox with a pull-off lid. The lid is enriched with the repoussé Arms of the Chevalier Bartholomew Ruspini. Charles Mieg, London 1786 (AGG 363). 2¼in (5.7cm) in diameter by ⅝in (1.6cm) deep.

The Chevalier Ruspini was both a distinguished Freemason and a noted dentist. He founded the Royal Masonic Institution for Girls in 1788, and this box has passed into the possession of the Grand Lodge Museum. He invented and sold tins of dentifrice closely resembling this box. The coat-of-arms and address exactly imitate one of these base metal receptacles, and it is therefore probable that this silver specimen was made for Ruspini himself to be used as a snuffbox, and not as a dentifrice box, as has been believed hitherto. A full account of the Chevalier Ruspini and his philanthropic work can be found in J Menzies Campbell's *Dentistry Then and Now* (published privately by the author, 1963).

*Courtesy the Board of General Purposes, Freemasons' Hall*

**Plate 201**

*Above*. George III oval elliptical snuffbox: the lid with an inserted mother-of-pearl plaque enriched in the centre with a silver oval plate which is engraved with Masonic subjects: squares and compasses, an arch composed of two Doric columns and further Masonic symbols in a squared pavement. The lid is enriched with a band of reeding and with a scrolling thumbpiece. Thomas Bowen II, London 1800. 3½in (8.9cm) by 2½in (6.3cm) by 1in (2.5cm) deep.

Thomas Bowen entered his mark at Goldsmiths' Hall in 1770. He worked at 5 Naked Boy Court, Ludgate Hill in 1782.

*Courtesy the Board of General Purposes, Freemasons' Hall*

*Centre*. George III silver-mounted cowrie-shell snuffbox, the lid with an 'integral-hinge' and engraved with Masonic subjects – square and compasses, sun, moon and stars, the All-Seeing Eye, and other Masonic emblems of symbolic significance. Joseph Taylor, Birmingham 1810. 2¾in (7cm) by 2in (5.1cm).

Cowrie-shell boxes from the workshop of Joseph Taylor are uncommon. *Courtesy the Board of General Purposes, Freemasons' Hall*

*Below*. George III oval vertical tobacco box, the inserted domed plaque of the lid enriched with Masonic subjects – the All-Seeing Eye within an arch, resting on Corinthian and Doric columns, on which stand figures representing Faith, Hope and Charity, clasped hands symbolic of friendship, a 'Star of David' containing the 'G' for geometry, and other Masonic symbols on a squared pavement. The skull in the far background symbolises mortality. John Robertson, Newcastle *circa* 1790. 4in (10.2cm) by 3in (7.6cm) by 1¼in (3.2cm).

*Courtesy the Board of General Purposes, Freemasons' Hall*

you wish for relieving the figures… (directions are given for testing the quality of the casting)… when it has become so (sound, and reliable to work on) see beforehand that the anvils and your hammers, with which you should work, are quite smooth and polished; and take care that the gold or silver plate be so equally thinned everywhere, that it be in no place thicker than in another. And when it has been thinned so that the nail, slightly pressed upon it, may show upon the other side, and it is perfectly sound, directly portray the figures you may wish, according to your will… you will then with a curved iron, well polished, gently however, rub the head in the first place, which must be more raised; and so turning the plate upon the right side you will rub around the head, also with the smooth and polished iron so that the ground may descend and the head be raised, and you will directly beat around the head with a middling sized hammer upon the anvil, gently, and you thus cook it before the furnace, until it glows, coals being superposed in that place. Which being done, and the plate cooled by itself, you will again rub it with the curved instrument on the underneath part, inside the hollow of the head, slightly and carefully, and turning the plate you will again rub with the smooth iron upon the upper part, and you depress the ground that the relief of the head may be raised, and again gently striking it with the middling hammer about this, you recook it, by applying the coals; and thus you act often, by carefully raising it inside and outside and frequently hammering, as often cooking until the relief is brought to the height of three or four fingers, or more or less, according to the number of figures'. The remainder of Theophilus' instructions concern the design and execution of the details – the mouth, nose and eyes – and methods of re-soldering fractures should these occur, and how to polish the plate and apply gilding to it.

*Birmingham Repoussé-Work*

How were the Birmingham dies for mechanical striking made and by whom? The first part of the question is easily answered: the subject, whatever it was to be, was first copied by an artist from a contemporary painting, engraving or print, probably the last. It was then passed to a craftsman-engraver, who scooped out the pattern in a block of hard steel and a refinement of Theophilus' method was then applied, the one important difference being the use of power-operated machines – water-power,

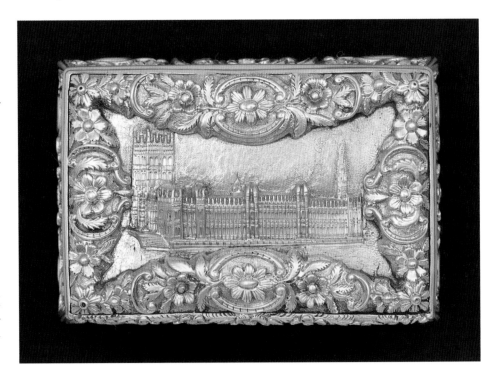

**Plate 202** Victorian large rectangular snuffbox, the lid with an inserted repoussé plaque of The Palace of Westminster. The plaque is set in heavy repoussé floral frames, the sides with floral enrichment. Edward Smith, Birmingham 1850. 4in (10cm) by 3in (7.5cm).

The old House of Commons was destroyed by fire in 1834, and Charles Barry (1795-1860) designed new buildings in the late Perpendicular style for the 'Mother of Parliaments'. The building was commenced in 1840 and concluded in 1860. This view shows the terrace of the Commons from the river, of with the partially finished Victoria Tower at the far left (it was finally completed in 1860). The tower at the far right is the unfinished clock tower which now houses 'Big Ben', the 13½ ton bell, cast in 1856.

**Plate 203** George IV large rectangular snuffbox, the sides and base enriched with engine-turning of the 'basketweave' motif, the rim with cast foliate motifs. The lid has an inserted repoussé plaque depicting Mrs Siddons playing Catherine of Aragon in Shakespeare's *Henry VIII* (Act II Scene IV). John Bettridge, Birmingham 1828. 3½in (8.9cm) by 2¼in (5.7cm) by 1in (2.5cm) deep. Sarah Siddons (1755-1831) was the sister of the great English actor John Kemble. The part of Catherine of Aragon was perhaps her most triumphant role, and the famous painter of historical subjects, George Henry Harlow (1787-1819), recorded the scene as she addressed Cardinal Wolsey while the King and the Bishops looked on. The painting was copied by the noted engraver George Clint (1770-1854) and it is probable that John Bettridge was inspired by this. It has already been stated in the text that engravings were the probable source for many of these box-lid subjects.

of course — and the box-lid was then 'chased up' by hand, to remove any excess metal and to heighten the effect of 'depth'. After being polished, it was trimmed and inserted into the box-lid.

Although William West's *The History, Topography and Directory of Warwickshire, 1830* lists forty-eight die-sinkers, only Edward Thomason is also identifiable as a silversmith, but he was no mere 'small-worker': he had, next to Matthew Boulton, the largest manufactory in Birmingham, and produced a bewildering variety of articles, among which were medals, so perhaps the dies were used for these. It is probable that, as in the case of the engravers mentioned above, die-sinkers who worked on seals also produced dies for the silversmiths; when a new subject was introduced, all the other die-makers copied it and distributed the motif to all who bought it.

Of the genre of the subjects, also, little can be traced, but there are a few slender clues, which coincidence has brought to light. Most boxes which have 'Sporting Subjects' enrichment are of the cast variety, probably because casting was more to the taste of the wealthy, as a symbol of opulence, but towards the middle of the 19th century, repoussé-top boxes with this type of subject may be found. One such box had a 'Hunting-scene' subject which, by pure chance, was also noted on an engraved box by Joseph Willmore, dated *circa* 1820, which was exhibited at the British Antique Dealers' Fair in 1954. This latter box was discussed in an article in *Apollo Magazine*, by G Bernard Hughes, who attributed the subject to Henry Alken, the great English etcher (1784-1851) who specialised in both sporting subjects and caricatures of them. The subject was 'In Full Cry', and the central figure was a mounted huntsman beckoning his fellows on. The same motif was subsequently noted on a Victorian

**Plate 204** George III vertically 'die-stamped' vinaigrette of 'Admiral Lord Nelson' with the motto 'England Expects Every Man Will Do His Duty' engraved in an oval. On a 'scored threaded' ground, with an integral-hinge and short scrolling thumbpiece. The grille is die-stamped with a view of *The Victory* and the date of the Battle of Trafalgar 'Oct 21 1805'. It is engraved on the base with a floral motif. Matthew Linwood V, Birmingham, 1806. 1¼in (3.2cm) by 1in (2.5cm)

**Plate 205** Victorian shaped rectangular vinaigrette of York Minster, die-stamped on a horizontally engine-turned ground, with hints of hand engraved foliage at rims. Nathaniel Mills, Birmingham 1850. 1½in (3.8cm) by 1¼in (3.2cm)

box, dated 1840, but this was a repoussé-top specimen. So a probable source for these 'Sporting Subjects' may be found among works on this type of painting. It is possible that further hitherto unknown subjects may be identified with the use of such books as Lord Lavington's *Sporting Pictures at Lavington Park* (printed for private circulation in 1927), which illustrates many pictures by various famous artists in this genre, and other similar works.

Another interesting ascription was discovered, again by pure accident, when a watercolour by Joseph Nash dated 1846, the subject of which was Buckingham Palace with the Marble Arch still in front (it was removed to its present site at Tyburn in 1851) was noted. On closer examination, the subject turned out to be the exact facsimile of the superb table snuffbox, illustrated on page 98 of *Investing in Silver,* which is by Nathaniel Mills. Subsequently, two other articles – a sweetmeat basket and the covers of an 'aide memoire' – were also observed to bear the same subject, all three dated 1846 and by the same maker.

Such fortuitous discoveries, however, are rare, and furthermore, artistic licence has also to be taken into account. Very often, a view of a castle or a famous country house or mansion is shown out of context, with only one aspect receiving attention. The Terrace at Windsor Castle, for instance, was for years mistaken for a view of the buildings at Hampton Court, because there was not enough detail to identify the scene with the former, but the subject seemed to comply with the architecture of the latter. For the most part, views in the 'Castles, Cathedrals and Country-house' series were probably struck (as was stated in *Investing in Silver,* pages 113-114) to serve as mementoes of visits to well-known places by a public which was just beginning to savour the delights of unlimited rail travel.

**Die-Stamping**

The realisation that there might be mechanical forces at work on what had hitherto been believed to be 'hand-engraved' ornament came gradually, following a series of fortunate coincidences. A number of the famous Matthew Linwood series 'Admiral Lord Nelson' vinaigrettes (which portray, on the lid, the Hero of Trafalgar in his characteristic pose with the sleeve pinned up and the motto 'England expects every man will do his duty') were observed over a period of about eight years. On noting that perhaps the second specimen had a peculiar 'vagueness' about one certain position near the top of the head, a watch was thereafter maintained, and subsequent examples revealed the same anomaly – a fact which could not be explained away by the convenient phrase 'wear and tear' – and it did not make sense for one particular spot to be so lightly engraved as to make the subject almost invisible. When this present work was being researched, therefore, a photograph of one of these 'Nelson Vinaigrettes' was submitted to the senior Birmingham engraver mentioned above, who immediately and unhesitatingly identified it as a specimen of 'Die-stamping'.

Were it not for the discovery of a contemporary patent for a method of *Cutting, Pressing and Squeezing Metals, etc.* taken out in 1804 by John Gregory Hancock of Birmingham, a die-engraver by profession, which was first noted in Bennet Woodcroft's *Subject-matter Index of Patents of Inventions,* London 1857, the attention of the writer would not have been focused on the method at all, but on reflection, Hancock's invention deals not so much with a completely new invention for stamping metal – after all, we have read Theophilus' method – as with a method of (to quote the official description on the patent-specification) 'Forcing or working the bolts of presses or of engines used for the purpose of cutting, pressing, and squeezing,' etc. Nevertheless, the method of die-stamping metal was refined, and it is odd that Linwood appears to be the first person to have used 'die-stamped ornament' on his boxes.

It ought, at this juncture, to be pointed out that when speaking of boxmakers, and the Birmingham craftsmen in particular, it should be borne in mind that with the exception of the very large manufactories (Thomason has been mentioned above)

**Plate 206** *Above left.* George III circular counter box, of a 'half-barrel' shape. The lid is struck with a portrait of 'Admiral Lord Nelson' in uniform and facing left. Below the bust is 'Born 29 Spr 1758'. The bottom states 'Conqueror of Aboukir 1 Augt 1798 Copenhagen 2 April 1801 Trafalgar 21 Octb 1805 Where He Gloriously Fell'. 1⅛in (2.8cm) by ⅞in (2.2cm deep).

This box is a rendering of the larger series of brass boxes marked 'M & P Fecit' – Lewis Pingo (1743-1830) and Nathaniel Marchant (1739-1816). From Lawrence Brown's *British Historical Medals*, we have the following comment to medal number 625, which uses as a reverse design the same as the top of the two boxes. The note reads: 'the reverse bust of Nelson is reminiscent of the discarded trial by Kuchler (M.H. 494 – *British Naval Medals*, Admiral the Marquis of Milford Haven, London 1919) with the lapels of the jacket folded open; it is almost identical to the obverse of No. 580 [which is a trial striking for the box components] see M.H. 523 [which depicts the box]. The obverse of the latter is signed M & P Fecit: according to Forrer (*Biographical Dictionary of Medallists* 1904) (III pp 560) Marchant was employed by Lewis Pingo and Thomas Wyon between *circa* 1782-1815.'

*Below left.* George III gold-mounted snuffbox, inscribed: 'The Gift of the 5th Batt Comp y 1st Regt Aberdeen Volunteers to Captain Thomas Burnett as a mark of their esteem'. Samuel Pemberton, Birmingham 1805. 2¾in (6.9cm) by 1¾in (4.4cm).

From information regarding the early days of the Gordon Highlanders it is noted that in Kincardineshire there were two corps of volunteers, the first formed in 1803 was known as the Mearnshire Volunteers and had, as one of their captains, Thomas Burnett. 'The above named officers continued to serve until 1808, and both corps volunteered into the Kincardineshire local militia in that year. Like other northern corps, they were repeatedly upon permanent duty, both at Stonehaven and in Aberdeen.' The Kincardineshire Volunteers later became the 1st Regiment of the Aberdeen Volunteers and from this corps would be drawn many men who would join the Gordon Highlanders.

*Above right.* George III snuffbox, the lid mounted with a piece of wood from the *Victory*. Henry Cornman, London 1816. This is a very early date for a *Victory* wood box. 2½in (6.4cm) by 1½in (3.8cm).

*Below right.* HMS *Victory* gold-mounted pine snuffbox. The label set into the lid reads: 'This is made from the Main Mast close to which the Immortal NELSON fell. October 21st. 1805 Alex r Davison'.

Alexander Davison was Lord Nelson's prize agent, business manager and very close friend. Upon news of the death of Lord Nelson, Alexander Davison proceeded immediately to Portsmouth and on Monday, 16th December 1805 made a copy of Lord Nelson's last codicil to his will. During this trip, he would have had the opportunity to receive some of the wood from the *Victory's* mainmast from which this box was fashioned.

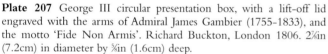

**Plate 207** George III circular presentation box, with a lift-off lid engraved with the arms of Admiral James Gambier (1755-1833), and the motto 'Fide Non Armis'. Richard Buckton, London 1806. 2⅞in (7.2cm) in diameter by ⅝in (1.6cm) deep.

This important relic was a personal gift from the Secretary of State for War, Lord Castlereagh (1769-1822). Engraved on the side: 'With regard and admiration on the capture of 18 Sail of the Line and 52 other vessels of war', and on the base, 'This presentation in recognition of the Courage and Determination shown by Admiral Gambier and his Expeditionary Force on the Bombardment and Capitulation of the Danish Fleet at Copenhagen, September 7th 1807'.

In 1807, Napoleon wished to close the Baltic to British trade, thus also depriving the Royal Navy of much needed supplies of timber for mainmasts and tar for caulking the vessels. Denmark was to be coerced into closing the Sound to Britain, and lending her navy to the French to further his ambitions. On 19th July 1807 the British decided to ask Denmark to hand over her fleet to Great Britain, upon the promise to restore the whole of it at the conclusion of the war, and, in the case of refusal, to seize it by force. On 26th July Gambier sailed from Yarmouth to the Baltic, the army accompanying the expedition being commanded by General Lord Cathcart (1755-1853). Denmark rejected the British proposals and on 2nd September Copenhagen was attacked by the British. The Danes surrendered the city on 7th September. The

British then took possession of a large part of the Danish Fleet and naval stores, which were then taken to England. For this important service Admiral Gambier was raised to the Peerage with the title 'Baron Gambier', and received the thanks of both Houses of Parliament. Lord Cathcart, who commanded the Army, was rewarded with a Viscountcy. Accompanying the silver box is a personal letter from Lord Castlereagh dated 'Downing Street, September 16th 1807, 6p.m.', warmly congratulating the Admiral for the conduct of the fleet and army and signed, 'Yours, my dear sir, In truth most sincerely and faithfully, Castlereagh'. Admiral Gambier married in 1788. He then retired to Iver, Buckinghamshire. As there was no issue, the title lapsed with his death in 1833.

*The author would like to thank Mr. Grayham Hunt for his assistance in the preparation of the historical background to the Gambier snuffbox.*

**Plate 208** George III blue and white jasperware portrait medallion in a gilt frame of Admiral Lord Nelson by John De Vaere (1754-1830). One of a series, including Admirals Howe, Duncan and St.Vincent, after the Battle of the Nile, 1798. 3½in (8.8cm) by 3¾in (9.5cm).

Josiah Wedgwood commissioned De Vaere in 1787, on the recommendation of John Flaxman. In 1788, De Vaere accompanied Flaxman to Rome to copy bas-reliefs. He was employed at Etruria from 1790.

most workshops employed 'outworkers' for all but the essential silversmithing work. Thus, a box would be made by Linwood, who sent it out to receive the hinge, which was made by a specialist hinge-maker, then to be engraved or bright-cut by another specialist. The grilles were pierced or (as has recently been discovered) die-stamped. A very fine caddy-spoon by John Bettridge of Birmingham, dated 1823, was found to have, as part of the enrichment in the 'shovel-bowl', a fully recognisable vinaigrette grille die-stamped in the centre. The grille had all the characteristics of the usual box-grille, namely, floral motifs and a central 'snowdrop' motif, but it was completely unpierced. A closer examination of some of Linwood's so-called 'filigree grilles' has also revealed that only the front looks like filigree, the back is quite flat, so that these, too, were struck in a die to simulate other methods of silversmithing. It should be emphasised that these latter specimens should not be confused with the 'simulated filigree' enrichment on caddy-spoons, where the ornament merely *looks like* filigree in its delicate piercing; in this case, the filigree-effect is so real that unless the back of the plate can be examined, the deception is complete.

When the various components were returned to the original maker, he assembled them and sent the article for assay: thus, only his mark appears. Hand-pierced grilles appear to have arrived *circa* 1840.

On reflection, Matthew Linwood's use of this form of 'mechanical ornament' is entirely natural: such great interest was shown in the Hero of Trafalgar and his great and victorious Battle, that any memento was eagerly sought. Linwood, or his engraver (the latter is the more likely to have introduced him to this early form of 'mass-production') had to resort to this method of keeping pace with the flood of orders, once the motif was introduced, and the temptation to 'strike while the iron was hot' (in more senses than one) must have been overpowering. The motif was accordingly die-struck on a flat surface and subsequently fashioned into the lid, and then 'touched-up' by hand to give it the authentic 'hand-produced' appearance.

Another later type of die-stamping was produced by Mills and his contemporaries, examples of which are shown, including one by George Unite, dated 1845 (Plate 212). The subject is a presently unidentified view, possibly the Barracks at Windsor Castle with the Round Tower in the background. This variety

**Plate 209** An unusually fine cast and pierced grille from a 'Nelson vinaigrette'. Matthew Linwood, Birmingham 1805. 2in (5.1cm) by 1¾in (4.4cm).

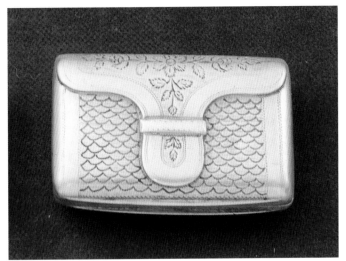

**Plate 210** George III cast-top rectangular vinaigrette formed as a silver-gilt wallet, with floral bright-cutting on the 'flap' and 'scale-motif' engraving on the lid. With a die-stamped filigree grille. Matthew Linwood V, Birmingham 1816. 1¾in (4.4cm) by 1⅛in (2.9cm).
Struck between the lion passant and the maker's mark is the figure '2', so Linwood probably had a team of workers making the vinaigrettes, as this is a 'workers' punch.

**Plate 211** George III hand-engraved vinaigrette, the lid with a vertical 'Nursery Rhymes' theme of *Little Boy Blue* and a finely die-stamped basket of flowers grille. Matthew Linwood V, Birmingham, 1808. 1in (2.5cm) by ⅞in (2.2cm).

**Plate 212** Victorian large rectangular vinaigrette, with shaped borders and stand-away hinge. Die-stamped on the lid with an architectural scene of an unidentified building, possibly the Barracks at Windsor Castle with the Round Tower in the background. Scrolling thumbpiece. George Unite, Birmingham 1845. 1¼in (3.2cm) by 1in (2.5cm).

was produced in much the same manner as Linwood's earlier specimens, with the exception that the detail – being architectural in content – is far vaguer, but also shows signs of 'touching-up' by hand. Another famous 'die-stamped' variety is the Mills' version of 'The Crystal Palace' issued in 1851, but this type is more complex: the delicate and very effective 'raying' background was first engine-turned in a radial form, and then the design was stamped on. This variation is almost always seen on 'architectural motif' subjects, so perhaps it was found to be most effective, when used in this context.

### Acid-Etching

Finally, the very last method of 'Applied Ornament' is reached. As has been hinted above, this is, perhaps, the most revolutionary of any of the devices examined. To obtain the best effect the silversmiths – Mills, Willmore, Unite and Taylor & Perry are among makers working in this medium – placed the acid-etched illustration within a cartouche of real 'hand-engraved' motifs, usually floral, and somewhat coarsely executed or, as in the instance of the Willmore subject 'The Good Samaritan', within a heavily enriched repoussé appliqué border. The artistic intent is obviously the same: to heighten the effect of the lightly etched plaques by placing them in elaborately conceived 'frames'.

As a well-known 19th century source put it: 'In the earlier part of this century etching was a defunct art, *except as it was employed by engravers to get faster through their work, of which 'engraving' got all the credit,* the public being unable to distinguish between etched lines and lines cut with the "burin" (a special tool for cutting on copper)'. As with 'die-stamping', the process was not a new invention: many great painters used it as a variation of their work, and Rembrandt and Van Dyck stand out as masters of their craft. Etching was particularly successful where chiaroscuro effects were required. P G Hamerton, in *The Etcher's Handbook,* defined the qualities of a successful etcher thus: 'I would ask the reader to think of etching simply as a kind of highly concentrated drawing… the first step towards becoming an etcher is to become a good draughtsman with any kind of pointed instrument. The second step is to master the relations of light and dark in nature. The third and final stage of an etcher's education is to obtain a technical mastery over copper so as to make the

**Plate 213** William IV acid-etched snuffbox depicting 'The Good Samaritan'. Set in a heavy foliate and scroll border and with a foliate thumbpiece. Joseph Willmore, Birmingham, 1832. 3⅞in (9.7cm) by 2½in (6.3cm).

*Courtesy of the Birmingham Assay Office*

**Plate 214** Victorian acid-etched rectangular vinaigrette, the lid embellished with a superb love-birds motif, the base with a butterflies and foliage motif. It has a slightly projecting thumbpiece. Colen Hewer Cheshire, Birmingham 1878. The firm existed until 1927. 1⅜in (3.5cm) by 1in (2.5cm).

metal yield the precise tone he requires, whether in the space of a single line or in the shading of a space'.

Singer and Strang's classical textbook *On Etching* contains an interesting view: 'Line engraving was learned from the goldsmiths (the early goldsmiths made *nielli,* or silver plaques engraved with a "burin" to be set in shrines, small coffers, etc, for decoration; these were then filled with a black alloy of silver, copper and lead) and etching from the armourers. The practice of ornamenting guns and arms with etched ornaments is a good deal prior to the oldest printed etching that we have been able to find'.

Two pre-19th century examples of acid-etched ornament on silver have been observed. The first, one of the exhibits at the 1952 British Antique Dealers' Fair, was an oval Charles II tobacco box dated 1682. On the apparently 'hand engraved' lid, it bore the Arms of King, County Devon and on the base was an acknowledged (by the exhibitor) etching of the painting 'The Money-lenders'. The Arms here, on closer examination, greatly resembled the Victorian acid-etchings, both in their elaborate attention to detail (the scrolling foliate manteling was particularly fine) and the quality of the 'shading', the subtlety of which by far exceeds anything which could be accomplished by the 'burin'. The etching on the base is far cruder in execution, and though the two subjects might not have come from the same hand, there is no reason to doubt that the acid-etching method was not applied to both.

On mature reflection, it is possible that the superbly 'engraved' oval tobacco box which appeared in *Investing in Silver* (facing page 19) in which the subject was Archbishop Sancroft, and which was, by implication, attributed to the hand of Simon Gribelin, could also be an acid-etching, as Gribelin is known to have worked in the medium for his engraved plates. The intention here, of course, was not 'mass-production', but quality of delineation. By the use of an engraved copper plate, bitten by acids, a much more dramatic effect could be obtained, as well as, perhaps, that elusive 'depth' for which all engravers appear to have striven, than could be achieved with hand-engraving.

The second example is even more interesting. It is illustrated in the May, 1938 issue of *The Connoisseur,* where a brilliantly 'engraved' oval tea-caddy by Andrew Fogelberg, London, 1772, appears. The editorial comments 'Its execution is exceptional for a piece of silver, on which as a rule the conventional character of the ornament requires a somewhat heavy and even incision. This, however, is cut in lines of extraordinary fineness, showing a much more delicate tool has been employed. In addition to the difference in execution as compared to the usual ornamentation of silver, the design itself is a noteworthy one, and is so reminiscent of Morland, with its group around the inn door (the engraving shows an innkeeper proffering a tankard to an obviously inebriated gentleman, while a lady tries to restrain the latter from accepting it) that it is baffling to find an origin for it at a time when the great genre painter was only nine years old. The whole has the appearance of an *etched plate, designed and executed by the same hand'*. After a full description of the subject, the editorial probes the possible identity of the artist who was also an etcher skilled enough to have accomplished this fine piece of enrichment, and suggests the Alsatian artist, Philippe Jacques de Loutherbourg, who came from Paris to London in 1771, became an ARA in 1780 and an RA in 1781.

To return to the Birmingham acid-etching period: two patents associated with the process were granted within the first half of the 19th century. The first was issued to John Ham, Vinegar Maker, of Bristol in December 1826, for 'An improved process for promoting the actions of the Acetic Acid on metallic bodies'. The invention primarily consisted of improved cisterns for the acid vapours to circulate 'by presenting an extensive surface to the atmosphere air, so that the acidification of the vinous fluid, and the corrosion and solution of the metal shall proceed simultaneously'.

The second patent was granted to Charles Hullmandel, lithographic printer of London, in September 1838 and consisted of 'A new mode of preparing certain surfaces for being corroded with acids in order to produce patterns and designs for the purposes of certain kinds of printing and transparencies'. The specification in this instance consisted of improved methods of preparing the 'mordant', that is, the fluid used to 'bite in' the lines, to Mr Hullmandel's own recipe, and in preparing the surfaces to accept this, by means of various gums and the 'best lamp black'. This last is a pigment consisting of almost pure carbon in a state of fine division, made by collecting the soot produced by burning oil; an early mention of the process occurred in Henry Peacham's *The Gentleman's Exercise,* 1612, speaking of the 'art of drawing and limming' [sic]: 'The making of ordinary lamp blacke. Take a torch or linke, and hold it vnder the bottom of a latten basen, and as it groweth to be furd

**Plate 215** Victorian cheroot case: of rectangular form with rounded corners, acid-etched with a hunting-scene on the lid, set in hand-engraved scrolling foliate motifs. It has an integral-hinge and a push-piece opener. Nathaniel Mills, Birmingham 1855. 6in (15.2cm) by 3½in (8.9cm) by 1in (2.5cm) deep.
This article was made in Mills' last years but lacks nothing in beauty of design.

and blacke within, strike it with a feather into some shell or other, and grinde it with gummewater'. The Birmingham engraver who was instrumental in uncovering this process also stated that the Victorian 'acid-etchings' were produced with wax and lamp-black.

Bearing all the above in mind, namely, that patented inventions (as well, perhaps, as trade secrets of the older methods) were available at the time that the first 'acid-etched' boxes appeared – the earliest observed was dated 1830 – it is no longer surprising that craftsmen of Mills' calibre did not hesitate to use the method to embellish some of their finest boxes. Far from detracting from their value (as has already been stated, in the preamble to this long survey on 'Applied Ornament'), the process would appear to have enhanced these fine *objets d'art*: any clever silversmith could employ an engraver, but who would have thought that corrosive elements could produce such beautiful effects with pictures and designs?

**Plate 216** George III oval elliptical toothpick case fashioned in filigree and set in the middle of the lid with an oval escutcheon containing a wheatsheaf under a domed glass. The filigree is placed on top of an inner lining of silver. Unmarked, *circa* 1790. 3¾in (9.5cm) by 1in (2.5cm) by ¼in (6.3mm) deep.

# Filigree

It has been said that the origins of filigree are notoriously difficult to define. Perhaps so, but within the past decade there has been a revival of interest in this attractive medium, and a number of books and articles have opened the subject much wider.

Firstly, a description of the methods involved: An ingot of silver was drawn through a 'draw-plate'. Thinner wire for compactness, heavier for a twisted 'cable' to serve as a *cloisson* (chamber) for enamels and jewels. An Indian trade list itemises 'a herd of graduated elephants – *with their trunks raised or lowered* and – a couple of grazing giraffes', and illustrates a fine selection of caskets, salvers and trays, cups and vases, and spoons – all created from tightly curled silver and gold wire.

There is a detailed account of how the threads were made, also from an Indian source: 'The metal was purified by melting sixteen parts of silver with one part of lead. It was then cast into moulds, beaten into plates and drawn into wire. The pattern was formed by placing the wire on sheets of mica, to which it was cemented and soldered. The mica sheets provided a rigid and flame-proof backing for the cemented wire while soldering took place.' In ancient times, the worker heated the wire, annealed it and used an amalgam of gold, silver and mercury instead of solder. Another method was to hammer the drawn threads into shape without soldering. Later craftsmen worked with soldering tubes, blowing the flame of a paraffin lamp through it. All these processes required manual dexterity as well as skill, and a late 19th century account says 'The work is generally done by children, whose sensitive fingers and keener sight enable them to put the fine silver threads together with rapidity and accuracy.'

Manuel de Freitas in his finely illustrated *Filigrana Portuguesa* tells us 'A gram of gold can be spun into a very thin thread of 10 thousand feet and an ounce can be expanded to form a surface of 33 square feet', and adds 'the most ancient filigree ornamented piece is about four thousand years old and was discovered in the Chaldean city of Ur'.

Among British vessels from the 10th-11th centuries enriched with a form of Celtic filigree is the famous 'Ardagh Cup' – a sacred Irish gold chalice which Sir Charles Jackson's *History of English Plate* describes thus: 'This magnificent cup combines classical beauty with the most exquisite examples of almost every variety of Irish ornamentation... possessing the interlaced work of various patterns.' This early work is not, however, of the familiar openwork wire type, but appliqué repoussé frames which accommodated the beautiful enamelled 'chambered' settings for enamels and jewellery, in much the same manner as the *objets* created by the 19th century Russian masters. Sometimes in this early period, zoomorphic (animal) shapes were also added.

Some important places of origin were the 'China Export Trade' workshops centred around Canton, mainland China, Persia, Cuttack, near the Indian city of Orissa, and coming nearer to Europe, countries as widespread as Turkey, Malta and Italy, Scandinavia and, of course, Russia.

Probably the finest object made in filigree may be seen in the tranquillity of the 'China Export Trade' gallery at the Victoria & Albert Museum. This is a superb silver-gilt bombé shaped George III type tea caddy, *circa* 1760. it is encased in the finest silken web of knotted diaper and scroll work, and set within a rococo cartouche.

Filigree is uncommon in 17th century Britain, and appears to be limited to smaller *objets* – thimbles and thimble cases, ladies' purses, mirror frames, travel *etuis* containing knives, spoons and forks. Among other rarities noted were a pair of short 'cluster column' candlesticks on square bases, domed lid caskets and oval and circular boxes, and a few mysterious items – alleged without any supporting evidence to be 'serving spoons!'

Birmingham would seem to have produced the majority of late 18th-early 19th century filigree objects. The famous Boulton and Fothergill partnership at Soho in the 1770-80s employed George and Thomas Caldecott (father and son) and the firm's Letter Books for 1773 mention sales of buttons, buckles, hair ornaments, toothpick cases, snuffboxes and sword fittings. No B&F snuffboxes appear to have survived, unless they are in privately held collections.

A charming note on which to end: the well-known Russian silver authority, Mme. Postnikova-Losseva's peroration to a fine little Moscow exhibition catalogue: 'Filigree work does not take great physical strength but only exceptional patience, attention and precision. That is why this has always been largely a female occupation.'

# CHAPTER 4

# The Birmingham Boxmakers

Some sort of minor industry in the working of precious metals existed in the city long before Birmingham became nationally famous for the excellence of its wares, thanks largely to Matthew Boulton's determined stand over the establishment of its own Assay Office, which aim, when realised in 1773, organised the industry into a prosperous and healthy body. It needs to be stressed, however, that Birmingham had long been a producer of base-metal wares, chiefly iron and brass, and the late Arthur Westwood, Esq., Assay Master of Birmingham in the early part of this century, read a very learned and important paper to the *Birmingham Archaeological Society* in March 1904, in which the following interesting statement appeared: 'The traveller Misson (a French Huguenot lawyer who became a travelling tutor and journeyed through Italy, and died in London in 1721), visiting Milan towards the end of the 17th century, speaks of the fine works of rock crystal, swords, heads of canes, snuffboxes, and other fine "works of Steel" he saw there, but remarks that "they can be had cheaper and better at Birmingham".' It should be added that this masterly paper with its mass of valuable data has been the 'spur' which initiated the present writer's interest in the old Birmingham craftsmen, and finally prompted his investigations into the genealogies of the five craftsmen, namely, Samuel Pemberton, Matthew Linwood, Joseph Willmore, Joseph Taylor and Nathaniel Mills.

Before these are undertaken, it is imperative that some mention, at least, be made of the two progenitors of the Birmingham Silver Trade – Matthew Boulton and James Watt – the celebrated industrialist on the one hand, and the inventive genius on the other, through whose combined business acumen and engineering prowess Birmingham became the centre of a large manufacturing empire. Boulton was born in Birmingham in 1728. On his father's death in 1759, he inherited the family metal manufacturing business, and in 1764 removed the works from Snow Hill to a much larger area at Soho in the north of the city. Here, he manufactured various 'toys', and as Dr Erasmus Darwin, the famous physician and man of letters, wrote in 1768: 'Here are toys and utensils of various kinds, in gold, copper, tortoiseshell, enamels, and many vitreous and metallic compositions, with gilt, plated, and inlaid works, all wrought up to the finest elegance and perfection of execution'.

Matthew Boulton was an adventurous trader, and in 1762 he began to

**Plate 217** George III oval rectangular bright-cut vinaigrette, the lid with cross-hatching in a plain rectangle, and a finely pierced floral grille. In a contemporary red morocco leather case, the bright-cutting so sharp, the article could hardly have had any use. John Shaw, Birmingham 1807. 3⅛in (3.9cm).

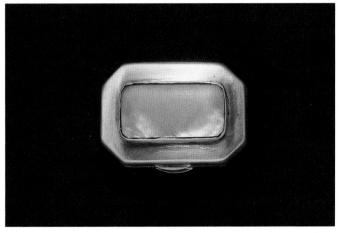

**Plate 218** George III small rectangular vinaigrette, set with a mother-of-pearl plaque in the lid. Wardell & Kempson, Birmingham, 1812. 1¼in (3.2cm) by 1in (2.5cm).     *Courtesy of the Birmingham Assay Office*

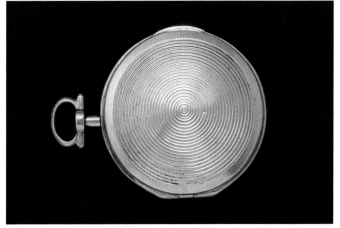

**Plate 219** George III circular vinaigrette, with a cast concentric motif on the lid and base, formed as a 'watch'. Samuel Pemberton VI, Birmingham 1808. 1½in (3.8cm) diameter.

*Courtesy of the Birmingham Assay Office*

**Plate 220** Large Victorian shaped rectangular parcel-gilt (partially gilt) vinaigrette, the coat-of-arms was finally attributed to William Leigh of Braby Hall, Co. Lancaster, and his wife Caroline, whom he married on 1st April 1828. (Previously attributed to Chandos, 1st Baron Leigh.) Nathaniel Mills, Birmingham 1841. 2½in (6.3cm) by 1⅜in (3.5cm).
*Courtesy of the Birmingham Assay Office*

**Plate 221** George III rectangular cast-top, silver-gilt vinaigrette of 'Hare in Reeds' designed by Thomas Bewick. The grille is pierced with a 'Greek Key' motif. Thomas Newbold, Birmingham 1820.
*Courtesy of the Birmingham Assay Office*

**Plate 222** Matthew Boulton (1728-1809). School of Peter Paillou, Paris *circa* 1790. *By courtesy of Messrs. Sotheby*

manufacture solid silver plate in association with John Fothergill, and in 1778-80 to reproduce oil paintings by a mechanical process in association with Francis Eginton (1737-1805). Both ventures, however, were doomed to failure. As H W Dickinson says, in his absorbing work *Matthew Boulton*, 'The partnership of Boulton and Fothergill was an unsuccessful one. From a misleading statement prepared by Zaccaeus Walker, the clerk to the firm, it appears that on a capital of £20,000, the excess of losses over profits for the twenty years of the partnership ending in 1782 was upwards of £11,000. Had it not been for the sales of his wives' estates (Boulton married twice, first Mary Robinson, and secondly his deceased wife's sister, Anne, whose combined fortunes he inherited) the firm must inevitably have gone bankrupt, because the profits from the steam engine business had not yet materialised'.

Boulton was not, it would appear, a silversmith himself, but the driving force behind the scenes of a busy, progressive, and thriving enterprise. The masterpieces bearing his famous mark – in association with John Fothergill he headed the entries in the first Register of the newly founded Assay Office in 1773 – were produced by the many craftsmen and apprentices whom he attracted to his great 'Soho Works'. In his learned article in the autumn 1995 issue of the Silver Society's Journal, Mr Kenneth Quickenden lists no fewer than forty-seven specialist silversmiths, chasers, engravers and designers. Outstanding among these craftsmen are Francis Eginton (1737-1805) (*vide ultra*), known as the 'Chief Designer', who also produced mechanical paintings and japanned wares, and the Caldecotts, see page 136.

As was mentioned above, *inter alia*, Edward Thomason was another Boulton apprentice. He commenced work with him at the age of sixteen, remaining at Soho until he was twenty-one years old. In 1793, he started in business on his own and eventually produced gilt and plated buttons, jewellery, medals and tokens, and later, silver plate. Next to Soho, his premises in Church Street (very near his master's) were the largest in Birmingham. An advertisement of 1830 is illuminating for the detailed list of the items produced, and is of interest at the present juncture because it provides the reader with a good insight of the stock which had to be carried by a

**Plate 223**

*Above left.* A George III vinaigrette grille showing the national emblems – rose, thistle and shamrock. Matthew Linwood V, Birmingham 1812, 1in (2.5cm)by ⅜in (1.9cm).

*Above right.* George III vinaigrette grille of a pair of lovebirds in a hand-pierced foliate frame. Lawrence & Company, Birmingham 1818. 1½in (3.8cm) by 1in (2.5cm).

*Below left.* George IV vinaigrette grille showing Phoenix in a hand-pierced scrolling foliate frame. James William Garland, London 1828. Goldworker, 16 Bridgewater Square, off Aldersgate Street. Entered August 1826 (AGG p.370). 1½in (3.8cm) by 1in (2.5cm).

*Below right.* Victorian vinaigrette grille with 'crossed quills and a book' in hand-pierced foliage. Edward Edwards, London 1846. 1½in (3.8cm) by 1in (2.5cm).

**Plate 224** Victorian 'cartouche-shaped' vinaigrette enriched with barleycorn motif engine-turning, with a cast foliate thumbpiece, and stand-away hinge. The hand-pierced floral grille opens upwards. William Simpson, Birmingham 1840. 1½in (3.8cm) by 1in (2.5cm) by ¼in (6.3mm) deep.
William Simpson entered his mark at Birmingham in 1825.

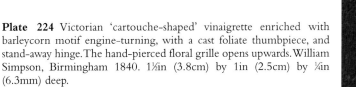

Plate 225 Tapering elliptical Victorian scissor-case, hand-engraved with scrolling floral motifs, the suspensory loop at the narrowest point. David Pettifer, Birmingham 1849. 2¾in (7cm).

Plate 226 A pair of 'presently unique' vinaigrettes formed as silver-gilt veined leaves (possibly birch). Both by Joseph Willmore, Birmingham but dated 1825 and 1831 respectively. Of shallow form and with 'wire-loop' handles, and integral three-lugged hinges. There are no grilles – the sponge being held in position by a wire frame – and the marks are on the loop-handles. 1½in (3.8cm).

*Courtesy of the Birmingham Assay Office.*

Plate 227 George III vertical rectangular cut-corner vinaigrette, both lid and base die-struck. The lid with 'lovers' meeting by a stone column topped by an urn, the base with rocaille scrolls. The mark-striker at the Assay Office has been careful to place the marks inside the column. Samuel Pemberton, Birmingham 1814. 1¼in (3.2cm).

large contemporary manufactory. It is thus given in full:

'Silver Services of all descriptions.
Plated        Do   Do   Do
Plated cutlery, Spoons &c. on Steel.
Fine Cut Glass for the Table.
Bronzed or Mulu [ormulu] Figures and Lustres
Papier Mache Trays & Cabinets
– Exclusively –
A Great Variety of Patent Articles and Mechanical
Inventions – and His Majestys Royal Letters Patent for
the Making of Gold and Silver Mounted Medals
And Coins – The Medal Dies of the Kings – of Celebrated
Men – of the Victories of the Late war – of The
Elgin Marbles [brought to England in 1816] – of Science
and Philosophy – of Society and other Medals. Jewellery
and Gold and Silver Snuff Boxes. Brass and Bronzed
Staircases.
Communion Plate, Cups and Vases in gold and Silver.'

Edward Thomason entered his first mark in 1809-10. He was a leading figure in Birmingham commerce, the Vice-Consul for Russia, France, Prussia, Austria, Spain, Portugal, Brazil, Sweden and Norway, and held the Knighthood of nine countries, including Great Britain, the latter being granted to him in 1832. He married Phyllis

**Plate 228** William IV walnut shaped vinaigrette of cast and chased form simulating the natural fruit, with a florally pierced hinged grille. Taylor and Perry, Birmingham 1834. 2in (5.1cm) by 1½in (3.8cm).

**Plate 229** George IV shaped vinaigrette formed as a 'beehive'. The tubular container has die-struck concentric rings, a domed pull-off lid and a pull-out grille. Thomas Willmore, Birmingham 1822. 1¼in (3.2cm) by ¾in (1.9cm) in diameter.

Bowan Glover, the daughter of Samuel Glover of Abercarn, near Newport, Monmouthshire, and had one son, Henry Botfield who died in 1843, aged forty-one. The 'John Thomason' who partnered John Hilliard, and whose joint mark was 'H & T', entered at the Assay Office in 1847, might have been a nephew, the son of Sir Edward's brother James. This latter partnership, according to Jackson, was still active in 1882. Sir Edward retired from business in 1835, wrote his memoirs in two volumes in 1845, and died in May 1849.

Matthew Boulton's partnership with James Watt (as opposed to that with John Fothergill) was blessed with success. Watt, born at Greenock in 1736, the son of a merchant and town-councillor, came to Glasgow in 1754 to learn the trade of a mathematical-instrument maker, and set up in business there. As early as 1759, his attention had been directed to steam as a motive-force, and he made a series of experiments, which, however, led to no positive results. In 1763, while he was working at Glasgow University, a working model of Thomas Newcomen's Engine (adapted by Newcomen before 1698 from an earlier engine by a Captain Savery) was sent for repair from a college class-room. Watt soon repaired it, and, on seeing the defects in the design of the machine, made a number of improvements. Watt's great invention, which revolutionised the production of cheap steam-driven power, and brought eventual prosperity to Birmingham was, according to Dickinson, 'to install a separate condenser. The effect of this was a saving of from two thirds to three quarters of the coal, as compared with the old engine doing the same work'.

The remainder of Watt's life-story is one of success, and he died at Heathfield Hall, his seat near Birmingham, in 1819. In 1824, his Memorial was erected in Handsworth Church, where he is buried, at a cost of £2,000, which was raised by public subscription. The sculptor was the great 19th century artist Sir Francis Legatt Chantrey, and the great inventor is shown seated, in thoughtful mien, contemplating a plan. This very fine sculpture was copied by the Mills workshop in 1838, and appears on the superb vertical lid snuffbox illustrated (page 91). The quality of the casting is absolutely supreme, and the original model must have been carved by a master-craftsman. The box is Number One in the Birmingham Assay Office Collection, and is justly admired. It is the apotheosis of the

**Plate 230** George III small rectangular snuffbox, the surfaces with alternating 'zig-zag' motifs interspaced with a band of 'wriggle-engraving', the facets of diamond face appearance, with concealed hinge. Cocks & Bettridge, Birmingham 1803. 4in (10.2cm).

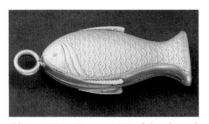

**Plate 231** George III fish shaped vinaigrette, the lid and base hand-engraved with scale motifs. The projecting fins form thumbpieces, It has a stand-away hinge and a suspensory loop at mouth. The grille is also of 'piscatorial' form. Joseph Taylor, Birmingham 1818. 1½in (3.8cm) by ½in (1.3cm).

Silversmith's craft.

Matthew Boulton's enterprises were very widespread. According to Dickinson, he had no fewer than thirteen different businesses between 1759 and 1809, including Plated and Silver ware, Steam Engines, Buttons, Medals, the Mint for government copper coins and an Iron Foundry. His biographer leaves us with this picture of him: 'In appearance Boulton was above the medium height with a fine figure and erect carriage. He had a handsome face, with somewhat receding forehead, a firm chin and grey eyes with a humorous twinkle in them under well-arched eyebrows. Boulton's manners were charming and easy as if accustomed to wealth and habitual command. Doubtless this arose from his intercourse with persons in high places in a period when manners certainly were polished. This address secured for him entrée to the very highest in the land. Boulton was always well dressed, and we must not forget what an addition to a man's appearance was afforded by the picturesque dress of the period: the grey peruke, the embroidered coat, set off with some of his own buttons, the lace jabot and lace at the wrists, the flowered waistcoat, the knee-breeches, the silk stockings, the inlaid buckles, again his own, on the polished shoes; we even hear, on one occasion, of his wearing a sword' (see Plate 222).

Boulton died on 17 August, 1809 in his eighty-first year. The funeral was attended by thousands of people. The cortège was followed by a procession of 600 workmen from the Manufactory and Foundry, and a Memorial Medal, in copper, was presented to each individual invited to attend the funeral, which, on the obverse read: 'Matthew Boulton, died August 17th 1809 aged 81 years', and on the reverse, in a palm-wreath, the words: 'In memory of his obsequies August 24th, 1809'. For further details see *The Great Silver Manufactory*, Eric Delieb and Michael Roberts, Studio Vista, 1971.

# The Famous Five

Confusingly for the researcher, the five leading Birmingham 18th-19th century silversmiths (with the exception of Joseph Taylor) used the same Christian name in each succeeding generation. There were four Samuel Pembertons, six Matthew Linwoods, three Nathaniel Mills, two Joseph Willmores and a Joseph Taylor.

In order to avoid a plethora of genealogy, they are here greatly curtailed by omitting their family histories, and listing only the silversmiths.

These great Birmingham craftsmen created a fine legacy of *objets de vertu* and splendid workmanship and fascinating artistry of designs in the use of precious metals, and something about them should be told.

### The Pembertons

The founder of the business was Samuel III (1704-1784) of 110 Snow Hill, 'jeweller and toymaker', who was not registered at the Birmingham Assay Office (henceforth designated the BAO).

His son was Samuel IV (1731-1803) of 'Edgbaston and Five Ways' who in 1773 entered six punches at the BAO. The rarest (1f) is the small 'SP' with a line through the 'S' (very similar to the London date-letter for the year 1793 which might be found on smallwares, such as caddy spoons) entered between 1 July 1774 and 30 June 1775.

Another uncommon mark is (1c) Gothic initials struck in a cut-corner punch. This and the plain rectangle punch with larger letters (1a) were both not recorded by Jackson.

The rest were the familiar ovals. To complicate matters, another Pemberton, Thomas, described in the register as a 'Toy Maker' (1775-1808), entered his 'watchmaker's punch' between 1 July 1803 – 30 June 1804 (Mark 2) when he worked at St Paul's Square, Birmingham. He took as a partner Robert Mitchell,

**1**

**2**

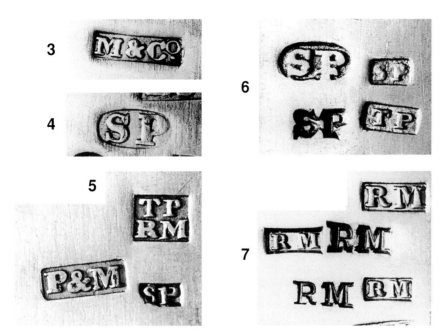

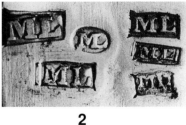

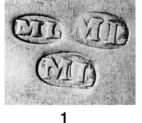

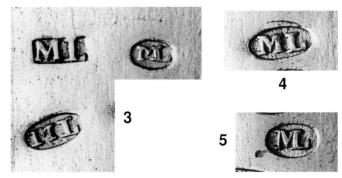

whereupon the firm became 'Robert Mitchell & Co (late S. Pemberton & Son)', Goldsmiths of Snow Hill (mark 3).

On 6 May 1812, the firm was registered as 'Samuel Pemberton Son & Mitchell', continuing on 14 October 1812 (Mark 4). Marks 5 and 6, however, struck 18 December 1816 and 28 February 1821, were for Pemberton & Mitchell (a punch for watchcases), and S. Pemberton & Son (late Pemberton, Son & Mitchell), respectively.

The last Mitchell sequence was struck on 23 May 1821 in the name of Robert Mitchell, Silversmiths, St. Paul's Square, Birmingham, removed to Bishops Gate Street, 27 March 1822 (Mark 7).

## The Linwoods of Cogenhoe

The Linwoods came from the Northamptonshire town of Cogenhoe (pronounced 'Cookno'). There were six Matthews, but the first Matthew to register as a silversmith at the BAO was Matthew IV (1726-died Leicester 1793), who entered between 1 July 1783 and 30 June 1784, when the letters appeared in an oval (Mark 1). A subsequent entry for 1 July 1800 to 30 June 1801 (Mark 2) has him as a 'plater and buckle-maker'. The familiar 'ML conjoined' first appears in this sequence.

Marks 3 and 4 belong to Matthew V (1754-1826), the linchpin of the Linwoods, whose beautifully conceived confections brought such prominence to Birmingham. These marks consist of rectangles and ovals, struck 19 May 1813 and 29 March 1820.

The fifth Mark, entered 19 April 1820, is that of Matthew VI (1783-1847). He had been apprenticed to his father, but when his infant son and daughter died tragically in 1815, he and his wife went to live at Hoxton Old Town, London. He opened a shop in Bouverie Street, off Fleet Street, probably selling his father's wares. Again, the mark is 'ML conjoined'. Whenever this mark appears alone, usually on silver-mounted items such as exotic shell-bowled caddy spoons, it indicates Matthew VI.

1

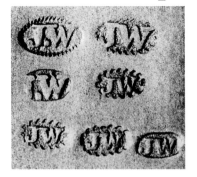

2

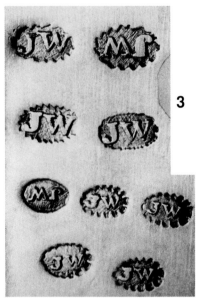

3

4

### The Willmores of Birmingham

As well as being a silversmith, Joseph Willmore I (1792-1865) was an engineer and inventor. His nephew, Joseph II (1790-1855), was *the* silversmith. Joseph I entered his first mark, a 'serrated rectangle' at the BAO between 1 July 1804 and 30 June 1805 (Mark 1).

In 1810 Joseph II took the young George Unite (spelt 'Unitt' in the Indenture) as an apprentice. Unite, then aged twelve years, received the sum of 3/- per week and his keep, the sum increasing by 6d. per annum until his Freedom was attained in 1818.

Joseph II's marks are a series of seven oval serrated-edge punches, three with stops between (Mark 2) were entered on 4 July 1832, when he worked at 13 Bread Street, Birmingham.

On 5 September 1834, Joseph II, John Yapp and John Woodward formed a partnership, working at 13 Bread Street, Birmingham and 11 Thames Street, London, although the registration names only Willmore. (See the sequence of nine, Mark 3.)

Joseph II was also entered at the London Goldsmiths' Company. He registered in 1808 when he had a showroom in Bouverie Street, off Fleet Street, and again in 1823 when he was at Thavies Inn, Holborn. Joseph retired from business in 1851, and lived at Withwood Cottage, King's Norton in Worcestershire, until his death. He was buried at Key Hill Cemetery, Birmingham.

The final mark recorded at the BAO on 16 August 1836 (Mark 4) retains the serrated oval 'J.W.'. The registration is still for 'Joseph Willmore, John Yapp and John Woodward, Goldsmiths, Silversmiths and Jewellers', but it is probable that by this time, Willmore took no further active part in the business.

His former partners, Yapp & Woodward, entered their first mark as independent silversmiths in May 1845, but it seems that with Joseph's death, the silversmiths' connection eventually petered out.

### Joseph Taylor

Fortunately there was only one Joseph Taylor, 'Silversmith of Birmingham' (as he is described in his will), for the name is common to so many British families, and the search for his genealogy was difficult enough!

Little is known about his background. Taylor (1767-1827) was born in Birmingham, and entered at the BAO between 1 July 1789 and 30 June 1790. He was working at Aston, near Birmingham. Mark 1, as shown, has a series of 'skeleton letters', probably case-makers' punches.

Between 1813 and 1825, he entered two more sequences (Marks 2 and 3). On 22 July 1829, the Mark became 'T&P', for his brother John, and his brother-in-law, John Perry (who had married his sister, Dorothy), who jointly inherited the business.

John Taylor and John Perry were both left substantial sums in the will, for Joseph left £18,000 altogether. The names given with Mark 4 are 'John Taylor, John Perry (late Joseph Taylor), Silversmiths, 8 Newhall Street, Birmingham'.

The last entry, a large oval, for 11 April 1832, was for John Taylor & John Perry (Mark 5).

1

2

3

4

5

## The Mills Family of Birmingham

In the first edition of this pioneering work, the attempt to create a genealogy of this famous Birmingham silver manufacturing firm virtually comprised all that was known of Nathaniel I and II, and ended with the death of the father.

However, the data then known was incomplete, and it was not until the 1970s when a fortuitous letter arrived from a great, great-granddaugher of yet another Nathaniel, offering a family tree and listing a number of Mills' possessions, that new vistas were opened. This lady was Mrs Myra Louisa Waterson, member of an old Birmingham family. The letter was then mislaid, not to surface until the 1990s, when the daughter of the late Mrs Waterson, Miss Juanita Waterson, a retired BBC costume designer and artist, was traced.

This family tree (see page 158), in addition to citing dates of birth for both Nathaniel I (1746-1840) and Nathaniel II (1784-1843), names the eleven children of Nathaniel II, among whom is Nathaniel, born 1810, died 1873, and five other brothers.

The Waterson tradition, lovingly built up over two centuries, concentrates on this third Nathaniel as the head of the great box and *objets de vertu* manufactory, all of which appear under the umbrella of 'Nathaniel Mills' and later, 'Nathaniel Mills and Sons'. Miss Waterson also possesses a sampler by her great-aunt 'Ann Mills aged 8 1820'; a silver-plated half-fluted teapot given as a wedding present by a fourth generation Mills – Emily Maria Leerhoff; an engine-turned silver card case by Alfred Taylor *circa* 1850, and a number of rudimentary sketches of castles, cottages, towers and gateways and other decorative motifs from the hand of Edward Barnett, a Birmingham steel engraver and die-stamper who worked in the workshops. He married Ann, one of the five daughters. Sadly, these sketches are not clear enough for reproduction.

Family tradition includes personal anecdotes of Nathaniel born in 1810. He was careful with money, and it was rumoured that he would pick up coals from the hearth with ember tongs and replace them on the fire. He wore an old black jacket for years, and spent little or nothing on himself.

Thus far, the Waterson version. In the meantime, Mr Peter Cameron, the distinguished London antique silver dealer and writer, was consulting Birmingham census returns of the 1840-50s was well as trade directories. He found no evidence that the third Nathaniel had any part in the silversmithing firm of Nathaniel Mills and later, Nathaniel Mills and Sons. Mr Cameron, using the 1851 census return, records that Nathaniel (III) aged 41, living at 57 George Street, Lozells [Aston Manor], gives his occupation as 'general agent', and the 1864 Post Office Directory has him – Nathaniel Mills, merchant and importer of swords, bayonets and gun stocks, 25 Mary Ann Street. By that time he was in partnership with his son-in-law, Henry Leerhoff Müller, a German who had come to work in the Mills Manufactory and, to quote a relative's sniping remark, 'married the daughter'. Mills' business must have been successful, for when he died in 1873, he left his widow £30,000.

Mr Cameron's researches show that in 1841, Mills II is described as head of the house with two of his sons – Thomas, a silversmith, and John, an apprentice silver engraver. In 1842 William Mills, the eldest brother, and Thomas Mills were partners in Nathaniel Mills and Sons, silversmiths.

William died in the autumn of 1853. The firm of Nathaniel Mills and Sons effectively ended upon William's death – although another NM mark was entered on 30/1/1854, giving an address at 72 Northwood Street, removed from 42 Caroline Street. The mark appears to represent a new partnership. Directories of this year list 'Mills and Owen, silversmiths, 72 Northwood Street'. Mr Cameron believes *that* Mills to have been Thomas, for he is still listed as a silversmith in the directories. This partnership certainly did not last and is not mentioned further in directories after 1854.

Listed in his will were the two children of his late brother James Gordon Mills: Nathaniel and William. 'I believe these cousins set up in 1855 as silversmiths and

*[The illustrations of the Makers' Marks appearing here are shown by courtesy of the Birmingham Assay Office. They are shown slightly larger than real life.]*

**Plate 232** Large Victorian rectangular table snuffbox, the lid applied with a cast scroll and foliate border and fruit and scroll motifs around the body, engine-turning on the base. Finely engraved with a view of the mansion built in 1725 by Sir Gregory Page at Wricklemarsh, Kent (then known as 'Blackheath'), demolished in 1787 and bequeathed by him to his nephew Sir Gregory Turner of Ambroseden, Oxon. The building took just eleven months to erect. Yapp & Woodward, Birmingham 1845. Weight: 12ozs. 14dwt (395gr.) 4¾in (12.1cm).

**Plate 233** William IV vertical rectangular card case. Repoussé with foliate shell and scroll motifs, the centres with bright-cut 'double dot' scoring, the centre with 'sunburst' in an oval cartouche. The bright-cutting reminiscent of the 1790s, the repoussé worthy of the 1830s. Taylor & Perry, Birmingham 1830. 3½in (8.9cm).

jewellers', says Mr Cameron. Yet another NM mark was entered at the Assay Office on 16/8/1855 with 11½ Howard Street as the address. An advertisement from the 1865 Post Office Directory shows 'Nathaniel and William Mills, 11½ Howard Street, Birmingham – listing most of the familiar silver objects associated with these workshops – Snuff Boxes, Card Cases, Vinaigrettes, Ladies Tablets, etc., Agents for Henry Bye of Whitby, Jet Ornament manufacturer.'

Finally, Mr Cameron picks up the Alfred Taylor who in 1847 married Sarah Mills, 'daughter of Nathaniel Mills, silversmith'. Although listed as a coal dealer he was, from *circa* 1850, a gold spectacle maker and silversmith, employing 24 men according to the 1851 census.

Mr Cameron concludes with a question: 'I don't know if you may have seen a piece of silver bearing the NM after 1853, but I haven't.' Well, perhaps so, but illustrated within these pages are a fine deeply die-struck vinaigrette with a view of Ely Cathedral, dated 1858, and a small shaped finely engraved gold vinaigrette dated 1866.

## The Birmingham Repoussé and Die-stamped Silver Box and a Guide to Topography

'The Box', in all its forms, uses, styles and ornament was fully discussed in *Investing in Silver*, 1967, pages 84–120, and of course in the first edition of this work. These books were aimed at features which had not received ample coverage in previously published works and the new treatment attempted to adjust this anomaly. Over the past thirty years, through painstaking research and the emergence of new material, the scope has appreciably widened.

For instance, the wide variety of castles, country houses, cathedrals and abbeys which adorned boxes, was originally attributed to the spread of the railways. This could well have been true, for from the 1830s, Stephenson's 'Rocket', Braithwaite and Ericsson's 'Novelty', Hackworth's 'Sanspareil', and other locomotives traversed the length and breadth of Britain, and mementoes were avidly sought by travellers. Subsequent study,

however, has revealed that the development of the silver repoussé or die-stamped vinaigrette, snuffbox, or card case, had little to do with the spread of the rail network.

Years before the Industrial Revolution, the workshops of Staffordshire and Warwickshire, including Bilston and Birmingham, introduced a wide range of the little oval enamel patchboxes which were favourite relics of a visit to a cathedral, a fine city or a country mansion. These were the 'Trifles from' – Bath, Lincoln, Sidmouth, Bridgwater, Aberystwyth Castle, etc, all bearing topographical transfers on their lids.

Well-illustrated works on the subject are few, but the catalogue of the outstanding collection of the late Mrs Irma Harris of Atlanta, Georgia, sold at Sotheby Parke Bernet, New York in June, 1974, forms a treasure-filled manual for the connoisseur, identifying many splendid silver, porcelain, gold and enamel bonbonnières and boxes.

In addition to the superb array of repoussé and engraved vinaigrettes, snuffboxes, and patch-boxes, there are over seventy oval enamel transfer-lidded patch-boxes, dating from the 1760s. Many possess finely printed topographical views. Thus, Sir Robert Walpole's great mansion at Strawberry Hill, Twickenham, built to his taste in the Gothic manner, could be the forerunner of any crenellated Gothick castle from the hand of Nathaniel Mills, struck almost a century later.

There are three 'three-dimensional' views of the west front of Bath Abbey; Royal Crescent, Bath; a north-east view of Lincoln Cathedral, showing its towers, gateways and turrets; Cheltenham Spa 'From the Serpentine Walk'; the full length of Ramsgate Pier with a view of the harbour, and the spectacle of an ascending balloon, possibly a memento of Blanchard and Jeffries' first aerial crossing of the English Channel in 1785. These are all prototypes of the early 19th century silver box-lids.

Arriving at Georgian and Victorian repoussé and die-stamped box-lids, it should be pointed out that the so-called 'die-stampers' were not mere shop-workers, but highly skilled artists who created *objets d'art* from a skilfully incised die. It was truly said that a specialist engraver needed the wrist action of a violinist for preparing steel dies for the stamping of silver.

The head of the design department of a Birmingham silver manufactory would have given much thought into selecting these subjects. He would have sought topographical views at the local print-seller's, where for a few pence he might obtain

**Plate 236** Victorian fluted walnut-shaped nutmeg grater, with a blued steel grater. Hilliard & Thomason, Birmingham 1878. 1½in (3.8cm).

**Plate 237** George III rectangular silver-gilt cast-top vinaigrette, with 'L'Amour' in a floral border. Samuel Pemberton, Birmingham 1814. 1½in (3.8cm) by 1in (2.5cm).

**Plate 238** Small George III raying shell vinaigrette. Joseph Willmore, Birmingham 1802. ⅞in (2.2cm) by ⅝in (1.5cm).

pictures taken from old broken-up almanacs, county histories, and drawings by noted architects. Other sources included the fine sketches of Windsor Castle and its environs by the noted watercolourist Paul Sandby, and views of landed seats and mansions anthologised by his pupil William Watts from the hands of gifted artists and engravers.

Similarly, finely engraved horticultural manuals by Dutch and English artists would have provided him with inspiration for floral and artificially constructed foliage, particularly the popular acanthus and laurel leaves for festoons, swags, and other foliate motifs which framed and enriched the boxes.

If the silversmith required more formalised books of ornament, the works of Thomas Bewick for English motifs and Joseph Beunat's *Empire Styles, Designs and Ornaments*, *circa* 1813, might have been consulted and, from 1856, the magnificently lithographed *Grammar of Ornament* by Owen Jones, published by Day & Son, 'lithographers to the Queen, illustrated with a hundred folio plates drawn on stone by F. Bedford'.

In an attempt to create a wider range, makers issued differing versions of the same subject. There are at least three varying panoramas of Wells Cathedral – the West Front, a north-eastern view, and an oblique angle. Windsor Castle has at least five variations: the Round Tower, the East Terrace, the Castle as seen from the Long Walk, the Castle as seen from the side of St. George's Chapel, and the South Front facing the Broad Walk, sometimes showing the Pool amid foliage. Warwick Castle also appears in its great expanse and another version shows the River Avon, and most frequently found are St. Paul's Cathedral, Crystal Palace and York Minster.

Small Victorian boxes – for snuff, aromatic vinegar and vestas – are frequently embellished with finely 'engraved' scrolling and floral motifs. Engraving the articles by hand was a costly process, even when mass-production brought the prices down. The Birmingham boxmakers hit on John Ham and Charles Hullmandel's decorative invention of acid etching. This inexpensive method brought 'engraved' boxes within most people's grasp.

### Boxes by Nathaniel Mills

This particular workshop, one of the many flourishing Birmingham enterprises, is discussed at length for no other reason than that the name 'Mills' somehow elicits general admiration and is noted for boldness, ingenuity and quality.

From the 1830s a wide range of snuffboxes, vinaigrettes, card cases and vesta cases were thus attractively enriched with topographical views. Among the most popular were Windsor and Warwick Castles, and Abbotsford House. All the illustrated pictures were, in reality, carefully created optical illusions in the art of perspective. The artist die-sinker packed finely detailed vistas on to the surface, paying particular attention to studies of buildings, gardens, gateways, crenellated towers, trees and foliage, and fluttering pennants. Elaborate scrolls, floral motifs and inverting florally enriched frames and sides, especially around the views, were a particular feature of Mills' boxes.

**Plate 239** *Clockwise*: **a** Victorian shaped rectangular snuffbox, with heavy cast border, engraved with the ruins of an unidentified abbey. Nathaniel Mills, Birmingham 1842. 3¼in (8.2cm).

**b** Victorian vertically engraved vinaigrette depicting the City or Butter Cross, Winchester, set within a scrolling cartouche and with incurving sides and floral scrolls on the base. George Unite, Birmingham 1846. Size 1¾in (4.4cm).

**c** Victorian engraved top vinaigrette showing Drummond Castle in the Perthshire town of Crieff, the seat of the Earls of Perth. The castle was built in 1490, demolished in 1689 after the siege by Cromwell and rebuilt after the Jacobite Rebellion. Nathaniel Mills, Birmingham 1852. 2in (5.1cm).

**d** Victorian vertical vinaigrette engraved with the Scott Memorial, Edinburgh, and foliate motifs. Frederick Marson, Birmingham 1876. 2⅛in (5.4cm).

*Centre*: Victorian shaped rectangular engraved top vinaigrette showing Warwick Castle from the River Avon. With raying engine-turning. Nathaniel Mills, Birmingham 1838. 2¼in (5.7cm).

**Plate 240** The Henry Ellis 'Shawl Brooch', named 'The Patent Safety Chain Brooch', patented by Ellis at Exeter in 1847. Formed with pin and toggle attached, fastening into a sheath with two large scrolls enclosed by a buckle, engraved with scrollwork. Following Queen Victoria's purchase of five brooches, some were also ordered by the Duke of Cambridge and the Queen of the Belgians. The firm was invited to send a case of its wares to the Great Exhibition. This article is illustrated because it comes from the workshop of Nathaniel Mills, dated Birmingham 1847, and shows two unidentified die-stamped castles, towers and castle keeps, or follies, either side of the pin.

The brooches were also made under licence in Birmingham and marked at the Birmingham Assay Office. A number were manufactured by Francis Clark, here a Nathaniel Mills piece, also crept past the patentee's scrutiny.

The silver used for this object came from the Coombe Martin mines on Exmoor, and it was stamped 'Combmartin Silver'. Birmingham 1847. 4⅞in (12.2cm).

**Plate 241** Victorian card case, with a view of Bath Abbey, and the Guildhall from the High Street. By Nathaniel Mills, Birmingham 1852.

**Plate 242** Victorian shaped rectangular snuffbox, the lid acid-etched with a scene of the Good Samaritan, engine-turned on sides and base with basketweave motif. Nathaniel Mills, Birmingham 1840. 4in (10.2cm).

**Plate 243**

*Above left.* William IV oval vinaigrette, the base cast with scroll work, set in a cast foliate border, the lid applied with a carved cameo plaque depicting Eros on a cloud, wreath in hand, escorted by doves. Nathaniel Mills, Birmingham 1836. 1⅜in (3.5cm).

*Right.* Victorian shallow vinaigrette formed as a fold-over wallet, with 'tuck-in' flap and extra inside double lid, engine-turned in basketweave motifs, an oval escutcheon on the lid. Gervase Wheeler, Birmingham 1858. 1½in (3.8cm).

*Below.* Victorian rectangular fine cast-top vinaigrette, the lid with an unusual view of Abbotsford House, built 1811-24 by Sir Walter Scott on the south bank of the Tweed, two miles west of Melrose. Nathaniel Mills, Birmingham 1840. 1⅞in (4.6cm).

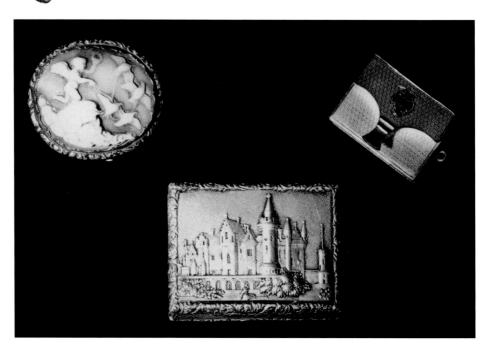

**Plate 244** *Clockwise:* Victorian repoussé top shaped rectangular vinaigrette of Worcester Cathedral, set on a mount. The grille is pierced with 'starburst and patera' within a scroll in the spandrels. Nathaniel Mills, Birmingham 1851. 1¾in (4.4cm).

Victorian silver-gilt repoussé top Westminster Abbey vinaigrette, engine-turned on the base. Nathaniel Mills, Birmingham 1842. 1¾in (4.4cm).

Victorian oval rectangular repoussé top vinaigrette applied with cast thumbpiece. The subject is Liverpool Collegiate High School, designed by the architect Harvey Lonsdale Elmes (1813-1847). Nathaniel Mills, Birmingham 1849. 2in (5.1cm).

A Victorian repoussé-top vinaigrette of Ely Cathedral. Nathaniel Mills, Birmingham 1858. 1¾in (4.4cm).

Rectangular Victorian York Minster snuffbox with scrolling border and thumbpiece and deep repoussé lid. Nathaniel Mills, Birmingham 1841. 3in (7.6cm).

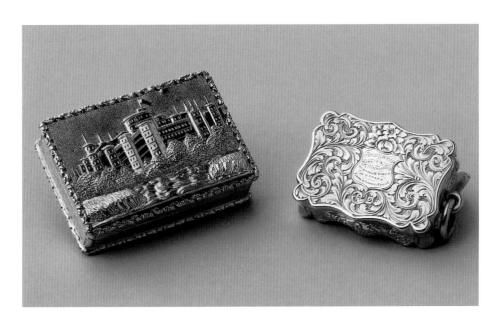

**Plate 245** Victorian silver-gilt vinaigrette with an alternative view of Windsor Castle from the River Thames, with a foliate grille and engine-turned base. Edwin Jones, Birmingham 1836. 1½in (3.8cm) by 1in (2.5cm).

Victorian 18ct gold shaped rectangular vinaigrette with a contemporary presentation inscription and engraved with foliate motifs. Nathaniel Mills. Birmingham 1866. 1¼in (3.2cm) by ⅞in (2.2cm).

**Plate 246** *Clockwise*: Victorian repoussé top shaped rectangular vinaigrette showing an alternate (closer) view of Warwick Castle. Taylor & Perry, Birmingham 1839. 1½in (3.8cm).
Silver-gilt shaped repoussé top vinaigrette of St Paul's Cathedral, with a florally engraved base. Nathaniel Mills, Birmingham 1852. 1¾in (4.4cm).
Victorian silver-gilt repoussé top vinaigrette of Windsor Castle. Nathaniel Mills, Birmingham 1837. 1¼in (3.2cm).
Victorian silver-gilt repoussé top vinaigrette of Abbotsford House, the base and sides encrusted with floral casting and engine turning. Nathaniel Mills, Birmingham 1836. 1¾in (4.4cm).

Among the favourite views were the British and Scottish royal palaces and mansions and follies of the Landed Gentry. In the mid-1850s came deeply struck views of Buckingham Palace, shown with the Marble Arch in front, as well as the pool, probably based on John Nash's famous 1846 watercolour.

Before examining the Mills and other noted Birmingham box-makers, it may be useful to list some of the rarer views. It should be pointed out that they are personally noted versions, and their inclusion here does not indicate absolute rarity.

Identities of ruined abbeys continue to mystify, but buildings with distinguishing features are easier to place, such as the Cistercian Fountains Abbey in Yorkshire, with its great square Gothic tower built by Abbot Huby (1494-1526), narrow perpendicular windows, gateways, cloisters, vaulted chapter house, and sometimes, an interior view from the Choir. Another reasonably identifiable ruin is the transitional Norman and Perpendicular style Cistercian Abbey at Kirkstall, near Leeds, founded 1152. Two versions of this ruin appear on Mills card cases.

Turning to snuffboxes and vinaigrettes, more obscure views include the Scottish Dryburgh Abbey, near Melrose, destroyed in the expedition of the Earl of Hertford in 1545. Sir Walter Scott and his family are interred at Dryburgh. Further uncommon Mills views are of Lulworth Cove, Dorset, dated 1840, shown with a harbour scene and steam packets and sailing ships, St Michael's Mount in Cornwall 1838, Birmingham Town Hall 1843, Edinburgh Castle 1837, Nottingham Castle 1844 and Tintern Abbey 1841.

Unusual angles can also confuse. The oft-cited *rare* view of Gloucester Cathedral, p.115 *Investing in Silver*, is sadly, another view of Durham Cathedral, of which at least three versions have been noted. Further, for 'Lincoln' read 'Worcester'. Such anomalies, chiefly the result of personal or communicated inaccuracies, continue to annoy and it is hoped that 'putting the record straight' will placate the reader.

Several views of ruined abbeys, cathedrals and mansions still remain to perplex the collector. Tintern, Bolton, Malmesbury, the rear of Worcester Cathedral, and Lanercost are complex scenes which often defy identification.

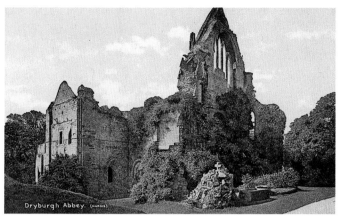

1. Dryburgh Abbey, near Melrose in Berwickshire.

2. Elgin Cathedral, Morayshire, west view of the nave.

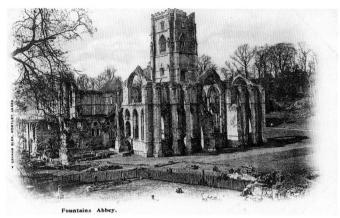

3. Fountains Abbey, Somerset.

4. Bolton Abbey, Ilkley, Yorkshire.

## Topographical Guides

There are many such works, but four important 18th century books which illustrate British Country Houses and Houses of Worship merit particular attention:

*Views of the Seats of the Nobility and Gentry* by William Watts (1752-1851), a pupil of Paul Sandby. Watts engraved the plates and published the work in 1779. Many mansions and houses illustrated are no longer in existence but the book is useful for identification.

William Byrne (1748-1805) in his *Antiquities of Great Britain*, published by Thomas Hearne, London 1807, shows many monasteries, castles and churches and Adam de Cardonnel's *Picturesque Antiquities of Scotland*, London 1778, has many finely etched views of castles and mansions.

Paul Sandby (1725-1809) was a distinguished watercolourist and genre artist. His particular interest was Windsor, the environs of the Castle, the woods around and various views of other castles and houses. Hundreds of his superb watercolours are in the Print Room at the British Library, as fresh as when they were painted, almost two centuries ago. Many others are in the Royal Collection at Windsor.

In addition, an attractive, informative modern publication, *The Country House Described* by Michael Holmes, published by the V & A Museum, 1986, lists over four thousand country houses. A copy is on the reference shelves in the National Art Library at the V & A. Some kind hand has annotated many of the entries with the V & A Press Marks for easy reference. REF: 728. 8. HOL.

Mills and their Birmingham contemporaries created numerous views of ecclesiastical buildings on their boxes. Further illustrations of ruins known to have been die-struck are shown here, using postcard views to assist readers in their quest. Melrose Abbey, a Columban monastery, was founded in the 7th century. Another notable ruin known to be a Mills subject is the 12th-13th century Jedburgh Abbey.

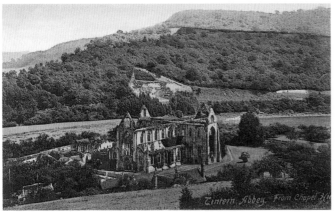

5. Tintern Abbey, near Chepstow, Monmouthshire.

6. Ruins at the back of Worcester Cathedral. The shrines of St Oswald and St Wulstan were destroyed at the Reformation.

7. and 8. Two views of Kirkstall Abbey, near Leeds, Yorkshire.

9. Melrose Abbey, Roxburgh.

10. Gloucester Cathedral, from the south-west.

11. Durham Cathedral, the West Front.

Why should Nathaniel Mills have selected an old city gate, the Bar Gate at Southampton, as one of his rarer subjects? The Hampshire historian, Peter Kilby's *Southampton through the Ages*, says: 'It was known as "The Gateway to England". Kings and Queens of England who passed through this space included Henry II when he came on foot in 1147 on his walk of penance to Canterbury. Henry V in 1415 *en route* to the Battle of Agincourt and Queen Elizabeth I in 1591 when she visited Southampton with her entire court to be greeted by the Mayor and Corporation and presented with a purse containing forty pounds.' The object atop the crenellated gateway is a furled flag. A further gloss dates the Norman archway from *circa* 1175, the two flanking towers from about a hundred years later. The upper floor was the medieval Guild Hall.

The Bar Gate, Southampton. A colour illustration taken from *The Graphic*, July 14, 1883.

The fine colour print showing the Bar Gate is taken from the Victorian journal *The Graphic*, dated 14 July 1883. It will be seen that the heraldic arms above the arch have vanished. Otherwise, the view of the jutting outbuildings to the left and right, shown here with groups of fashionably costumed ladies and gentlemen, is the same as on the Nathaniel Mills vinaigrette of 1842 (see page 120).

### Some important London boxmakers

This review of die-struck and repoussé box-lids concentrates on Birmingham, but there were also London silversmiths who produced fine 'strikings', notably the John Linnet Workshop, which specialised in reproductions of Flemish and Dutch genre paintings. These include the well-known 'Wine and Spirit Pedlar', the 'Toper', and other *Watteauesque* genre examples.

Other outstanding London box-top makers include the Rawlings and Summers partnership. Their die-strikings and castings were always in excellent taste and skilfully done, and Edward Edwards II also made sturdy finely cast and chased boxes, mainly of the 'table snuffbox' type.

Returning to Birmingham, John Shaw and his son Thomas, in the 1820s, were

**Plate 247** William IV rectangular Newstead Abbey snuff box with applied heavy cast scrolling border and thumbpiece. Rawlings & Summers, London 1835. 3½in (8.9cm).

early exponents of the shallow relief view. Other later specialists included John Bettridge, Edwin Jones, Joseph Willmore, Frederick Marson, Yapp & Woodward, Taylor & Perry, Hilliard & Thomason, Wheeler & Cronin, David Pettifer, John Tongue, Edward Smith, Thomas and William Simpson, Colin Hewer Cheshire and, working right up to the 1930s, the prolific manufacturers, George Unite.

## Addendum

It might prove of interest to mention a number of uncommon Georgian and Victorian snuffboxes, vinaigrettes, card cases and *aides memoire* seen since the issue of the first edition of this book in 1968.

The Nathaniel Mills pieces include: Birmingham Town Hall, 1843; The Mansion House, London, 1844; Eddystone Lighthouse, 1847; Nottingham Castle, 1845; Tintern Abbey, 1848, a large book-shaped table snuffbox, 1856; a large table snuffbox with a cast and chased 'Roman Battle' scene, 1826; a large table snuffbox with, under a glass lid, two songbirds executed in brightly coloured feathers, 1836 and an engraved sporting scene, 1842.

## Other Makers

*Aide memoire*, repoussé, The Dublin International Exhibition, with the clasp formed as a silver pencil. By David Pettifer, Birmingham, 1853.
A vinaigrette engraved with 'Battle Honours' by Matthew Linwood V, 1802.
Ditto, by Samuel Pemberton VI, 1810.
A vinaigrette shaped as a cornucopia by Samuel Pemberton VI, 1816.
A silver-gilt vinaigrette with repoussé 'Roman Matron' by Lea & Co., Birmingham 1817.
A vinaigrette shaped as a fox's mask, unmarked, *circa* 1840.
A vinaigrette inset with a Wedgwood blue and white jasper classical scene by James Fenton, Birmingham 1864.
A vinaigrette shaped as a strawberry by Richard Millington, Birmingham 1860.

## Some rare grilles

'Country Cottage', Birmingham 1830.
Masonic emblems, Birmingham 1870.

# Birmingham Gold Boxes

Illustrated in a group from a private source (Plate 245) is an 18 carat gold vinaigrette made by Nathaniel Mills, dated 1866. As very few Birmingham-made gold boxes appear in museum collections, reference works and sale catalogues, a concentrated search was made at eminent dealers, auction houses, museums and libraries. This revealed very little.

The two Nathaniel Mills gold snuffboxes that have so far been traced are in national museums. One, dated 1835, is in the collection of the National Maritime Museum at Greenwich. It was presented by passengers, after a difficult maiden voyage, to the Captain of the *Liverpool*, a three-masted paddle-steamer. The lid is finely engraved with a view of the ship and inscribed *Liverpool*. Inside the lid, which has the well-known Mills incurving chased border, is a long presentation inscription. The size is 3⅛in (7.9cm) long and it weighs 3.9 oz. (110.5g).

Another smaller, but slightly heavier, Mills snuffbox, also dated 1835, is on loan to the Victoria & Albert Museum. This fine box has a typical Mills view of Windsor Castle, standing within flowers and foliage struck in shallow relief, and has florally enriched encrusted edges and is otherwise engine-turned. The size is 3¼in (8.2cm) by⅞in (2.2cm) deep and it weighs 4.76 troy ounces (135g).

Occasionally one spots an interesting gold box in a sale catalogue. An *objet de vertu* sale at Zurich in November 1978 illustrated a large rectangular snuffbox, 3⅝in (9.2cm) long, cast and chased with foliate and floral motifs on the lid and sides, and with additional engine-turning. The maker was Joseph Willmore, Birmingham 1826. Another Willmore box, 2¾in (7cm) long, appears in a catalogue of June 1990, dated 1843 and engraved with wrigglework motifs.

One of the rarest gold specimens seen (for its size, it would be uncommon even in silver) was a Matthew Linwood, Birmingham 1805 snuffbox superbly engraved with a celebrated Nelson portrait and the 'England Expects' motto on the lid, with *H.M.S. Victory* engraved on the base. It is 4in (10.2cm) long and weighs 8oz (203g).

Perhaps the most remarkable Birmingham-made box noted was by the well-known boxmakers Yapp & Woodward, 1850, also on loan to the Victoria & Albert Museum. The rectangular base is made in silver. Its lid, however, is cast and chased in *platinum*. In 1850, Percival Norton Johnson, a member of the famous family of metallurgists and bullion dealers, which eventually became Johnson Matthey, succeeded in producing a larger than usual ingot of platinum and because the London metal workers were unable to 'roll' (flatten) such a size, Norton Johnson took it to Birmingham to be rolled. He approached Yapp & Woodward, the successors to Joseph Willmore at Bread Street, another workshop which also produced fine snuffboxes, vinaigrettes and card-cases. After the metal was rolled, a finely cast and chased platinum rectangular lid was made to fit the silver base. The subject struck in relief depicted a classical scene, the Roman Consul Lucius Junius Brutus (509BC) condemning his two sons to death for conspiracy. 'They were executed by sentence of their father, and in his sight.' (Livy i 59.)

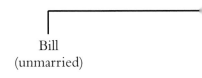

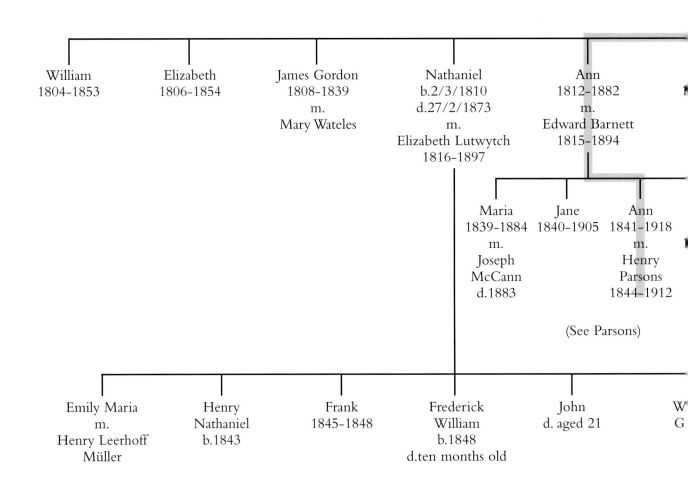

Bill
(unmarried)

| William 1804–1853 | Elizabeth 1806–1854 | James Gordon 1808–1839 m. Mary Wateles | Nathaniel b.2/3/1810 d.27/2/1873 m. Elizabeth Lutwytch 1816–1897 | Ann 1812–1882 m. Edward Barnett 1815–1894 |

Maria 1839–1884 m. Joseph McCann d.1883

Jane 1840–1905

Ann 1841–1918 m. Henry Parsons 1844–1912

(See Parsons)

| Emily Maria m. Henry Leerhoff Müller | Henry Nathaniel b.1843 | Frank 1845–1848 | Frederick William b.1848 d.ten months old | John d. aged 21 | W G |

# Family Tree

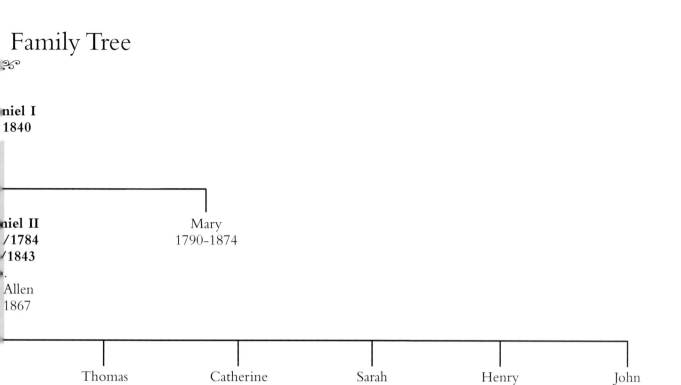

**niel I**
**1840**

**niel II**
**/1784**
**/1843**
**.**
Allen
1867

Mary
1790-1874

Thomas
1815-1892?
m.
Sarah Ann Bowdler
d.1859

Catherine
(Kate)
1818-1899
m.
Thomas Doyle

Sarah
1820-1902
m.
Alfred Taylor
b.1815

Henry
1822-1824

John
1824-1850

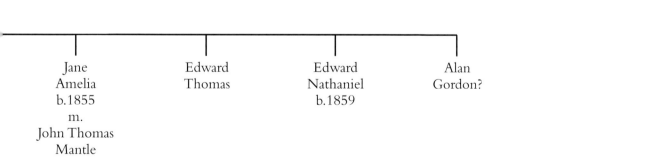

Jane
Amelia
b.1855
m.
John Thomas
Mantle

Edward
Thomas

Edward
Nathaniel
b.1859

Alan
Gordon?

# Bibliography

Bagshawe, Thomas W.: 'Souvenirs of Tight-Lacing: Stay-busks for the Lass who Loved a Sailor', *The Antique Collector*, November 1937.

Banfield, Edwin: *Visiting Cards and Cases,* Baros Books, Trowbridge 1989.

Bennett, Douglas: *Irish Heritage Series,* Eason & Son, Dublin 1976.

Berry-Hill, Henry & Sidney: *Antique Gold Boxes,* Abelard-Schuman, New York 1960.

Beunat, Joseph: *Empire Styles, Designs and Ornaments,* circa 1813.

Boesen, Gudmund: *Danish Museums,* Copenhagen 1966.

Brooke, Nathaniel: *A Queen's Delight,* R. Wood, at the Angel, Cornhill 1660.

Brown, Lawrence: *British Historical Medals,* Seaby 1980.

Bryant & May: Catalogue of the Exhibits & Supplement, Bryant & May, Bow, 1926-1928.

Byrne, William, FSA: *Antiquities of Great Britain. Monasteries, Castles and Churches,* 50 plates, two volumes. Engraved by Byrne from drawings by Thomas Hearne, FSA. Printed for T. Cadell & W. Davies, Strand, London 1807.

Cardonnel, Adam: *Picturesque Antiquities of Scotland,* London 1778.

Christy, Miller: 'Concerning Tinder Boxes', *Burlington Magazine,* No.1, March-December 1903.

Clomas, C (ed.): 'Chinese Export and Design'. Victoria & Albert Museum 1987. p.107. Item registration number: M.114 – 1919.

Country Life: *The Book of Castles and Houses in Britain,* 1986.

Culme, John: *The Directory of Gold and Silversmiths,* Antique Collectors' Club, 1987.

Currie, Ian: *Frosts, Freezes and Fairs,* Frosted Earth, 1996.

Curtis, Mattoon, M: *The Book of Snuff and Snuffboxes,* Liveright Publishing Corporation, New York 1935.

de Freitas, Manuel: *Filigrana Portuguesa.* Bon Amigos, Portugal, 1994.

Delieb, Eric: 'The Silver Vinaigrette', *The Saturday Book,* Hutchinson 1965.

Delieb, Eric: *Investing in Silver,* Barrie & Rockliff, 1967.

Delieb, Eric, with Michael Roberts: *The Great Silver Manufactory,* Studio Vista, 1971.

De Quincy, John: *English Dispensatory,* 1782.

*Encylopaedia Britannica:* 11th edition, New York 1910.

Evans, George: *An Old Snuff House 1720-1920,* privately published.

Exhibition catalogue: 'Filigree in the Order of Lenin State History Museum', Moscow 1990. Edited by Postnikova-Losseva.

Forrer, Leonard: *Biographical Dictionary of Medallists,* Spink & Son, 1904.

Gilbert Collection: 'The Art of Mosaics'. Exhibition Catalogue, Los Angeles County Museum of Art, 1982.

*Graphic, The*: Magazine, July 14th, 1883.

Grimwade, Arthur G., FSA: *The London Goldsmiths 1697-1837,* Faber & Faber, 1976.

Handbook to the Industrial Art Collections. City of Birmingham Museum and Art Gallery, n.d., p.139.

Hare, Susan M: 'Paul de Lamerie', Exhibition Catalogue, The Worshipful Company of Goldsmiths, 1990.

Heavisides, Michael: *The True History of the Invention of the Friction Light,* Stockton-on-Tees, 1827.

Holmes, Michael: *The Country House Described,* V & A, 1986.

Hyatt Major, A: 'Old Calling Cards'. Bulletin of the Metropolitan Museum, New York, 1943.

Jackson, Sir Charles: *The History of English Plate,* Country Life and Batsford, London 1911.

Jones, Owen: *The Grammar of Ornament,* Day & Son, 1856.

Kelly, Francis M. and Schwabe, Randolph: *A Short History of Costume and Armour – 1066-1800,* Batsford, London 1931.

Kent, Timothy Arthur, MA, Cantab: *The London Silver Spoonmakers,* The Silver Society, 1981.

Kilby, Peter: *Southampton through the Ages,* Computational Mechanics Publications, Southampton, UK, 1997.

McDonald, D and Hunt, L. B: *A History of Platinum and its Allied Metals,* Johnson Matthey, London 1982.

Miles, Elizabeth B: *English Silver – The Miles Collection,* The Wadsworth Atheneum. Hartford, Conn, 1976.

Milford Haven, Admiral the Marquis of: *British Naval Medals,* National Maritime Museum, Greenwich, 1919.

Opie, A. P.: *Paul and Thomas Sandby. The Catalogue of Prints and Drawings in the Collection of H.M. the King at Windsor Castle,* Phaidon Press, 1947.

Pickford, Ian: Ed. Third Edition *Jackson's Silver and Gold Marks,* Antique Collectors' Club, 1989.

Porter, Roy: *Health for Sale: Quackery in England 1660-1850,* Manchester University Press, 1989.

Quickenden, Kenneth: 'Boulton and Fothergill's Silversmiths'. The Autumn 1993 *Journal of the Silver Society*, p.350.

Reilly, Robin: 'Wedgwood Portrait Medallions', Exhibition Catalogue, National Portrait Gallery. Barrie & Jenkins, 1973.

Reports of the Juries: The Great Exhibition', William Clowes & Sons, 1852.

Rimmel, Eugene: *The Book of Perfumes*, Chapman & Hall, 1868.

Schofield, Robert E: *The Lunar Society of Birmingham,* Clarendon Press, Oxford, 1963.

Sotheby Parke Bernet, New York: June 19th 1974. The Collection of the late Mrs. Arthur I. Harris.

Spink, Michael: 'Silver from Cuttack'. The Winter 1991 *Journal of the Silver Society*.

Thornhill, Walter & Co: Prices. *The Queen* magazine, November–December 1876.

Watts, William W: *Views of the Seats of the Nobility and Gentry,* Kemps Row, Chelsea, London 1779.

West, William: *History, Topography and Directory of Warwickshire,* R. Wrightson, Birmingham 1830.

Wootton, A. C: *Chronicles of Pharmacy,* Macmillan & Co, 1910.

And many sale catalogues: Bonhams, London; Christie's, King Street, Christie's, South Kensington, London; Christie's, New York; Christie's, Geneva; Christie's, Amsterdam; Phillips, London; Phillips, Geneva; Sotheby Park Bernet, New York; Sotheby, Bond Street, Sotheby, Belgravia, London; Sotheby, Monaco. – dating from 1900 to the present day.

**Plate 254** Modern hand engraved copper plaque which was especially commissioned to illustrate the process, pioneered by Mills, of hand engraving on an engine-turned ground. The choice of the Post Office Tower in London is deliberate, to show the way in which a contemporary subject would have been treated.
This article was made in collaboration by two Birmingham craft workshops, Messrs. F L Lancaster and V Joliffe, Birmingham 1968. 4in (10.2cm) x 3¼in (8.3cm).

# Makers' Index

George Reid, London, Plate 190
John Reily, London 1797, Plates 43, 83
RG, Plate 32
Charles Robb, Edinburgh, Plate 58
John Robertson, Newcastle, Plates 121, 201
RS in heart, London, Plate 156

James Scott, Dublin, Plate 110
John Shaw, Birmingham, page 155; Plates 55, 217
Thomas Shaw, Birmingham, Plate 124
William Simpson, Birmingham, Plate 154, 224
Simpson & Son, Birmingham, page 156; Plates 161, 167
W R Smiley, London, Plate 165
Edward Smith, Birmingham, page 156; Plates 150, 193, 202
Edward H Stockwell, London, Plate 69
Stokes & Ireland, Birmingham, page 54
Alexander James Strachan, London, Plate 78
William Summers, London 1871, page 52

Taylor and Perry, Birmingham, Plates 44, 48, 49, 228, 233, 246
Alfred Taylor, Birmingham 1866, page 52
Joseph Taylor, Birmingham, page 144; Plates 19, 39, 122, 133, 188, 201, 231
Edward Thomason, pages 127, 138, 140
Thropp and Taylor, Birmingham, Plate 163
TN, Plate 30

John Tongue, Birmingham, page 156; Plates 90, 169
TT crowned, London, Plate 160

George Unite, Birmingham, pages 51, 144, 156; Plates 198, 212, 239
Samuel Urlin, page 23

Charles Wallingford and Shirley Deakin, Birmingham, page 50; Plate 14
William Wardell and Peter Kempston, Birmingham 1817, Plates 130, 218
Wheeler and Cronin, page 156
Gervase Wheeler, Birmingham, Plates 139, 243
Starling Wilford, London, Plate 165
Henry Wilkinson & Co, Sheffield, Plate 57
David Willaume, London 1720, page 29
Joseph Willmore, Birmingham, pages 91, 127, 144, 156, 157; Plates 22, 37, 47, 127, 163, 213, 226, 234, 235, 238
Joseph Willmore II, Birmingham, page 144, Plates 177, 185
Thomas Willmore, Birmingham, Plate 229
John Woodward, page 144

John Yapp, page 144
Yapp and Woodward, Birmingham, pages 156, 157; 1845, Plate 232

# Topographical Index

# Abbreviations

AGG     *London Goldsmiths 1697-1837*, Arthur G. Grimwade, FSA, Faber & Faber, 1976.

J3     Third edition, *Jackson's Silver and Gold Marks*. Edited by Ian Pickford. Antique Collectors' Club, 1989.

JC     *The Directory of Gold and Silversmiths*, John Culme. Antique Collectors' Club, 1987.

# Antique Collectors' Club

THE ANTIQUE COLLECTORS' CLUB was formed in 1966 and quickly grew to a five figure membership spread throughout the world. It publishes the only independently run monthly antiques magazine, *Antique Collecting*, which caters for those collectors who are interested in widening their knowledge of antiques, both by greater awareness of quality and by discussion of the factors which influence the price that is likely to be asked. The Antique Collectors' Club pioneered the provision of information on prices for collectors and the magazine still leads in the provision of detailed articles on a variety of subjects.

It was in response to the enormous demand for information on 'what to pay' that the price guide series was introduced in 1968 with the first edition of *The Price Guide to Antique Furniture* (completely revised 1978 and 1989), a book which broke new ground by illustrating the more common types of antique furniture, the sort that collectors could buy in shops and at auctions rather than the rare museum pieces which had previously been used (and still to a large extent are used) to make up the limited amount of illustrations in books published by commercial publishers. Many other price guides have followed, all copiously illustrated, and greatly appreciated by collectors for the valuable information they contain, quite apart from prices. The Price Guide Series heralded the publication of many standard works of reference on art and antiques. *The Dictionary of British Art* (now in six volumes), *The Pictorial Dictionary of British 19th Century Furniture Design*, *Oak Furniture* and *Early English Clocks* were followed by many deeply researched reference works such as *The Directory of Gold and Silversmiths*, providing new information. Many of these books are now accepted as the standard work of reference on their subject.

The Antique Collectors' Club has widened its list to include books on gardens and architecture. All the Club's publications are available through bookshops world wide and a full catalogue of all these titles is available free of charge from the addresses below.

Club membership, open to all collectors, costs little. Members receive free of charge *Antique Collecting*, the Club's magazine (published ten times a year), which contains well-illustrated articles dealing with the practical aspects of collecting not normally dealt with by magazines. Prices, features of value, investment potential, fakes and forgeries are all given prominence in the magazine.

Among other facilities available to members are private buying and selling facilities and the opportunity to meet other collectors at their local antique collectors' club. There are over eighty in Britain and more than a dozen overseas. Members may also buy the Club's publications at special pre-publication prices.

As its motto implies, the Club is an organisation designed to help collectors get the most out of their hobby: it is informal and friendly and gives enormous enjoyment to all concerned.

*For Collectors — By Collectors — About Collecting*

ANTIQUE COLLECTORS' CLUB
Sandy Lane, Old Martlesham, Woodbridge, Suffolk, IP12 4SD, UK
Tel: 01394 389950 Fax: 01394 389999
Email: sales@antique-acc.com
Website: www.antique-acc.com
or
Market Street Industrial Park, Wappingers' Falls, NY 12590, USA
Tel: 845 297 0003 Fax: 845 297 0068
Email: info@antiquecc.com
Website: www.antiquecc.com